CW00662456

SOMERSET & DORSET

Life on the Bath to Bournemouth Line

SOMERSET & DORSET

Life on the Bath to Bournemouth Line

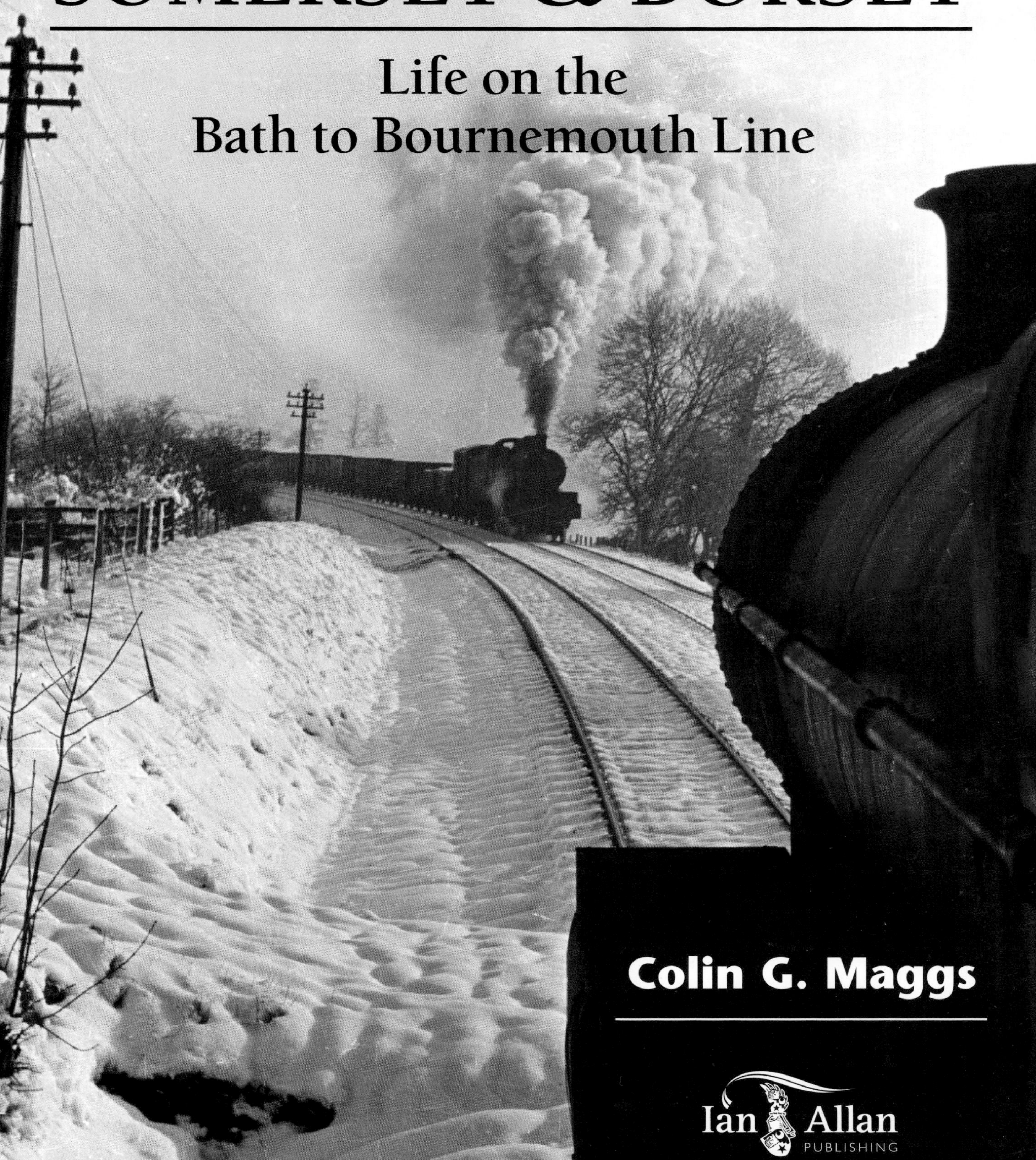

Colin G. Maggs

Ian Allan PUBLISHING

Above: Class 7F 2-8-0 No 53804 passes Midford with a down freight on 19 August 1959. The line here is on a hillside ledge. *Author*

Front cover: BR Standard Class 5 4-6-0 No 75052 with a down train at Chilcompton. The water column, well protected against frost, is to the right of the locomotive. *R. E. Toop*

Back cover: 'West Country' class Pacific no 34006 Bude being turned at Bath, 5 March 1966. *Author*

Half title: Binegar down platform *c*1905, with the station staff posed for the camera. The barrow has but a single wheel. *Author's collection*

Title page: In January 1955, between Prestleigh Viaduct and Cannard's Grave cutting, Class 7F 2-8-0 No 53803 on the right (Driver Norman Gibbons and Fireman John Stamp), working the 9.5am from Bath to Evercreech Junction, approaches sister engine No 53807 (Driver Vic Hunt and Fireman Arthur Turner), heading the 1.45pm Evercreech Junction to Midsomer Norton empties. *John Stamp*

First published 2007

ISBN (10) 0 7110 3185 1
ISBN (13) 978 0 7110 3185 2

Published by Ian Allan Publishing

an imprint of Ian Allan Publishing Ltd, Hersham, Surrey KT12 4RG

Printed in England by Ian Allan Printing Ltd, Hersham, Surrey KT12 4RG

Code: 0707/B1

Visit the Ian Allan Publishing website at www.ianallanpublishing.com

Contents

Author's note and acknowledgements

This book does not set out to be a complete history of the Somerset & Dorset Joint Railway, but is intended to offer fascinating information and photographs, most of which I hope will be new.

The material is slanted towards the northern end of the line because that is where I have always lived and find it the most interesting.

Grateful acknowledgement for assistance is due to a multitude of ex-S&DJR railwaymen. Especial thanks are due to Colin Roberts for checking and improving the manuscript.

Colin G. Maggs
Bath
March 2007

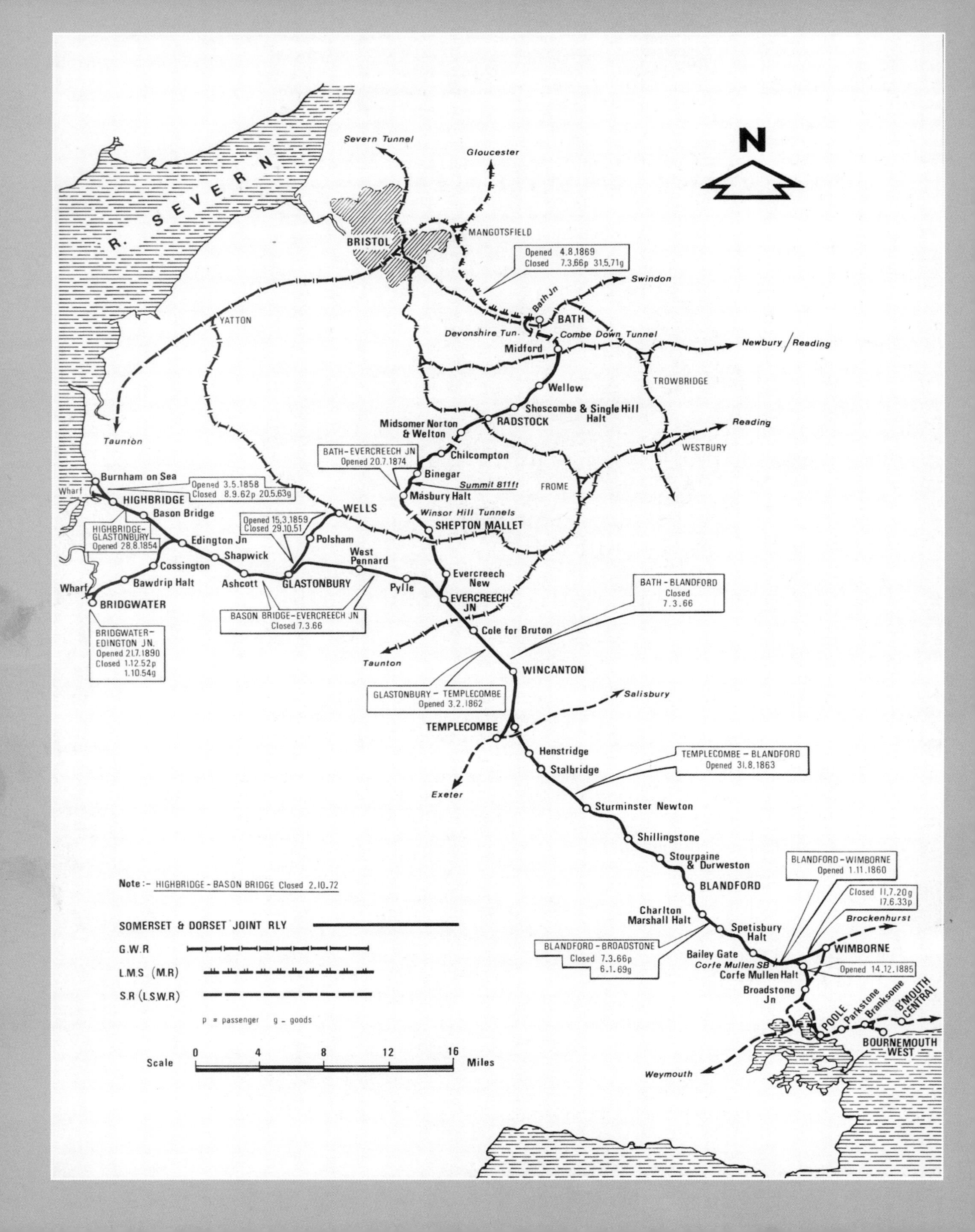

N
R. SEVERN
Severn Tunnel
Gloucester
MANGOTSFIELD
BRISTOL
Opened 4.8.1869
Closed 7.3.66p 31.5.71g
Swindon
Bath Jn
BATH
Devonshire Tun.
Combe Down Tunnel
Midford
Newbury / Reading
YATTON
TROWBRIDGE
Wellow
Shoscombe & Single Hill Halt
RADSTOCK
Midsomer Norton & Welton
Reading
Taunton
WESTBURY
Chilcompton
BATH-EVERCREECH JN
Opened 20.7.1874
Binegar
Summit 811ft
FROME
Burnham on Sea
Opened 3.5.1858
Closed 8.9.62p 20.5.63g
Wharf
HIGHBRIDGE
Masbury Halt
Winsor Hill Tunnels
WELLS
Bason Bridge
SHEPTON MALLET
Opened 15.3.1859
Closed 29.10.51
HIGHBRIDGE-GLASTONBURY
Opened 28.8.1854
Edington Jn
Polsham
Shapwick
West Pennard
Cossington
Evercreech New
Bawdrip Halt
Ashcott
GLASTONBURY
Pylle
Wharf
BRIDGWATER
EVERCREECH JN
BATH-BLANDFORD
Closed
7.3.66
BASON BRIDGE-EVERCREECH JN
Closed 7.3.66
BRIDGWATER-EDINGTON JN.
Opened 21.7.1890
Closed 1.12.52p
1.10.54g
Cole for Bruton
Taunton
WINCANTON
GLASTONBURY - TEMPLECOMBE
Opened 3.2.1862
Salisbury
TEMPLECOMBE
Henstridge
TEMPLECOMBE - BLANDFORD
Opened 31.8.1863
Stalbridge
Exeter
Sturminster Newton
Shillingstone
Stourpaine & Durweston
BLANDFORD-WIMBORNE
Opened 1.11.1860
Note:- HIGHBRIDGE - BASON BRIDGE Closed 2.10.72
BLANDFORD
Closed 11.7.20g
17.6.33p
Charlton Marshall Halt
SOMERSET & DORSET JOINT RLY
Brockenhurst
Spetisbury Halt
BLANDFORD - BROADSTONE
Closed 7.3.66p
6.1.69g
G.W.R
Bailey Gate
WIMBORNE
Corfe Mullen SB
L.M.S (M.R)
Corfe Mullen Halt
Opened 14.12.1885
S.R (L.S.W.R)
Broadstone Jn
POOLE
Parkstone
Branksome
B'MOUTH CENTRAL
p = passenger g = goods
Scale 0 4 8 12 16 Miles
BOURNEMOUTH WEST
Weymouth

— 1 —

A brief history

Opposite: The route of the Somerset and Dorset Railway with opening and closing dates of each section indicated.

Left: S&D seal: depicting train, St John's Church and Tor at Glastonbury, and the seal of Dorchester. *Author's collection*

THE Somerset & Dorset Railway had a most complicated history. It comprised two lines: the Somerset Central Railway (SCR) and the Dorset Central Railway (DCR), the former being the older partner.

The SCR was a concept by Glastonbury and Street businessmen to link with the outside world via the Bristol & Exeter Railway (B&E) and the sea wharf at Highbridge. From the earthworks point of view, construction was easy as the terrain was flat, but the peat bogs were not conducive to supporting permanent way and many faggots had to be laid to create a foundation. The first sod was cut on 18 April 1853 and the line formally opened 16 months later, on 17 August 1854. Somerset was in 7ft 0¼in, broad gauge territory, so to follow suit the SCR was broad gauge and indeed was worked by the B&E. In due course extensions were opened westwards to Burnham-on-Sea (1858) and northwards to Wells (1859), the diocesan centre.

Meanwhile, the DCR was being planned to link Blandford with the London & South Western Railway's line at Wimborne Junction and its first sod was cut on 13 November 1856. The LSWR being a standard gauge line meant that the DCR was too.

Now for a railway to be really profitable it needed to be a through route, whereas a local line usually enjoyed only a small income, so what could the directors do to make the SCR and DCR profitable?

Looking at the map it was obvious that if the DCR could be extended north west to Cole and the SCR south east to there, an end-on junction could be made and if powers were sought to run over the LSWR to Poole, a through route would be created from Burnham to Poole. Furthermore, these far-seeing directors believed that if they ran steamers from Burnham to Cardiff and from Poole to Cherbourg, the line would attract international traffic.

However, there was one big problem: the gauges of the SCR and DCR were different, but two solutions were available. A third rail could be added to the broad gauge track to give access to standard gauge trains, or broad gauge could be converted to standard. The latter course was chosen, and on 1 November 1860 the DCR opened its line between Wimborne and Blandford, and on 3 February 1862 the SCR reached

Cole, as did the DCR from Templecombe. This left a 16-mile gap between Blandford and Templecombe, which the DCR filled on 31 August 1863.

Gauge conversion meant that the B&E was no longer able to work the line, so the SCR took over the working shortly before the two companies amalgamated to form the Somerset & Dorset Railway (S&D) on 1 September 1862. The new company's seal depicted, on the left, Glastonbury Tor and St John's Church, and to the right, the seal of Dorchester.

Although the S&D was a through route, cash failed to fall like a torrent into its coffers, the problem being that only a very limited number of passengers wished to travel from South Wales to France and vice versa.

The directors donned their thinking caps once again, looked at the map and saw 26 miles to the north from Evercreech was the Midland Railway's new branch line to Bath. If they built a connecting line, it would place Evercreech to Poole on the shortest through line from the North and Midlands to the South Coast between Portsmouth and Plymouth. It would therefore offer a standard gauge link between the MR and the LSWR and as a significant bonus, would tap quarries and collieries *en route* where over 500,000 tons of coal had been mined in 1870 alone. The only problem was the topography: the Mendip Hills and their outliers lay at right angles across the line's path.

Skilful planning enabled gradients not to exceed 1 in 50 and the four tunnels to measure a total distance of less than 2,600yd. In addition, seven major viaducts needed to be constructed. Messrs T. & C. Walker built this impressive extension in only two years and it was opened on 20 July 1874.

Although the building of the Bath Extension proved to be an admirably wise move, it unfortunately caused the company to overstretch itself. There was insufficient rolling stock for the traffic, and too few sidings and crossing loops, and furthermore, no finance to amend matters. The only solution was to sell the whole railway.

At it was a standard gauge line, one would have thought that the MR or LSWR would have been

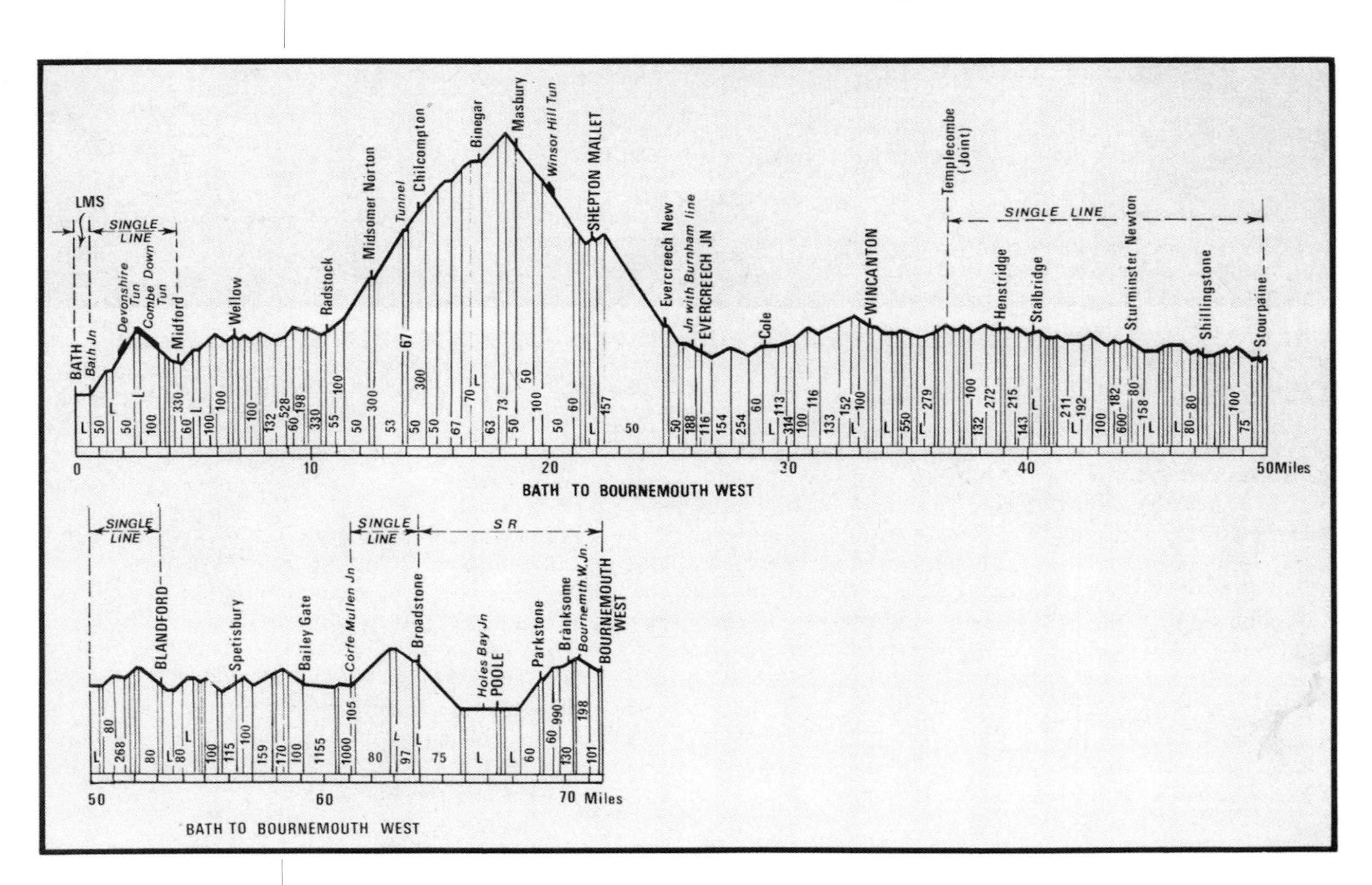

Gradient profile of the complete line.

the most likely purchasers, but instead, the S&D directors approached the GWR. Perhaps their reasoning was that it would pay generously to keep the S&D out of the hands of the two standard gauge parties.

In May 1875, the S&D approached the Great Western board, which then sought B&E approval which was given. Discussions rambled on until 12 August when Archibald Scott, the LSWR manager, was brought into the talks with the idea that the LSWR might take over the S&D south of Templecombe.

This was the first that Scott had heard about the S&D being for sale. He informed his directors who asked him to meet Sir James Allport, the MR manager. This he did on 14 August; the S&D and its accounts were inspected on the 15th and 16th, and on the 19th the MR and LSWR directors met and made a definite offer for the line. On 20 August the S&D directors accepted the terms proposed by the MR and LSWR which were superior to those suggested by the GWR and B&E.

The GWR had only itself to blame for missing this opportunity to purchase: it should not have behaved in such a dilatory manner. Frustrated, it opposed the Bill for confirming the lease. In order to avoid conflict, the GWR and MR had, by an Agreement of 1863, pledged to agree to the leasing or working of any new lines in the districts in which they were both interested and that the MR should make its branch 'to Bath but not beyond'. The GWR directors contested that the S&D lease broke this Agreement. The case was heard by the Railway Commissioners in March 1876, but they upheld the lease and the Act passed on 13 August 1876, and so from this date the S&D became the Somerset & Dorset Joint Railway (S&DJR). (This was the second largest joint line in the country, the biggest being the Cheshire Lines Committee.) The lease permitted the two operating companies to raise £100,000 in share capital to improve the line.

The S&D being taken over by the MR and LSWR was certainly the best decision for the public. Time proved that the MR and LSWR did their utmost for the district and developed the S&D, whereas the GWR most likely would have stifled traffic as it did when it took over the Midland & South Western Junction Railway, disliking any route which competed with its own lines. The S&DJR was managed by three members from the board of each owning company as well as a committee of two general managers — Sir James Allport, MR, and Archibald Scott, LSWR, plus S. W. Johnson, the MR's locomotive superintendent, and E. Andrews, the LSWR's chief engineer.

On 30 September and 1 October 1876, Allport and Scott inspected the S&D accompanied by Robert Reid, S&D secretary, Benjamin Fisher, S&D locomotive superintendent, Samuel W. Johnson, together with the MR and LSWR engineers. Their report among other things proposed the company's principal offices be moved

SUBSCRIPTION FOR

£50,000 PERPETUAL FIVE PER CENT. DEBENTURE STOCK,

BALANCE OF £110,000,

SECURED UPON THE

EXTENSION TO THE MIDLAND RAILWAY

OF THE

SOMERSET AND DORSET RAILWAY COMPANY,

Authorized by an Act of the 37 & 38 Vict., Sess. 1874.

The Directors of the Somerset and Dorset Railway Company are prepared to receive Subscriptions for £50,000, balance of £110,000 of Perpetual Five per Cent. Extension Debenture Stock, 1874, in sums of £50 and upwards *at Par*. This Debenture Stock is secured upon the Extension to the Midland Railway at Bath, and the interest, which ranks next immediately after the interest (namely £6,000 a year) on the £120,000 of Extension Debenture Stock already issued, is payable out of the **gross receipts** of that Extension, as hereafter mentioned.

The Line was opened for public Traffic on the 20th of July last, and a through service of Trains has been established between the **system of the Midland Railway and Bournemouth, Weymouth,** and the whole of the South and West of England. (*See Map.*)

The original Line is 66 miles in length, and the Extension to Bath is about 26 miles, making a total of 92 miles.

The total capital expended upon the whole undertaking, exclusive of the £110,000 (of which the balance of £50,000 is now offered for subscription), amounts to upwards of £2,200,000.

Special advantages are secured to the Extension Capital by the terms of the Act of Parliament under which the original Line is charged, not only with the payment of its own working expenses, but also with the working expenses of the Extension Line, and (together with the Extension Line) with an annual charge of £17,000.

The **gross receipts** of the Extension Line are therefore available (subject to the above) for payment, in priority to all other interest or dividend, of the interest at 5 per cent. on the Extension Debenture Stocks of £120,000 and £110,000, amounting together to £11,500 per annum, or **£8 10s. per mile per week of gross receipts, while the actual average gross receipts already amount to nearly double that sum,** although the traffic is naturally in so short a time quite undeveloped.

The working of the Railway since it was opened strengthens the opinion that the original estimate **of £48,882 per annum, or £36 per-mile per week,** will be more than realised when the arrangements in progress for securing the traffic of the Coal Basin, through which the Line passes, and other local traffic are completed.

Applications, accompanied by a deposit of £10 per cent. on the amount of Debenture Stock applied for, may be made in the form annexed, and should be forwarded either to Messrs. Robarts, Lubbock & Co., 15, Lombard Street, E.C., London; or to the Secretary, at the General Offices of the Company, Glastonbury, Somerset.

The balance will be payable on Allotment.

The Interest is payable half-yearly at the Bank of Messrs. Robarts, Lubbock & Co., 15, Lombard Street, London; it commenced on the 1st of September last, and Subscribers will have the benefit of the three months' interest since accrued.

The Debenture Stock will be registered in the names of the applicants free of expense.

If no allotment is made, the Deposit will be forthwith returned in full.

General Offices:
Glastonbury, Somerset,
1st December, 1874.

CHARLES WARING, *Chairman.*
ROBERT A. READ, *Managing Director.*

Prospectus for Extension shares.

FIVE PER CENT. PERPETUAL EXTENSION DEBENTURE STOCK, 1874,
Secured upon the
EXTENSION TO THE MIDLAND RAILWAY
OF THE
SOMERSET AND DORSET RAILWAY COMPANY.
FORM OF APPLICATION.

To the DIRECTORS OF THE SOMERSET AND DORSET RAILWAY COMPANY,
GLASTONBURY, SOMERSET.

GENTLEMEN,
Having paid the sum of £ .... being the deposit of £10 per Cent on an application for £ .... of the 5 per Cent. Extension Debenture Stock, 1874, I request you to allot me that amount, and I hereby agree to pay up on allotment the balance due thereon, or on any less sum which may be allotted to me

Name (in full) ....
Address ....
Profession (if any) ....
Date .... 1874.
Signature ....

SOMERSET AND DORSET RAILWAY COMPANY.
EXTENSION TO THE MIDLAND RAILWAY.
FIVE PER CENT EXTENSION DEBENTURE STOCK, 1874.
BANKERS' RECEIPT.

Received *of* ....
the Sum of .... *Pounds, being the Deposit of £10 per Cent upon an application for £* .... *of the 5 per Cent. Extension Debenture Stock,* 1874.

For ....

£ : :

Form of Application for Extension shares.

from Glastonbury, which had been relegated to branch status since the opening of the Bath Extension, to Bath. In 1877 an office was made at 14 Green Park Buildings close to Queen Square station, this move bringing 70 officials and their families to Bath, while the superintendent of the line and the crossing agent were accommodated at Bath station. (The 'crossing agent' was the man responsible for determining where trains crossed, the S&D consisting of a single line with passing loops. He sent crossing instructions by single-needle telegraph.)

S&D locomotives were the responsibility of Johnson, although general repairs continued to be carried out at the S&D's Highbridge works, also the base for the carriage and wagon department. Heavy locomotive repairs were executed by the MR at Bristol, while new locomotives were to be built at Derby.

The Joint Committee appointed Robert Armstrong Dykes superintendent of the line and he was largely responsible for raising standards so that it became efficient, and to quote his words from a March 1899 *Railway Magazine* article: 'on a par with any in the Kingdom'. Much of the line north of Templecombe had been doubled by the end of the 1890s and a fair proportion of track relaid with heavier rail. In 1886, Tyer's electric tablet system was installed to safeguard single-line working.

In 1899, Dykes explained that the S&D was a separate railway; each of the owning companies stated its requirements and the S&D accommodated them. The MR and LSWR were treated as 'foreign' lines. Each owning company placed all the traffic it could over the line and between 1876 and 1899 traffic almost doubled regarding train mileage, tonnage and the number of passengers carried. On one occasion the S&D had exchanged 1,000 wagons in a single day. At Bath MR staff dealt with S&D trains, the MR stationmaster being responsible for passenger traffic and the MR goods agent for goods. Similarly, the LSWR was responsible for traffic at Templecombe and Bournemouth West stations.

In the 1881 blizzard, the 11.45am Bournemouth West to Bath train was snowed up on 18 January at Sturminster Newton until 7pm and the line was also blocked near Masbury. The thaw following the blizzard caused floods near Sturminster Newton which rose to the level of the S&D track. On 13 February 1888, when 14½ inches of snow fell in Bath, and probably more on the Mendips, although GWR and MR trains were delayed, the S&D was almost unaffected due to its use of two snow ploughs. In 1891, there was a very heavy fall of snow on 9 March and no trains ran on Tuesday the 10th between Bath and Bournemouth because the line was blocked completely at Shillingstone by drifts 10 to 12 feet deep, while cuttings in the Shepton Mallet area were also blocked and where an up goods was embedded at Bath Road Viaduct, as was a down goods at Cannard's Grave.

It was decided that no attempt would be made to clear the snow until the weather began to

Snow was a threat, so each winter a locomotive had its buffers removed and a snow plough fitted. Here, Class 3F 0-6-0T No 47623 (82F Bath) stands outside the timber-built S&D shed at Bath, 30 January 1964. *Rev. Alan Newman*

improve. Clearance was done in due course by a labour force of over 200 who were diverted from their task of doubling the single line. The drift north of Shepton Mallet was over a mile in length and had an average depth of 12 feet. Four locomotives and a snowplough left Shepton and took 1½ hours to thrust through a 400ft-long drift at Cannard's Grave. From there they continued fairly easily down the line to a mile north of Sturminster Newton where they became stuck part way through a drift and had to dig themselves out. On Tuesday, 17 March the S&D was clear of snow.

In 1891, by a rearrangement of the capital sanctioned, the original S&D shareholders were granted the option of having MR debentures in exchange.

During 1892 and 1893 a considerable quantity of goods worth several hundred pounds was stolen in transit over the S&D. The railway police investigated and on 7 March 1893 search warrants were issued for the homes of four engine drivers who lived at Bath. Stolen goods of great variety were found, sufficient to fill a large MR van and included butter, cheese, bacon, ham, cloth, silk, serge, cigars, corsets and cutlery. As S&D goods trains tended to travel at night, these goods had been abstracted from wagons under cover of darkness and any wooden boxes incinerated in locomotive fireboxes. Seven men were arrested, all were found guilty and most sentenced to a year's imprisonment with hard labour. The sentences were relatively light as, until the offences were committed, these men had good characters and they had to suffer the shame of detection and loss of their jobs.

Reversal at Wimborne proved a bugbear to through trains, so a cut-off was opened from Bailey Gate to Broadstone on 14 December 1885 to goods, and on 1 November 1886 to passengers. On 16 April 1905 the 4¾ mile-long section was shortened by opening a signalbox at Corfe Mullen Junction.

In June 1914, the S&D stock of 1,136 goods wagons was divided equally between the MR and the LSWR, the 221 wagons in service stock remaining joint property.

The line proved a vital north to south artery in both world wars, carrying men and supplies to the south coast and hospital trains running north. The first ambulance train ran over the S&D on Easter Monday, 24 April 1916, travelling from Wimborne, hauled by LSWR 'C8' class 4-4-0 No 229 and an S&D locomotive. It was believed to have been the first time for 30 years that an LSWR engine had been seen north of Templecombe. At Bath, a large crowd of sightseers assembled in the vicinity of the MR station and was contained by about 80 members of the Somerset Volunteer Regiment. A fleet of private motor cars, together with a Red Cross ambulance, was drawn up on the ramp adjacent to the arrival platform to transport the 100 wounded to the Bath War Hospital, Combe Park. On 2 January 1918, the 50th train of wounded arrived at Bath, carrying 164 men comprising 83 cot cases and 81 sitting. They were removed from the train in 39 minutes and conveyed to the War Hospital in motor ambulances and private cars. This made a total of about 7,300 wounded that had arrived at the station.

From 1 August 1916, lodging expenses were raised from 1s 0d to 1s 6d per night to cover the increased cost of living, while on 17 January 1917 the locomotive superintendent's notice stated: 'Drivers must avoid blowing off steam and whistling in the event of enemy air attack.' The following month German prisoners-of-war *en route* from Calne to Dorset marched from Bath GWR station to that of the MR. As there was a 1½ hour wait, to help deter any plans for escape, they were placed in empty coaches at Queen Square and shunted away from the platform. From 9 February, to ease the food shortage, land beside the S&D was allowed to be cultivated rent-free for the first year in order that employees could grow vegetables. To replace men who had joined the Forces, five women engine cleaners started at the Bath S&D shed at the end of January 1918.

During the 1919 rail strike, a motor charabanc brought a load of passengers to Bath on 30 September. Rather than return empty, the proprietor rang round Bath hotels to seek passengers and his enterprise filled 14 seats.

On 10 November 1920 the locomotive superintendent issued a notice:

'It is the wish of His Majesty the King that,
as on the last anniversary of Armistice Day,
there should be a complete suspension of
normal business and locomotion for two
minutes at 11am on November 11th 1920
as far as this may be practicable, together
with the cessation of sound from engines etc;
as a simple Silent Service in reverent
remembrance of the Glorious Dead.
In order that all men may be afforded this
opportunity:
(a) All work will cease in offices, and
locomotive sheds etc, at 11.00 o'clock for
two minutes, the shop engines at Highbridge
workshops and Bath repair depot being
stopped for 5 minutes.
(b) Trains ready to leave a station or Signal
at 11.00 o'clock to be detained for 2 minutes.
(c) Trains in motion at 11.00 o'clock to be
brought to a stand as near as possible to that
time, but in complying therewith enginemen
must avoid bringing the train to rest on a
steep rising gradient, in a tunnel, or on a high
Viaduct or Bridge.
R. C. Archbutt
Resident Loco Supt'

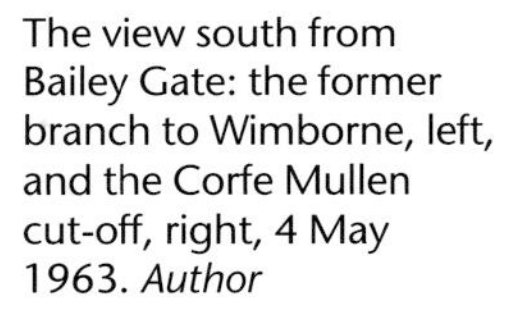

The view south from Bailey Gate: the former branch to Wimborne, left, and the Corfe Mullen cut-off, right, 4 May 1963. *Author*

Following the First World War, the S&D met its first serious rival — road transport. A notice was issued on 22 February 1921:

'Consequent upon the present depression in trade causing trains to be cancelled, there is a surplus of staff. Some Junior Cleaners have already been paid off and more will have to follow unless men are willing to adopt an alternative scheme.
The best alternative is for sufficient numbers of drivers, firemen and cleaners to take their Annual Leave at once.
This will mean no loss of pay to anyone, and will leave more men available for traffic working in the busier summer months.
A second alternative is for all men to agree for the available work to be shared out, which would mean men would be booked off about one day every two weeks.
I wish to know which scheme is most agreeable by Monday 28th instant. Men willing to take Annual Leave should apply at once in writing.
R. C. Archbutt'

German prisoners-of-war at Bath MR station, February 1917, *en route* from Calne to Dorset. *Author's collection*

Two months later it was announced that: 'The guaranteed week is suspended on and from May 2, 1921 due to the miners' strike. Work available in each particular grade at each shed will be distributed as far as possible in such a manner as to equalise the number of days' work for each man, no regard being paid to age or seniority in the service.' On 20 October 1921, Archbald asked drivers and firemen to try to prevent blowing off 'as the railway is at present working at a loss'.

Although long distance and excursion traffic continued to bring in good, steady revenue, people were turning to cars and buses for local journeys, while white collar workers were buying a car rather than a season ticket. Receipts from ordinary passenger tickets, season tickets, merchandise, mineral and livestock traffic, coal and coke, consistently fell during the 1920s, only parcels and miscellaneous traffic remaining steady. On 25 June 1929, H. V. Mosley and W. V. Wood sent a memorandum to Sir Josiah Stamp, President of the LMS. They suggested economy could be made by the physical division of the S&D between the two companies, or else by merging it into one or other of the companies. If divided physically, the abnormal costs of working the Bath–Evercreech Junction section would not be shared. Merging the line with one company would create maximum economy as it would abolish records for Clearing House divisions.

It was the LMS view that the S&D was more important to the LMS than it was to the SR — for example, carrying coal to the SR at Templecombe and heavy passenger traffic to Bournemouth, so it recommended that an offer be made to the SR for the LMS to take over the S&D.

Mosley wrote a memorandum to J. H. Follows, LMS chief general superintendent, on 27 September 1929, saying that if a physical division was made at Templecombe, the LMS would have a greater portion of mileage: the main line over the Mendips plus the Burnham, Wells and Bridgwater branches, these latter being useless to the LMS with so little traffic on them. He believed there was no advantage in physical division.

At a meeting on 3 October 1929 Morton, of the LMS chief general manager's department, put forward a different perspective. He said that at present the parent companies had an obligation to improve traffic on the joint undertaking, whereas if the S&D was controlled by the LMS, the GWR might demand the transfer of traffic at present passing from the LMS to the West of England via the S&D. For example, LMS traffic from Nottingham to Plymouth was sent via the

S&D and Templecombe due to this obligation, whereas if the obligation was removed, the GWR could ask the LMS to send Plymouth traffic via Bristol and the LMS would lose receipts from Bath to Templecombe.

The LMS decision was to place the S&D under direct operational and commercial control from 1 June 1930. The coaching stock was divided, all locomotives going to the LMS; Highbridge Works was to close and repairs transferred to Derby; management of the line transferred to Birmingham, and the committee's offices at Green Park were closed and the building sold. It is noticeable that in these reports officials showed no enthusiasm for developing the line.

From 1 January 1930 the LMS took over the stock of 80 S&D locomotives, in due course repainting them in its own livery. The SR took responsibility for the track and signalling, civil engineering and accounts. On 1 July 1930, 200 or so S&D coaches were divided between the LMS and SR. Although some of the stock was less than 20 years old, it did not last long with its new owners, probably due to being gas lit. Highbridge Works closed on 30 May 1930, throwing 300 men out of work, which was particularly serious as Highbridge was largely dependent on the railway for employment, and laying off men affected not only the families directly concerned, but also the town's tradesmen. On 1 July 1930 the traffic superintendent's office at Bath was closed and the staff transferred to the LMS which worked the line on behalf of the joint committee. The former traffic superintendent, G. H. Wheeler, was appointed commercial assistant to the SR traffic manager at Waterloo. The S&D Joint Committee continued to consist of three directors from each company.

Despite these economies it was believed that further action could be taken. On 8 January 1931, a joint conference was held of SR and LMS officials and the possibility considered of pooling traffic with the GWR at Joint line stations in competition with the GWR. At a further meeting on 21 May 1931 the possibility was put forward of certain S&D and GWR stations being supervised by one stationmaster and sharing clerical duties and cartage. As economies of the previous year had involved a staff loss of 300 at Highbridge, it was considered best that their own staff, and also the GWR, remained unaware of this investigation, so Messrs J. P. Euington, J. Davies and E. W. Green carried out the survey covertly.

On 15 and 29 July 1931 the three reported and made recommendations regarding stations on the main line of the S&D:

Bath — no change to the existing arrangements.
Midford — as the S&D Midford stationmaster was also in charge of Wellow, and the GWR Limpley Stoke stationmaster in charge of Monkton Combe, no change.
Radstock — the S&D stationmaster supervises traffic from four collieries and canvasses. Propose one stationmaster for GWR and S&D stations.
Midsomer Norton & Welton — S&D stationmaster visits Norton Hill colliery daily and also 'does the town work'. Proposed one stationmaster for S&D and GWR probably saving £230 per annum. GWR cartage was by one motor lorry, while S&D employ a carting agent at an average cost of £20 a month. Proposed amalgamation of carting.
Shepton Mallet — proposed one stationmaster; S&D cartage lorry not fully occupied, so combine cartage.
Evercreech Junction — the station was a regulating point for S&D traffic, the stationmaster responsible for yard working and also supervised Pylle. In view of this, and the distance to the GWR Castle Cary station, there was no advantage in combining.
Cole — Principal traffic was milk from the Co-op at Bruton, and bacon. Until recently milk traffic had exceeded 100 churns per day, but had shrunk to 10 churns. Believed milk tankers would return traffic to S&D. Cartage for S&D and GWR done by same local agent. No advantage in combining stations.

An SR/LMS meeting, 24 September 1931, concluded:

Bath and Midford: recommended no change.
Radstock, Midsomer Norton and Shepton Mallet: possible economy with one stationmaster and joint carting.
Evercreech Junction and Cole: recommended no change.

If traffic was pooled the total estimated saving would be small and it was conceivable under such a scheme that the GWR might carry additional traffic with an allowance for working expenses and this would swallow economies on the S&D without effecting any appreciable saving in train working, or other operating costs. The meeting did not recommend the pooling of traffic to and from GWR and S&D competitive stations.

Some improvements to the line were made in 1933: the junction site at Midford was moved, enabling a higher speed through the station; the curve at Cole was eased, lifting the speed restriction from 25 to 40mph, and the Wimborne branch closed on 18 June 1933 and the rails lifted except at Corfe Mullen where the track was left to give access to Carter's clay siding. The engine shed, turntable and junction signalbox at Wimborne were dismantled.

It was not all doom and gloom. To meet bus competition, halts were opened at places which offered traffic, but insufficient for a full-blown station. On the main line, halts had been opened in 1928/9 at Shoscombe & Single Hill, Stourpaine & Durweston, Charlton Marshall and Corfe Mullen, the SR's Exmouth Junction concrete depot supplying kits of parts for building them.

In the 1930s, with the average worker being given a week's holiday, more and longer through trains were worked from the North and Midlands to the sunny Bournemouth area.

WITH war clouds threatening again, on Sunday, 13 August 1939, 20 empty coaches were taken to Bournemouth in case people needed to be suddenly evacuated, or taken home at the outbreak of war. They were drawn to Bath by Standard Class 2P No 660 from Carnforth shed, and ex-MR Class 3P No 740 from Hellifield.

The beginning of the Second World War saw the withdrawal of the 'Pines Express' and all but one through train, and also the 'Black Fives'. The S&D again proved of the utmost strategic value, carrying ammunition from Bath to Poole, petrol from Avonmouth, coal from the Midlands, cattle from the Midlands to Dorset farms, beer from Burton-on-Trent and timber from Avonmouth to Radstock and Midsomer Norton for shed manufacture. The S&D also brought material for making concrete for tank traps and blockhouses, some of the latter disguised as cow sheds, making a line of defence southwards from Combe Down Tunnel to Evercreech Junction. Rail-mounted guns were kept in Moorewood sidings.

Fortunately, the S&D was largely undamaged by air raids. In May 1941 a high explosive bomb fell at Paglinch Farm, Shoscombe (site of the 1876 Foxcote disaster), severing S&D telephone wires. In the three serious Baedeker raids on Bath, 25/6 April 1942, the locomotive foreman had the foresight to disperse his engines in case the depot received a direct hit. On the second night of the blitz, S&D railwaymen who lived in Oldfield Park took their families, flasks and sandwiches to Devonshire Tunnel. They stood outside until the sirens sounded, then entered. They were aware that normally no trains ran on a Sunday.

Had the line been blocked between Mangotsfield, Bath and Templecombe, arrangements were in place for LMS trains to Bournemouth to run via Yate South Junction, Dr Day's Bridge Junction, Bathampton and Salisbury. LMS engines and men would have worked through, with GWR pilot drivers and guards between Yate and Salisbury, with the SR taking over from there.

Some women were employed on what had hitherto been men's duties. For instance there were two signalwomen at Radstock, one on early and one on late turn.

Italian prisoners-of-war were employed, chiefly on coal stacking: five at Bath from 22 December 1943, five at Templecombe from 28 December 1943, and 16 at Evercreech Junction from 11 April 1944.

The Rev Warren, Rector of Binegar, had nine children. His third son emigrated to Australia to take up farming. Following the outbreak of war, he joined the Australian army and was posted to England. His unit was moved south by S&D and when his train stopped he looked out of the window and down to Binegar Rectory, where he had grown up.

US troops transported across the Atlantic by the *Queen Mary* and *Queen Elizabeth* disembarked at Larne, crossed the Irish Sea and travelled to Bournemouth via the S&D and at 1 o'clock one morning, Bath station was full of Native Americans.

Nationalisation was unhelpful to the S&D. From 2 February 1948 it came under the aegis of the SR, but Bath, in the London Midland Region, was responsible for the locomotives. Then, in January 1950, the S&D north of Cole was placed under the commercial supervision of the WR, but was operated by the SR to which the LMR loaned locomotives. In January 1963 the SR main line between Salisbury and Exeter was transferred to the WR and the S&D north of Blandford placed under WR control. BR's changes completely wrecked the north-south importance of the S&D and it was startling, although not altogether surprising, that all through trains were withdrawn from the S&D on 10 September 1962. The Beeching Report published in March 1963 recommended closure.

On 2 August 1965, engineering work in connection with the Bournemouth electrification

Western and Southern Regions

British Railways Board
Transport Act 1962

Withdrawal of railway passenger services

**BRISTOL — BATH (Green Park) — BOURNEMOUTH
and
HIGHBRIDGE — EVERCREECH JCN.**

**Passenger services will be withdrawn
from the above sections of line on and from**

Left: The closure notice displayed at Shillingstone. *Christopher Steane*

Upper right: The end of the line at Wellow, 2 November 1967: a Ruston Bucyrus on caterpillar tracks is rail lifting. *Author*

Lower right: Isabel (Hawthorn, Leslie 3437 of 1919, 0-6-0ST) at the abortive preservation project, Radstock, May 1972. *R. J. Cannon*

Below: The view from the top of the water softening plant, Bath, on 6 March 1966, the last day of S&D passenger working. The large MR goods shed is at the top of the picture, with Bath Station signalbox in front of it, while left is the coaling plant. 'West Country' Pacific No 34006 *Bude* carries the Locomotive Club of Great Britain 'Somerset & Dorset Rail Tour' headboard. *John Stamp*

required closure of Bournemouth West station so S&D trains were either terminated at Branksome, with a bus link provided to Bournemouth Central, or run to Bournemouth Central. Although closure of the S&D was announced for 3 January 1966, one of the replacement bus operators withdrew, so closure was deferred until 7 March 1966.

Apart from a couple of excursions, DMUs never ran over the S&D and nor did diesel locomotives. A man with a highly responsible position in the Divisional Manager's office, at Bristol, Temple Meads, said that DMUs were banned from the S&D in order not to give any ideas for modernisation, because the WR was anxious to close the route.

5 January 1963, Class 7F 2-8-0 No 53807 piloted by Class 8F 2-8-0 No 48737 reverse ready to haul Class 3F 0-6-0T No 47276 (behind the photographer) out of a drift. A chain is drooped round the buffers and coupling hook. Jack Taylor, head of the permanent way gang, wears a trilby hat. Driver Bill Gunning is on the '7F' and Driver Charlie Hamilton on the '8F'. *John Stamp*

WEATHER sometimes caused the S&D problems. Early on 26 January 1939 an up goods became trapped in a snow drift between Masbury and Binegar. A. H. Whitaker, locomotive superintendent, went out with the plough and it took an hour to clear the up line, but the down was unaffected by snow. This was the first time the plough had been used for seven or eight years. At Masbury snow had drifted level with the platform and the 7.15am ex-Templecombe which should have arrived at Bath at 8.58am was delayed for over an hour. Railway officials thoughtfully telephoned schools, apprising heads of the late arrival of their pupils.

In 1940, the snow was so deep in Masbury cutting that people could walk across the roofs of passenger coaches snowbound there. Snow and ice that year brought down 200 telegraph poles on the S&D and disorganised the block system between Midsomer Norton and Evercreech Junction. In consequence, a series of emergency posts were established and permissive working at five-minute intervals was introduced. The weight of each train was reduced to give engines a greater margin of power. The freezing of points, preventing their operation, necessitated longer runs by bank engines assisting goods train over Masbury Summit before a workable crossover could be reached. In the hard winter of 1947 Masbury cutting was almost snow-free as the wind was in a different direction.

The blizzard of Saturday, 29 December 1963 caused problems. The snow plough was sent out on Sunday the 30th to free the line for the 2.40am 'Mail' on Monday the 31st, but the plough became wedged in a huge drift at Winsor Hill and had to be dug out. Trains were cancelled, but as the down line was fairly clear between Midsomer Norton and Shepton Mallet, it was decided to run the 2.40am 'Mail' and two other freight trains, with single-line working between these stations as much of the up line was covered with snow which had been cleared from the down line. The snow plough piloted the 'Mail', but at 6.03am it became trapped in a drift between Shepton Mallet and Evercreech New. The engines eventually arrived at Evercreech Junction in the late afternoon and the rest of the mail train the following afternoon. The two succeeding freight trains also became snowed up for three days and it was not until a fortnight after the blizzard commenced that double-line working was restored between Bath and Evercreech Junction.

Some S&D personalities and service conditions

R. C. Archbutt was appointed resident locomotive superintendent on 1 October 1913 at a salary of £250 pa. He came from the MR and returned to the Midland Division of the LMS when his SDJR office was terminated. On the S&D he introduced locomotive power classification. He was absent from the S&D when serving with the Railway Operating Division from February 1915 until January 1919.

At Shepton Mallet in January 1963 Fireman Ian Bunnet is on the tank of snow plough-fitted Class 3F 0-6-0T No 47276 (82F Bath). Heat from the 'devil' beyond the water column prevented the water from freezing.
John Stamp

Alfred Colson, son of Thomas Colson, engineer of the Croydon Canal, started work with his brothers as railway contractors and their firm was engaged in the construction of the SCR. After its completion, Alfred joined the SCR engineer's staff and when the line became a joint railway, he was appointed resident engineer.

A. R. Collier who had been employed by the S&D for many years, was appointed its chief accountant in 1913.

Abraham Difford was appointed traffic manager in 1863, but following the head-on crash at Foxcote, he was demoted to goods manager.

Robert Armstrong Dykes had distinguished ancestors. He was the grandson of John Armstrong Dykes who had been connected with the construction of such important works as St Katherine's Dock, London, the Thames Tunnel, and the Menai Bridge, finally becoming engineer to the City of Bristol. R. A. Dykes' father was employed for many years by the Bristol & Gloucester Railway and subsequently by the MR until his departure in 1855 to become chief superintendent of the B&E.

Robert began his railway career as a lad clerk for the MR in 1849 at Bristol, later being attached to the outdoor staff of the Superintendent of the Line at Derby. In 1865 he was appointed S&D traffic manager in succession to Difford whose shortcomings had been revealed by the Foxcote disaster. Dykes retired in 1902.

George Henry Eyre was appointed Superintendent of the Line in 1902, the year that the office accommodation expanded into No 13 Green Park Buildings, adjacent to the existing No 14. He retired on 31 July 1920. In the 18 years he was in charge, no passenger trains were involved in a fatal accident on the S&D.

B. S. Fisher, who came from the Taff Vale Railway, was appointed locomotive superintendent on 27 August 1875 at a salary of £300 pa. An excellent manager, within a month he knew the Christian names of all his staff. In 1876 his salary was raised to £400, and to £450 in November 1881. He was killed on 10 May 1883 when he became trapped between the buffers of goods wagons at Highbridge.

William H. French was appointed resident locomotive superintendent on 17 May 1883 at a salary of £300 pa, having been previously employed by the MR at Leicester. Unhappy at Highbridge, he asked for a transfer back to the MR in 1889, but was refused. He resigned and was believed to have taken a post with the Southampton Docks Company.

H. Leaker, chief accountant, grew up with the S&D and retired in 1913. A. S. Redman succeeded Eyre as Superintendent of the Line in 1920 and held the post until 1922.

M. F. Ryan was appointed locomotive superintendent on 24 July 1911. He came from the District Locomotive Department, Derby, and was responsible for the introduction of the successful class of 2-8-0s. It was through his suggestion that this wheel arrangement was adopted rather than an 0-8-0, since this reduced the weight on the coupled wheels and thus avoided an expensive bridge rebuilding programme, eased running round curves and reduced track wear. Ryan reorganised the boiler shop at Highbridge and instituted the pleasant practice of painting the name of the driver in the cab of his express engine. He resigned on 13 September 1913 on becoming assistant to Robert Urie, the LSWR's locomotive superintendent. Eventually, he became general manager of the Buenos Aires & Pacific Railway.

Driver Andrew Wesley Thomas was the first working man to be appointed a JP. A painting of him was hung on the wall of the Bath Trades & Labour Institute, No 23 Green Park, Bath. (By 2006 it had been 'mislaid'.) Quite a character, at work he wore a top hat and tails and refused to step on his engine until the foreman had the hand rails wiped.

George H. Wheeler took office as traffic superintendent on 2 January 1922. He had entered LSWR service in 1897 and for some time had been employed in various sections of the Superintendent of the Line's office. On the outbreak of the First World War he was transferred to the Military Department dealing with the movement of troops and supplies. In June 1917 he was appointed assistant to Major G. S. Szlumper, secretary to the Railway Executive Committee (REC) and on Major Szlumper's appointment as Docks & Marine Superintendent at Southampton in June 1919 Wheeler became secretary of the REC. In December 1919, following the resignation of the REC, Wheeler was appointed secretary to the Standing Committee of General Managers. He stayed with the S&D until 1 April 1930 when his office was abolished and he was appointed commercial assistant to the SR traffic manager at London Bridge.

Alfred Whitaker's photograph, autographed on the occasion of his retirement, 22 July 1911. *Author's collection*

Alfred W. Whitaker was born in July 1846 at Derby where his father was mayor. Alfred joined the MR in 1860 as a pupil of Matthew Kirtley, locomotive superintendent 1844-1873. On completing his training at Derby, Alfred was appointed initially to locomotive depots at Lancaster and then Bradford before becoming the first district locomotive superintendent at Carlisle when the MR extended there in 1875. He was subsequently appointed to Leeds where he remained until he attained the post of resident locomotive, carriage and wagon superintendent of the S&D on 1 November 1889 at a salary of £375 pa. When he retired on 22 July 1911 at the age of 65, he received 130 birthday cards from the Highbridge Works staff in addition to many gifts. At the farewell ceremony, guards' flags were imaginatively utilised as bunting.

On retirement from the S&D, Whitaker joined the board of directors of Whitwick Colliery, Leicestershire, and served on it for 23 years. He returned temporarily to the S&D from February 1915 to January 1919 as acting locomotive superintendent while R. C. Archbutt was serving with the Railway Operating Division.

Platelayers at Cole *c*1920.
Author's collection

Whitaker died on 5 March 1938, aged 91, at Lancaster Villa, Beechen Cliff, Bath. On 9 March, many former colleagues gathered at Bath Midland station to pay their last respects as his coffin was placed in a van attached to the mail train for transport to Leeds for interment.

On the S&D, Whitaker had been responsible for the rebuilding and modernisation of Highbridge Works and installing new machinery. Of inventive mind, he had several patents to ease railway working, including one dated 25 May 1887 for extension rails hinged to a turn table, counterbalanced and coupled together so one movement brought both extension rails into action. These extension rails, known as 'crocodiles', were used on the MR for many years.

Other patents were for a tender water indicator, an inclined traverser for locomotive workshops avoiding the use of more than one overhead crane, and best known of all, his apparatus for automatic tablet exchange. In addition to being used in Britain, it could also be found in Ireland, India and South America.

When one driver was on the carpet before Alfred for speeding, his excuse was that the faster he ran, the less time there was to come off the road, while another driver before him for making a slight technical slip was told by Alfred what he should have done in the circumstances. The driver paused for a few moments, turned to him and while still walking to the office door replied: ''Tis alright for thee to have foresight afterwards, but thee wasn't there' and so saying, opened the door and left.

When proposing a toast at the annual staff dinner in 1913, Alfred sagely observed that the MR and LSWR were foster parents of the S&D and had done their best to straighten the kinks of the 'child' which had been born with curvature of the spine.

Two other facts about Whitaker: he was churchwarden of St Andrew's, Burnham-on-Sea, and had a complete set of *The Railway Magazine*.

A. H. Whitaker, the son of Alfred, was assistant S&D locomotive superintendent, Bath, before appointment as Bristol District locomotive superintendent. He lived at Perrymead View, Greenway Lane, Bath, overlooking Lyncombe Vale between Devonshire and Combe Down tunnels.

Loyalty to the company, at least for some grades, was encouraged by such annual events as a staff annual dinner and an annual outing. For example, on 28 June 1897 clerical staff from the general offices, wives and friends making a party of 50, left Bath by special train in a saloon. They arrived at Blandford at 10am and were conveyed in a charabanc and brakes to Larmer Grounds where they enjoyed a hot luncheon and a 'substantial tea' before returning to Blandford in a thunderstorm. Bath was reached at 11pm.

The inquest and Board of Trade report of the 1876 Foxcote accident revealed details of S&D staff: Caleb Percy, the crossing agent, was on duty Bank Holiday Monday. He started work at 9am

Staff in front of the S&D offices, 14 Green Park Buildings, Bath, on 15 January 1928 before the accountant's and general manager's office moved to London. *Author's collection*

and would have finished at 11.30pm, but due to the accident, stayed until 5am the next day.

The salary of John Jarrett, stationmaster at Radstock, was £120 pa. The Wellow stationmaster, James Sleep, was paid £1 3s 0d per week. On the day of the accident he was on duty from 5.30am until 6.30pm, leaving the telegraph clerk and signalman in charge.

Signalman Alfred Dando, at Foxcote box, aged 20, was paid 15s per week. Arthur Hillard, telegraph clerk at Wellow, aged 15, was paid 7s 6d a week. He worked from 8am until the passing of the last passenger train which was due at 9.34pm. Like most S&D staff, he had Sundays off. His duties were to take messages and crossing orders and inform engine drivers whether or not to proceed. On the day of the accident he came on duty at 8am and was still on duty at 11pm. He booked passengers when the stationmaster was absent and also helped with luggage.

LMS Home Guard Platoon at Bath LMS station, August 1943. *John Stamp*

Far left: Goods Guard Frank Staddon and right, Goods Guard Jack Lake, at Bath *c*1960. The shunters' poles were usually made of hickory. *R. J. Coles*

Left: S&D accounts office, Green Park Buildings, Bath, late 1920s. Front row: Miss L. Hockey, Tom Chamberlain and back row: Christopher Edwards, Harry Offer and Albert Chamberlain. Note the gas lighting. *Author's collection*

There was no stationmaster at Midford, which was in the charge of booking porter Joseph Morris. He started duty 7am Monday and in consequence of the accident, remained until 10.18pm Tuesday, giving over 39 hours of duty. He was assisted by telegraph clerk Edwin Hues, aged 17, whose normal hours were 7am until the last up passenger train passed at 9.55pm. It was often late, so it was sometimes 10.30pm before he left. On Wednesdays, Thursdays and Saturdays he left at about 5.30pm. He was allowed half an hour for breakfast, half an hour for tea and an hour for dinner.

Alfred Lance, aged 14, telegraph clerk at Chilcompton, was paid 5s per week. He worked from 7.30am to 9.15pm and if the last train arrived late, he was permitted to arrive on duty next morning at 8.30. He was granted two hours daily for meals. As well as looking after the single-needle telegraph, he booked passengers, helped with accounts and sometimes collected tickets. Edward Rhymes, telegraph clerk at Evercreech New, aged 14, was paid 6s per week; he arrived on duty at 7am and left between 9pm and 10pm. He was allowed 1½ hours for meals. He also collected tickets and assisted with luggage when the porter was not on duty. He booked all goods and parcels, but not passengers.

Gilbert Slocombe, aged 21, telegraph clerk at Bath ticket platform, generally worked about a 12-hour day and was paid 18s a week.

The accident also revealed that the S&D cared for relatives of the accident victims, giving jobs on the line to several children whose parents had been killed.

Some drivers were particularly interesting characters. One, named George, was always referred

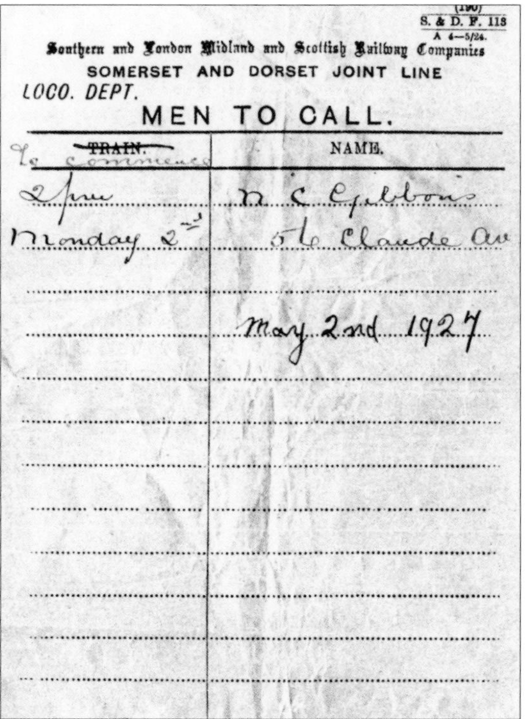

S. & D. F. 118
A 4—5/24.
Southern and London Midland and Scottish Railway Companies
SOMERSET AND DORSET JOINT LINE
LOCO. DEPT.
MEN TO CALL.

~~TRAIN.~~ To commence	NAME.
2 pm	N. C. Gibbons
Monday 2nd	56 Claude Av
	May 2nd 1927

Left: A call boy's instruction card, 2 May 1927. *Author's collection*

Right: S&D staff at Templecombe *c*1918. *Author's collection*

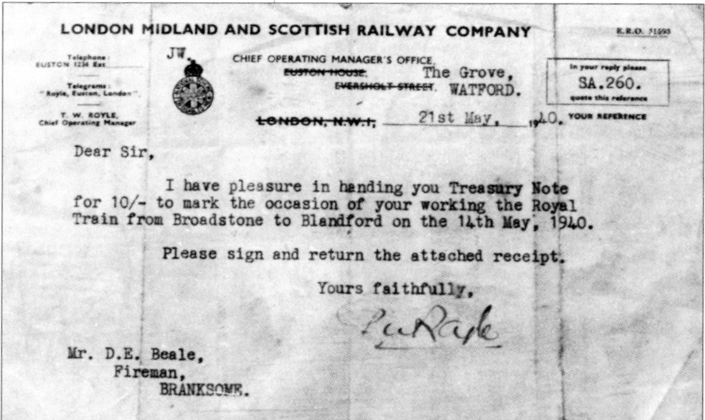

LONDON MIDLAND AND SCOTTISH RAILWAY COMPANY

CHIEF OPERATING MANAGER'S OFFICE,
~~EUSTON HOUSE,~~ The Grove,
~~EVERSHOLT STREET,~~ WATFORD.
~~LONDON, N.W.1,~~ 21st May, 1940.

In your reply please quote this reference SA.260.

T. W. ROYLE, Chief Operating Manager

Dear Sir,

I have pleasure in handing you Treasury Note for 10/- to mark the occasion of your working the Royal Train from Broadstone to Blandford on the 14th May, 1940.

Please sign and return the attached receipt.

Yours faithfully,

T. W. Royle

Mr. D.E. Beale,
Fireman,
BRANKSOME.

Below left: A letter to Fireman Donald Beale, 21 May 1940, from the chief operating manager, T. W. Royle. This payment was a non-taxable gratuity. All LMS letterheads carried the badge seen towards the upper left reading, 'National Scheme for Disabled Men'. This involved the railway in employing not less than 2% of disabled men. *Author's collection*

Southern and L. M. S. Railway Companies'

Somerset and Dorset Joint Line.

WILFUL DAMAGE.

£2 REWARD

The above Reward will be paid to any person giving such information as will lead to the discovery of the person or persons causing damage to the Fittings and Interior of Somerset and Dorset Joint Line Carriages.

BY ORDER.

Above right: An S&D notice. *Author's collection*

to as 'Gossle' for having purchased goslings at Wimborne and carried them home to Templecombe swimming in the tender tank. He always carried a gun on his engine and would shoot any game he saw, stop the train and retrieve it. He drove to Templecombe shed by donkey cart, drove it on the turntable, swung it round, and the donkey would return home by itself. It was said that the donkey was bought at Wimborne, hobbled and carried to Templecombe on the tender.

Tom, of the Bath locomotive department, was knocked over and rendered unconscious. As it was believed he was seriously hurt, the locomotive superintendent was called. He came, and with concern asked: 'What's up, Tom?' There was no reply. 'Just step into my office and bring out a glass of water,' he ordered an employee standing by. With this, Tom moved and spoke: 'The least I expected was a drop of brandy.'

Staff turnover between 20 October 1861 and 28 December 1899: periods of service ranged from 1 day to 57 years 2 months 24 days.

Number who completed:

Less than 1 year	494
1 to 10 years	762
11 to 20 years	139
21 to 30 years	93
31 to 40 years	113
41 to 50 years	182
51 years upwards	25
	1,808

– 2 –

The route: Bath to Bournemouth West

S&D 'Large' 4-4-0 No 69 at Bath *c*1920. The third coach from the front is an LNWR vehicle. Two wheel tappers are at work. *H. J. Patterson Rutherford*

MANY people assume that S&D began at the Midland Railway's Bath terminus, although strictly speaking, the S&D only had running powers over ½ mile of the MR, so its line really started at Bath Junction.

The Midland terminus had a splendid Georgian façade admirably matching Bath's main style of architecture. Opened on 4 August 1869, the platforms proved too short, so the following year they were extended to the river bridge. The platforms held eight bogie coaches on the south side and nine on the north, with a storage road and a runround road between. The platforms were inadequate for 12-coach trains running on summer Saturdays, but there was no economic method to lengthen them, the river bridge preventing any extension at reasonable cost.

Although officially named Queen Square, Bathonians always referred to it as 'The Midland Station', even after 18 June 1951 when BR renamed it Green Park to distinguish it from the former GWR station. As late as 1912, Bathonians still referred to the S&D as the 'new line'.

Leaving the terminus, an S&D train passed the locomotive sheds on the north side of the line and Boat Road leading to a riverside wharf used for rail/water exchange, S&D traffic to Trowbridge using the waterway until the 1920s. The MR goods shed and sidings stood to the south of the main line. West of the locomotive sheds were sidings where S&D goods trains were formed.

At Bath Junction, 41 chains from the terminus, the S&D curved south west from the MR, climbed at 1 in 50 and crossed the Lower Bristol Road directly in front of the Royal Oak by an iron bridge colloquially known, due to its colour, as the 'Red Bridge'. Erected in an incredibly short space of time, the metalwork was provided by the

Worcester Iron Foundry. Beyond was Twerton Viaduct, 74yd in length, with eight brick arches.

Continuing to climb, the line curved round through the suburbs of Bath, engines coating rafters of homes in Bellott's Road with 1½in of fine soot. The S&D crossed the GWR by a three-arch bridge, which in accordance with the Act, consisted of 'a centre opening sufficient for two lines of rails and two side openings, sufficient for one additional line of rails'. The bridge is of brick reinforced with steel girders over the central arch.

At 0 miles 41 chains (from Bath Junction) May's siding opened on 8 April 1890 to serve a brickworks, the name later changing to Bath Victoria Brick & Tile Co. Initially started to provide bricks for building homes in adjacent Oldfield Park, by 1910 the plant was capable of producing 20,000 bricks daily. Fine coal dust arrived at the siding, Radstock coal taken by banking engines making a special trip just to the

Above: Class 2P 4-4-0 No 40568 (71G Bath) leaves Green Park with the 4.25pm to Bournemouth West on 31 May 1954. Coach set No 348 is being used. Class 4F 0-6-0 and another engine stand on the right.
Rev Alan Newman

Right: Class 5 4-6-0 No 73047 crosses the Red Bridge, Lower Bristol Road, Bath *c*1960. The pipe on the side of the bridge carries water from Devonshire Tunnel to the locomotive depot.
John Hobbs

Right: Victoria Brick Works *c*1903; MR wagons in the siding. There is a double-track narrow gauge tramway in the foreground.
Author's collection

siding. Clay chimney pots and tiles were dispatched and occasionally bricks, but most of the latter left by road.

Railwaymen were given free allotments beside the railway, and one S&D guard who had his near the brickworks raised water from there. Suspecting another of stealing his water, he placed weed-killer in his water tank and the neighbour's row of beans died shortly after. When the works closed in September 1939 this source of water ended so he had to persuade drivers of returning banking engines to give him a supply. An engine could not be long about this as a driver would look at his watch and say: 'We'll have to go, we're two minutes late already.' (14 minutes was allowed for Bath Junction back to Bath Junction.)

When Claude Avenue cutting was made through blue lias clay covered with gravel, embedded in the latter was a large quantity of fossils and mammoth tusks. At 0 miles 66 chains was the Bath & Twerton Co-op siding, about 200ft in length on a short, level stretch, opened under a private siding agreement of 25 August 1911. Principal traffic was coal for household use and for the adjacent Co-op bakery, and also flour and salt. *Circa* 1947 if the 9.5am goods required banking from Bath, any vehicles for this siding were placed in front of the banking engine, the vehicles not coupled to the train's brake van. A guard or shunter travelled on the footplate when shunting this siding, and the key on the banking staff opened the ground frame. Rails in the siding were fixed in S&D chairs dated 1895, and the siding was probably last used in November 1967.

At 0 miles 69 chains on the south side of the line was the 200ft, long Bath Ticket Platform where tickets were collected from passengers of up trains, Queen Square being an open station.

In Bloomfield cutting leading to the 447yd-long Devonshire Tunnel, were found bones of a giant elk and also a human skeleton.

Most of the trackbed from the erstwhile Bath Junction to Devonshire Tunnel has become a linear park and a fair proportion of the rest of the S&D is becoming accessible to the public as a footpath.

A unique photograph of the brick-built signalbox which worked the Bath & Twerton Co-op siding opened in 1911. Coal wagons can be seen beyond the gate and the ticket platform was nearby. The fields in the background are now covered with housing. *Author's collection*

Class 4F 0-6-0 No 44096 banks the 12.35pm from Bath to Evercreech Junction towards Devonshire Tunnel on 1 September 1952. Nearly five years after Nationalisation the tender still bears the legend 'LMS'. The sixth wagon from the brake van has a load of overhanging timber so a runner wagon is utilised. *R. E. Toop*

Class 7F 2-8-0 No 53806 emerges from Devonshire Tunnel into Lyncombe Vale with the 12.35pm Bath to Evercreech Junction on 13 November 1954.
R. E. Toop

When Devonshire Tunnel, so named due to its burrowing near the adjacent Devonshire Arms and Devonshire Buildings, was cut through water-bearing oolite, numerous springs were tapped causing problems to nearby householders whose wells ran dry. To obviate this trouble they were granted a replacement piped supply. Using gravity, the S&D piped water from the former household spring issuing 75 gallons per minute, through the tunnel to a receiving tank. Some way in the tunnel on the north side was a door which led to a sump. This water was piped to the locomotive shed at Bath and thus eased the expense of pumping water from the Avon. The tank was 114ft above the locomotive depot and gave a pressure of 49.5lb. Periodically, sandy sludge was cleared out of the tunnel sump on to the ballast and this needed to be watched carefully to ensure it was not washed away.

Devonshire Tunnel has Bath stone portals and is doubly lined throughout. The line emerged, still climbing at 1 in 50, into the rural, picturesque Lyncombe Vale, less than a mile from the city centre, but double that distance by S&D. The arch by Lyncombe House, now the Paragon School, offered an early example of environmental care for '. . . by the aid of turf, plants and other garden accessories, has been made as pleasing an object from the house as a railway bridge, perhaps, could possibly be in the circumstances'. (*Bath Chronicle*)

Banking engines dropped off at the portal of Combe Down Tunnel and generally waited a few moments before returning in order to give some of the fumes in Devonshire Tunnel a chance to clear. In dry weather hot cinders ejected from hard-working engines caught the embankment in Oldfield Park alight, necessitating the fire brigade being called.

The northern portal of Combe Down Tunnel is 300ft below the down. The tunnel has a span of 13ft 6in, a height of 13ft 9in and is 1,829yd in length, being the longest single-bore tunnel in the country without a ventilating shaft. The tunnel is curved at each end and straight in the middle. At one point, about three-quarters of the way through, reflected light from both ends could be seen shining on the walls. The tunnel was cut through oolite so solid that it was initially believed that masonry was only occasionally required, although time proved otherwise and it was eventually brick lined, in some places completely, but others only partly and there were a few lengths of unlined stone. Bricks at the top of the roof arch were almost clean — kept so by the force of the blast. The stratum above the tunnel was fuller's earth and being impervious, stopped water entering the tunnel which was perfectly dry except for about 50yd at its southern end. Mr W. Lean (district engineer for the contractor) said that although having cut many tunnels, he considered Combe Down his pet and claimed there was not a better in England. A room midway on the east side reputedly was used for storing explosives when the tunnel was cut, and used latterly for permanent way purposes.

Just inside the north portal, the gradient changed from level to 1 in 100 down which continued most of the way to Midford. The fumes in the tunnel caused problems, crews having to crouch on the cab floor to get rather fresher air. Sometimes the engine of an up train slipped, drawing the weight of the train back out of the portal it had just entered and it was only on emerging into daylight that a driver knew of the problem!

Ex-S&D 0-6-0s Nos 59 and 60 as Nos 44559/60 emerge from the south portal of Combe Down Tunnel on 21 August 1954, with a Liverpool to Bournemouth West train. *R. E. Toop*

A very early fatal sufferer of exhaust fumes in the tunnel was the Rector of Bath Abbey. On Thursday, 5 August 1874 he caught a train to Binegar to stay with his son at East Harptree about 6 miles distant from that station. Passing through Combe Down Tunnel he experienced difficulty breathing — perhaps it was a hot day and he had omitted to close the windows. He suffered asphyxia and soon after arrival at East Harptree it was considered best to return him to Bath (daringly he returned via the S&D), where he died on 18 November 1874.

Class 2P 4-4-0 No 40509 emerges from the north portal of Combe Down Tunnel with the 2.25pm from Templecombe to Bath on 12 May 1951, and crosses the three-span stone Moger's Bridge. *Author's collection*

Right: Hoist used when widening Tucking Mill Viaduct in brick, *c*1894. *Courtesy BRB(R)*

Far right: Widening Tucking Mill Viaduct *c*1894: a steam travelling-crane is picking up an arch centre using rope, not chains. *Courtesy BRB(R)*

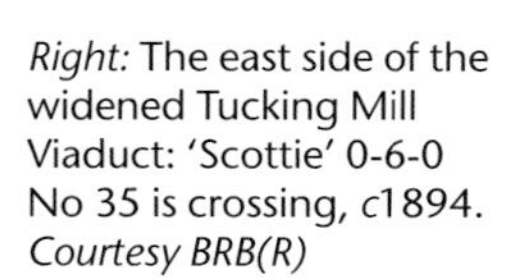

Right: The east side of the widened Tucking Mill Viaduct: 'Scottie' 0-6-0 No 35 is crossing, *c*1894. *Courtesy BRB(R)*

From Combe Down Tunnel the line emerges into a deep cutting, which, because of the steep hillside, within a few yards changes to a lofty embankment. At the end of the cutting, earthworks allowed for a station to be built. One never was — a very wise decision in view of the fact that its users would have had to climb laden with shopping baskets, 300ft up steps and steep paths to the village.

Carrying the line over Midford Ponds is Tucking Mill Viaduct, 96yd in length, 63ft high, its eight arches of 30ft span. In the 1890s it was widened, the original stonework being encased in brick, to take double track, although in the event this was never laid and with hindsight it seems curious that cash was spent on this work. On Park Bank the line skirts the grounds of Midford Castle and the Somerset Coal Canal could be seen many feet below.

Heavy rain on 3 and 4 December 1960 caused a landslip beneath the single line on the Bath side of Midford station. The embankment was rebuilt with stone from Grovesend Quarry, Tytherington, on the Thornbury branch. On Monday, 5th December and until the 10th, the 'Pines Express' was diverted via Salisbury, Bath and Stapleton

Road (Bristol) to regain its normal route at Yate. Radstock temporarily became the terminus for local traffic and brought a stranger, BR Standard Class 3 2-6-2T No 82039. (This echoed the events of 14 May 1951 when an early morning goods derailed between Shillingstone and Blandford damaging the track. The 'Pines Express' and its relief were diverted via Salisbury and the ex-GWR Bath Spa line.) On 22 December 1960, one set of wheels of a ballast wagon was derailed. Ramps were sent out on the banker which left Bath at 2.55am. The work was carried out and it arrived back at Bath at 5.15am. Chargeman H. Hiscox had to report that on the return journey a re-railing ramp had fallen from the engine. A ganger was sent out to search. It was not until the next day that it was located and returned on No 53807 heading an empty ballast train.

Midford station (3 miles 67 chains) was perched dramatically on a ledge cut into the hillside, a rising cliff on one side and a sheer drop on the other, its location making any doubling prohibitively expensive. Unlike other station buildings on the Extension, Midford was in wood. It became an unstaffed halt on 4 February 1964. Due to its precipitous location, there was no room for a goods yard near the passenger platform, but it could boast of two yards. The one to the north had its two sidings worked from Midford 'A' ground frame and was shunted by down trains after the key had unlocked the ground frame. This yard had a corrugated iron goods shed. Opened on 21 December 1894, it dealt with outwards, farm machinery using specialist railway wagons on existing wagon chassis, fuller's earth, sugar beet and other farm traffic. Inwards it received pit props for the earthworks, coal and, in the Second World War, boxes of ammunition for quarry storage. Between the yard and the station, the line passed below Tucking Mill Lane very obliquely through the tunnel-like 37yd, long Long Arch Bridge. Unusually, Midford Down Home and a backing signal were actually on this bridge. It is said that on Midford platform, behind a door in the gentlemen's toilet, was a 'fortified point' where guns and ammunition were stored in the Second World War and in the event of invasion would have commanded the valley towards Monkton Combe.

Immediately beyond the passenger platform was Midford Viaduct, 168yd in length, whose eight arches of 50ft span crossed the B3110, the Somerset Coal Canal, the GWR Limpley Stoke to Hallatrow branch, and the Cam Brook. The loftiest arch was 55ft high. In an agreement with landowner Gore Langton, the Midford to Wellow lane was diverted beside the viaduct and a new road built together with a new bridge spanning the Somerset Coal Canal.

From 28 August 1892 double track began at the down end of the platform, but from 9 April 1933 it was reduced to single track over the viaduct, double track beginning on the far side. This alteration enabled higher speeds to be run through the station, thus making climbing Park Bank that much more easy, and it also saved

Tucking Mill Viaduct *c*1894 after widening. The contractor's narrow gauge track is still in place to the right of the standard gauge. *Courtesy BRB(R)*

Class 4 4-6-0 No 75009 and Class 5 4-6-0 No 73051 pass Midford goods yard with a 12-coach down 'Pines Express' on 11 April 1962. *E. T. Gill*

'West Country' class Pacific No 34042 *Dorchester* north of Wellow with a semi-fast from Bournemouth West, 2 May 1953. *R. E. Toop*

maintenance of about 170yd of track. About a third of the S&D main line was single track and where the line was doubled, it was generally on a steep gradient. Two-thirds across the viaduct the gradient changed from 1 in 330 down to five-eighths of a mile at 1 in 60 up. Beyond the end of the viaduct was Midford 'B' ground frame controlling access from the up line to a single siding. The yard gate was interlocked with the points.

Between Midford and Radstock the line followed the route of the horse-worked tramway built on the Radstock arm of the Somerset Coal Canal, the tramway being sold to the S&D under its Act of Parliament. This was fortuitous for the canal company as by 1866 the tramway was 'not used by Radstock Collieries at all, and not much by any other' (McMurtrie's evidence on the Bristol & North Somerset Railway Bill), so the canal was being paid for something virtually useless. In parts the tramway was too sinuous to follow so the S&D made short cuts, but even so it was curvaceous and in later years flange oilers were frequent.

Bridge No 20, Twinhoe Bridge, is an interesting construction. It consists of two bridges set at an angle to each other: the original bridge on the up side being of stone and brick, while that carrying the down road is solely brick.

Before Wellow station (6 miles 20 chains) was a viaduct of four 30ft arches and between this and the station there was a siding where fuller's earth, farm machinery and wheelbarrows were loaded. The goods yard was at the other end of the station. The station building at Wellow, like all the others on the Extension except Midford, had blue lias walls with Bath or Doulting stone dressings and slated roof. The platform canopy had a Vandyked valance. The building contained a bay-windowed stationmaster's office, combined booking hall and waiting room, and a ladies' room. The platform was covered with gravel edged with two courses of blue bricks, the outer being rounded. Latterly, Wellow station was still well used as the village was served only by a weekly bus.

An S&DJR 0-6-0 enters Wellow with a down train *c*1910. The first vehicle appears to be an MR through coach. Porters on both platforms roll milk churns.
M. J. Tozer collection

Shoscombe & Single Hill Halt (8 miles 5 chains), a concrete construction, was officially opened on 21 September 1929 by the Rt Hon George Lansbury, a Labour MP and First Commissioner of Works. Public opening was on Monday the 23rd. As early as July 1874 the *Bath Chronicle* commented that Single Hill 'appears almost to deserve a station'. Petitions were made over many years, but one in January 1929 finally proved successful. George H. Wheeler, superintendent of the line when the halt was opened, said that the journey to Bath would take 22 minutes and he hoped local people would show their appreciation by using the halt as much as possible. He added that as far as possible local labour had been employed in its construction. Hubert Latcham was placed in charge of the halt, although for most of its 37-year life it was staffed by two sisters living in a railway bungalow. There were no shelters on the platforms, but one was provided by the lane adjacent to the office. Beyond was the 53yd-long Home Farm Viaduct. A nearby 36ft-deep cutting through blue, greasy, slippery clay caused the contractors trouble.

The first of the Radstock collieries was near Foxcote signalbox which was opened in May 1875, and where a siding served Braysdown Colliery on a hill to the north of the line, linked by a 2ft 6in gauge tramway. The colliery closed on 29 October 1959 and the sidings were taken out of use on 13 April 1962. When the line was doubled on 1 July 1894 the new signalbox was called Writhlington. Writhlington Colliery on the south side of the line remained open until 28 September 1973, the last train running on 16 November that year.

Shoscombe & Single Hill Halt: the view up in February 1966.
Christopher Steane

Just prior to Tyning Bridge, nicknamed 'Marble Arch', Ludlow's Wagon Works were to the south, while beyond were extensive sidings, engine shed, Radstock Coal Co wagon shops and a siding to Radstock Co-op bakery. 'Marble Arch' had a height of only 10ft 10in. One day a signalwoman argued with a guard for 'wasting time' when he suggested she could not shunt his train into Marble Arch siding, but should divide it between various sidings. She was quite unaware that box vans and high-sided coke wagons would foul the arch. Another guard who had an SR

Above left: Tyning bridges, Radstock *c*1894, shortly after the completion of track doubling. The low 'Marble Arch' is right, adjacent to Radstock East signalbox. *Author's collection*

Above right: At Radstock *c*1898 is special low-height goods brake van No 197 for passing through the 'Marble Arch'. *Author's collection*

brake van on the Arch road, had not screwed down the brake tightly and when wagons were shunted against it, it was pushed through the arch. A special low-height S&D brake van could pass through.

Radstock received a variety of goods traffic: buffers and springs for the two wagon repair shops; the Co-op received comestibles such as jam, vinegar, sugar and flour. Unloading these was a dirty job — porters needed old clothes for this as jam and flour went all over them.

Radstock (10 miles 11 chains) was renamed Radstock North on 26 September 1949 to distinguish it from the former GWR station alongside and renamed Radstock West on the same date. To the west of both stations was a pair of level crossings. To avoid the S&D crossing, a pedestrian subway was provided. On 24 November 1877 it became flooded to a depth of about 5ft and in the darkness two people had narrow escapes from drowning. A lady walking down the steps fell into the water and was rescued while a Mr Gulliford, seeing the gates closed, went down the steps, fell into the water and cried for help. In due course assistance arrived and he was pulled out exhausted.

Until the arrival of the S&D there was no rail connection to Radstock gas works, but following the line's opening, a standard gauge siding was laid from the Clandown branch. This branch served Middle Pit, Old Pit (facetiously termed

Right: The level crossing and Radstock North signalbox *circa* February 1966. Notice the gas lamp, left. *Christopher Steane*

A view of Radstock *c*1910: the Clandown branch curves left, the S&D line is centre, while the GWR's Frome to Bristol branch is right. *M. J. Tozer collection*

'Lord Chatham') and beyond the level crossing, which marked the end of the 44 chains of the S&D line, it continued up to Clandown Colliery, the branch some ¾ mile in length. Clandown Colliery closed on 11 November 1929 and Middle Pit in June 1933, but the branch continued to be used by the Anglo-American Asphalt Co. Disused after 1955, it was taken out of use on 5 February 1961.

Following closure of the S&D, a new chord line was opened west of the stations to enable Writhlington coal to be taken away via the former Bristol & North Somerset Railway (BNSR). The last rail movement over this chord was on 16 October 1975.

The gradient of 1 in 50 up resumed beyond this junction and an embankment 40ft high crossed Welton Bottom. North Somerset Viaduct, 128yd of five masonry and brick arches, crossed the BNSR and a colliery tramway. One day, in 1881, an S&D stone mason repairing this viaduct was ordered not to work above the BNSR as this would be an act of trespass.

Approaching Midsomer Norton station a branch came in from Norton Hill Colliery which had its own locomotive until closure on 12 February 1966. Midsomer Norton (12 miles 1 chain) was an extremely picturesque station, famous for its prize gardens and lawns. *Circa* 1902 the signalman grew a climbing rose round his box and up an adjoining telegraph pole and sold rosebuds in aid of the Royal United Hospital, Bath. Timber arrived for Pratten's which normally made sheds and greenhouses, but manufactured ammunition boxes during the Second World War. Gunpowder arrived for Casswell's, ironmongers, who supplied some of the quarries. For safety, a gunpowder van had to be marshalled at least six wagons from an engine. Rolls of paper arrived for making cheque books and bags.

The S&D–BNSR link in operation, spring 1966. The view is towards Radstock North as a shunter works Radstock West ground frame. *Christopher Steane*

The line went through Chilcompton cutting 44ft deep and almost half a mile in length, followed by the 61yd-long twin-bore Chilcompton Tunnel. The gradient eased from 1 in 50 to 1 in 300 through Chilcompton (13 miles 79 chains). The station was particularly busy at the beginning and end of term at Downside School when a special train was run from or to London via Templecombe, but this ceased after 1950. Members of Downside monastery also travelled by train to parishes all over England, particularly the Midlands and the North West. In the late 1870s the monastery made a new drive giving better

Right: A BR Standard Class 4 2-6-4T crosses 'Five Arches' with an up S&D train *c*1966. The GWR fixed distant signal for Radstock West is on the left. *Christopher Steane*

Above: BR Standard Class 5 4-6-0 No 73001 approaches Midsomer Norton with the 09.50 from Bath to Bournemouth Central on 5 October 1965, Bournemouth West having closed the previous day. *Rev. Alan Newman*

Right: Shortly after general overhaul, NCB 0-6-0ST shunter *Lord Salisbury* (Peckett 1041 of 1906) at Norton Hill Colliery on 8 September 1953. At one time this engine shunted at Coalpit Heath Colliery, north-east of Bristol. *Rev Alan Newman*

An 0-6-0 stands on the up line at Midsomer Norton & Welton *c*1900. The goods sidings are on the right. *Author's collection*

A pair of Class 2P 4-4-0s, Nos 40698 (71G, Bath) and 40601, climb through Midsomer Norton with the return working of the Ian Allan 'Trains Illustrated' excursion from Bath to Waterloo, 25 April 1954. *Rev Alan Newman*

Class 3F 0-6-0T No 47557 shunts on the goods shed road, Midsomer Norton. The goods guard raises his left hand signalling the driver to stop. He will then uncouple the wagons to be left in the shed for unloading. *R. E. Toop*

Above: Class 7F 2-8-0 No 53806 climbs the 1 in 53 between Midsomer Norton and Chilcompton, banked by Class 3F 0-6-0T No 47465. *R. E. Toop*

Right: 'Large' 4-4-0 No 71 leaves Chilcompton with an up train. *Author's collection*

Class 2P 4-4-0 No 40700 and BR Standard Class 5 4-6-0 No 73052 descending past Moorewood sidings with an up express, 19 June 1954.
The gradient post marks the change from 1 in 158 to 1 in 55. *R. E. Toop*

access to the station, which at one time was named 'Chilcompton for Downside'. The school's films arrived weekly as did Friday's fish from Grimsby. The station had water columns and from 9 November 1926 the stationmaster was responsible for the daily starting of the petrol-driven waterpump. Beyond the goods shed and sidings were those belonging to New Rock Colliery. Coal was brought ½ mile by road and tipped into a loading chute.

At Moorewood Sidings (15 miles 15 chains), engines and firemen enjoyed a brief respite from a rising gradient of 1 in 50. It was a busy place. On the down side were Moorewood colliery sidings, which until 1937, had coal brought to them by a 2ft gauge locomotive-worked tramway. From about 1930 output was insufficient for the tramway to be economic and it was replaced by a lorry. The standard gauge sidings were also used for stone traffic, the mineral transferred from quarry by aerial ropeway. On the up side a siding served a brick and tile works and also a fuller's earth and ochre works, the latter's quarry acquired by the Emborough Stone Co (later Roads Reconstruction Ltd). From 1914, access to these sidings was made by Moorewood signalbox opened in 1914, the last S&D box to be built. Locomotives were banned from entering the quarry sidings, so wagons were given a sharp push below the screens to enable quarrymen to let them roll back under the screens by gravity.

The line climbed at 1 in 67 across Nettlebridge Viaduct, 87yd in length with seven 30ft span arches. Before Binegar (16 miles 44 chains) stone sidings branched from the down line, while beyond the station was the large shed to which, from 1904 to 1921, a 2ft 6in gauge locomotive-worked tramway brought 'Invalid Stout' from Oakhill Brewery. Beer traffic from Binegar, Shepton Mallet and Blandford was carried in five-plank high-sided wagons with sheet support. Before the First World War the brewery had an output of 2,000-2,500 barrels weekly, but traffic declined in postwar years. Calf traffic for

Oakhill and a train of two bogie wagons cross Binegar Bottom Viaduct *c*1910.
M. J. Tozer collection

Peckett 1021 of 1904, 0-4-0ST *Oakhill* working a train of bogie wagons on the 2ft 6in gauge Oakhill Brewery Railway. The centre-door wagons have a hoop at each end to support a sheet and prevent it being damaged by the edges of the barrels.
M. J. Tozer collection

Bagnall 1701 of 1903, 0-4-0ST *Mendip* at Oakhill Brewery *c*1910 with centre buffers and the couplings below.
M. J. Tozer collection

Above: S&D five-plank high-sided wagon No 141 with sheet bar to support a tarpaulin, *c*1904. This type of wagon was used for Oakhill Brewery traffic. Brake blocks and lever are on one side only.
Author's collection

Class 7F 2-8-0 No 53808 approaches Masbury Summit with a down express, 28 July 1962. *R. E. Toop*

Scotland left the station, often in a calf box branded 'Return to Binegar'. Lime was brought to the station on an old Ford lorry and loaded into a wagon which required to be sheeted and roped. The staff were not keen on this traffic as lime caused their hands to chap with deep cracks. Lead, destined for Bristol, came by road from Priddy. From 1929, banking engines collected a key from the Whitaker tablet apparatus, this enabling them to return 'wrong line' to Binegar after assisting a train to Masbury Summit.

The line climbed at 1 in 63/73 from Binegar to a summit at the end of an eight-mile ascent from Radstock, 811ft above sea level in a cutting 40ft deep where there were about 40yd of level track before the descent at 1 in 50 to Shepton Mallet.

Passing over the summit the guard felt a tug as descending wagons pulled his van strongly. He waved a hand, or white light at night so that the driver would know that the complete train was on the down gradient. The guard always applied his brake before reaching the summit because some of the wagons ahead were already descending. Until the early 20th century the S&D used two 10 ton brake vans. A brakesman travelled in the inside van and the goods guard in that at the rear. The brakesman carried out shunting operations while the guard did the paperwork.

Masbury (18 miles 10 chains) in grey stone was of different design to other Extension stations; also the down platform was unusually wide. The station was originally to be called 'Dinder', but due to a wish expressed by Mr Lovell, a large landowner living nearby, it was called Masbury. The bay-windowed stationmaster's house displayed Lovell's coat of arms. The station became a halt when staff was withdrawn on 26 September 1938.

BR Standard Class 4 4-6-0 No 75009 and Class 9F 2-10-0 No 92223 pass Masbury Halt with the up 'Pines Express', 2 August 1962. *E. T. Gill*

At one time Masbury had an ardent Wesleyan stationmaster who held Sunday services in the waiting room. The congregation of 30-40 was accompanied by a harmonium. The station, only 3½ miles from Wells, took a share of traffic for that city. When coming from the north it was far quicker getting off at Masbury and travelling by road, rather than changing at Evercreech Junction and then at Glastonbury — making a rail distance of 22¾ miles. A stone crushing firm, Mendipadam, a subsidiary of the Emborough Stone Co, had a siding at the station, while War Department sidings were laid *c*1929 serving petrol tanks both above and below the surface. After the Dunkirk evacuation, when German invasion was expected, it was believed that to prevent an enemy landing, eight trains of petrol would be taken to Poole, the fuel floated on the water and ignited. Before D-Day the site was taken over by the US Army.

The line crossed Hamwood Viaduct, 72yd in length, with five arches 69ft high and of 35ft span over a very picturesque wooded ravine. Beyond, from 1845 until 1940, were Winsor Hill Quarry sidings on the east side and Hamwood Quarry siding, 1893-1940, on the west. Admission to the sidings was by Winsor Hill signalbox which closed on 3 August 1948.

There were two Winsor Hill tunnels: that on the down side being the original and 239yd in length and that on the up line opened on 20 November 1892, and 126yd long. The down tunnel was originally unlined except for short arches where the rock was unsound, but the up tunnel was lined throughout. The down tunnel was the site of a considerable slaughter of cattle which had broken through a lineside fence and taken shelter from a very violent storm. Driver George Darke on the 1.20am goods from Bath never forgot his experience. 250yd beyond the exit portal of the down tunnel was Downside Quarry siding used from 1900 until 1940 and worked from a ground frame, the key electrically released from Winsor Hill signalbox.

The approach to Shepton Mallet was across Bath Road Viaduct, 118yd with six arches, the largest being of 50ft span and 62ft high. When the line was doubled, a second viaduct was built abutting the original, but the two were not physically joined. Engineers were worried by slight movement between the two sections and on 29 January 1946 the shift was sufficient to cause such concern that the newer section was closed to traffic. Action was just taken in time, for at 10.55pm on 1 February 1946 people living nearby heard weird sounds, some evacuating their homes clad only in night attire. In a series of crashes 500 tons of masonry from two arches fell to the road. Two further arches deemed unsafe were also demolished.

A view of the north portal of Winsor Hill Tunnel *c*1891. The original tunnel centre, the new down tunnel is to the right of the signalbox. The timber-built signalbox opened in 1875, ceased to be a block post on 1 January 1887 and was replaced by a new stone-built box on 2 November 1892. The stone quarry siding is on the left. *Courtesy BRB(R)*

Widening Bath Road Viaduct, Shepton Mallet *c*1892. *Courtesy BRB(R)*

Bath Road Viaduct following its partial collapse on 2 February 1946, with suspended track still in situ. Trains continued to use the standing half. *Author's collection*

1966 view of the 22-arch Charlton Road Viaduct. The change in gradient is noticeable. *Christopher Steane*

Frank Staddon was the guard on the first train to pass over the viaduct after part of it fell. He was in a three-coach empty coaching stock set going to pick up men who had been working on the viaduct. As the train crossed over at about 2mph, bits of ballast fell. The SR inspector, who believed the rest of the structure safe, had the courage of his convictions to travel across on the footplate.

The trouble was caused by the hastily-built arches for the line's doubling having become waterlogged and disintegrated from top to bottom by frost action. While the fallen arches were rebuilt in mass concrete with brindle brick facing, all traffic used the original line which reverted to single-line working. The line reopened on 1 August 1946 just in time for the heavy Bank Holiday traffic.

Beyond Bath Road Viaduct was the curved Charlton Viaduct, 308yd long, the S&D's most impressive structure: 27 arches of 30ft span and almost 50ft high. On it the gradient falls at 1 in 55, eases to 1 in 130 and midway changes to 1 in 66 up.

Shepton Mallet (21 miles 27 chains) had 'Charlton Road' added to its title in October 1883 to distinguish it from the GWR's 'Town Street', later 'High Street' station. Apart from passenger traffic, the S&D station was important for the nearby bacon factory, lime works, two breweries, a quarry for track ballast and, until 1930, the S&D signal works was on the down side. Water was pumped from a deep well.

South of the station the GWR's Witham to Yatton line crossed the S&D, the overbridge above the original, later down, line, being of brick and the newer up line, opened 6 February 1888, crossed by steel girders. The S&D line climbed to a summit at Cannard's Grave in a cutting 45ft deep where, unfortunately, excavation in 1887, preparing for doubling, destroyed the remains of a substantial Roman building. The descent at 1 in 50 to Evercreech New crossed the 121yd-long Prestleigh Viaduct of 11 arches.

Evercreech New (24 miles 31 chains) had a goods shed on the down side and a lime and stone siding on the up. To work traffic in and out of the goods shed siding, a raft of wagons had to be long enough to prevent the engine descending a steep slope. Evercreech New station was sited much more conveniently for the village than the original station, renamed Evercreech Junction on opening the line to Bath. The signalbox burnt down in October 1918 was not rebuilt until January 1920, a temporary ground frame being used during the intervening months. Between Evercreech New and Evercreech Junction the line crossed Pecking Mill Viaduct, 60yd long with five brick arches and a cast-iron deck over the A371. The Extension joined the Burnham line at Evercreech Junction North.

At Evercreech Junction (25 miles 73 chains) extensive sidings were laid on the up side between the passenger station and Evercreech Junction North, while more sidings were laid beside the Burnham branch. At the north end of the middle siding near Evercreech Junction North signalbox, the buffer stop was fitted with a three-link coupling to prevent vehicles standing in the siding from running down the 1 in 100 gradient. North of the passenger platforms was a Jewish slaughterhouse where daily traffic in kosher meat was sent to London markets in specially modified meat vans. From 1898 the Somerset Brick & Tile Co used a private siding.

Class 7F 2-8-0 No 53803 heads a down freight at Shepton Mallet in January 1955. *John Stamp*

Class 2 2-6-2T No 41307 and BR Standard Class 4 2-6-4T No 80138 call at Evercreech New on the last day of passenger working, 5 March 1966. *E. T. Gill*

Above: Class 5 4-6-0 No 73052 with a down train takes water at Evercreech Junction.
R. E. Toop

Right: Class 4 0-6-0 No 44235 at Evercreech Junction North with a down train as seen from the signalbox. The locomotive inspection pit and line of ashes from firebox cleaning are to the left of the stop block.
T. J. Saunders

Class 7F 2-8-0 No 13809 at Evercreech Junction. The siding between the up and down roads was used for holding pilot engines to assist trains over the Mendips. *M. F. Yarwood, Colin Roberts collection*

Ex-S&D No 60 as BR Class 4 0-6-0 No 44560 minus its shed plate shunts at Evercreech Junction, 28 June 1963. *Rev Alan Newman*

S&D meat van No 1203 c1904. *Author's collection*

BR Standard Class 4 4-6-0 No 75072 with an up freight crosses the main WR line to the West; the eleventh wagon is on the bridge. *R. E. Toop*

In 1913, monthly traffic at the station averaged 2,000 passengers, 1,300 tons of goods and coal, and 300 parcels. Milk was the principal traffic. A two-horse delivery van ran to Castle Cary. Evercreech Junction was manned by 24 staff in addition to the stationmaster. Six sets of enginemen covered 24 hours a day, three sets covering the down sidings and three the up: 6am–2pm; 2pm–10pm; 10pm–6am. The engines were allocated to Highbridge and changed daily with the 7.15am and 12.15pm goods. At weekends the engines were taken to Templecombe for stabling by Evercreech men working the late shift and then travelling back home. On Monday morning two sets of men rode on the 2.40am ex-Bath 'Mail Goods' and returned the engines to Evercreech Junction for shunting.

The first batch of '7Fs' with 48ft 11¼in wheelbase could just fit on the 50ft turntable, but the 56ft diameter table brought into use on 9 November 1922 allowed the later series with 50ft 1in wheelbase to be turned. They could be pushed round easily, but a Class 5 4-6-0 with 53ft wheelbase would only just fit and to get the correct balance, the front bogie wheels needed to be very close to the edge. Despite the fact that there was a length of rail beyond the table, some drivers were very nervous and failed to go on far enough. Consequently when they started to push the engine round, being unbalanced it halted. Although it was then dangerous to move the engine because a misjudgement could cause it to fall into the pit, a driver was forced to move it to get it balanced. When an engine was accurately balanced it could be pushed round with one hand.

Evercreech Junction was a draughty place to wait while changing trains, although latterly the waiting room was made pleasant with flowers, magazines and a fire in season. One man and his wife decided to walk the round trip of six miles to Castle Cary and back between trains.

Until the arrival of electricity on 21 June 1942, the locomotive department employed a water pumping engineman for the pump house about ½ mile south of the station on the banks of the tiny River Alham, the depth of which was controlled by mill owners who sometimes kept water back for their convenience. Evercreech Junction water tank had a capacity of 23,000 gallons. The two pumpers worked 12 hours each and latterly only one pumper was employed. He had a large family so to help feed them he laid down 'wires' to snare rabbits on the railway embankment. On at least one occasion a driver raided the wires, paunched the rabbit and left the remains in the snare. As no coal siding was provided, this was unloaded directly from the main line.

From Evercreech Junction southwards gradients were undulating and generally of short duration, though changes were frequent and quite a few were 1 in 100 or even steeper. At 2½ miles south of Evercreech Junction the S&D crossed the GWR's

Left: BR Standard Class 4 2-6-0 No 76065 working the 1.10pm from Bournemouth West to Bath on 28 October 1961 crosses the ex-GWR Westbury to Taunton line at Cole. *Author*

Left: Class 1P 0-4-4T No 1370 heads a Templecombe to Burnham-on-Sea train 3 June 1939, with part of the five-span Cole Viaduct visible on the right. *M. F. Yarwood, Colin Roberts collection*

Below: Class 1P 0-4-4T No 58086 (71J, Highbridge), with 'British Railways' spelt out on its side tanks, leaves Cole with a down train, 1954. *W. Vaughan-Jenkins*

Class 4F 0-6-0 No 44102 (82G, Templecombe) at Wincanton with an up train *c*1960.
Lens of Sutton

Frome to Castle Cary line. A spur was built giving access from Evercreech to the up GWR line, but this was never brought into use and was removed in 1878. The bridge was built by the DCR.

The five-span, 62yd-long Cole Viaduct was north of the Cole for Bruton station (28 miles 55 chains) of typical DCR design with high gables and tall chimneys. The signalbox was similar to those found on the LSWR. It is said that the S&D operated the first road/rail milk tank from Cole. The tank travelled to local farms collecting milk and was then placed on the milk train for Vauxhall. Four tankers were used: one collecting; one travelling home empty; one under washout; one unloading at the factory.

South of the station the three-arch Pitcombe Viaduct was crossed before the line reached Wincanton (32 miles 76 chains), which was lit by gas from its opening in 1862. In addition to regular traffic, races brought passengers and horse boxes, while two milk factories adjoined the station. A Cow & Gate siding was added to the goods yard in 1933 from where milk powder and dairy products were dispatched.

Wincanton: the view up on 4 May 1963, showing the staggered platforms. The original timber bridge has been replaced by a structure from the SR's Exmouth Junction concrete works. The platform edges are well whitened.
Author

Class 4 4-6-0 No 75073 heads a down train through Templecombe Lower *c*1965. *Christopher Steane*

Templecombe (36 miles 47 chains) — the name comes from the Knights Templars who had their home there — was complicated in both layout and history.

The original junction with the LSWR was only at the east end of the spur which connected with a short LSWR loop siding off the up line. Opened in November 1861, it closed in March 1870 and a stop block was inserted. When the through Burnham to Poole service started in September 1863 trains called at the S&D's lower station, the LSWR working a shuttle service from the lower to the upper station via this spur. On 1 February 1867 most S&D trains ran to the LSWR station using the LSWR up line in both directions. In March 1870, the west loop was opened giving the S&D direct access to the north face of the LSWR up platform. Until the end of the 1870s most S&D trains called at the lower station as well as the upper, but by the end of the decade, the lower station was almost disused. After 1870, trains from the upper station to Poole backed to No 2 Junction, proceeded to No 1 Junction and then reversed to the lower station before going onward to Poole. Except in the very early years, for safety reasons an additional engine was required so that there was always a locomotive at the leading end. The 7.15am passenger from Templecombe, the first train of the day, was for both Bath and Bournemouth. Like other passenger trains using the station it had an engine fore and aft, but on reaching Templecombe No 2 Junction the train was divided, some coaches running north and the others south. The lower station closed on 17 January 1887 and was replaced by Templecombe Lower Platform on the opposite side of the track and nearer the LSWR overbridge.

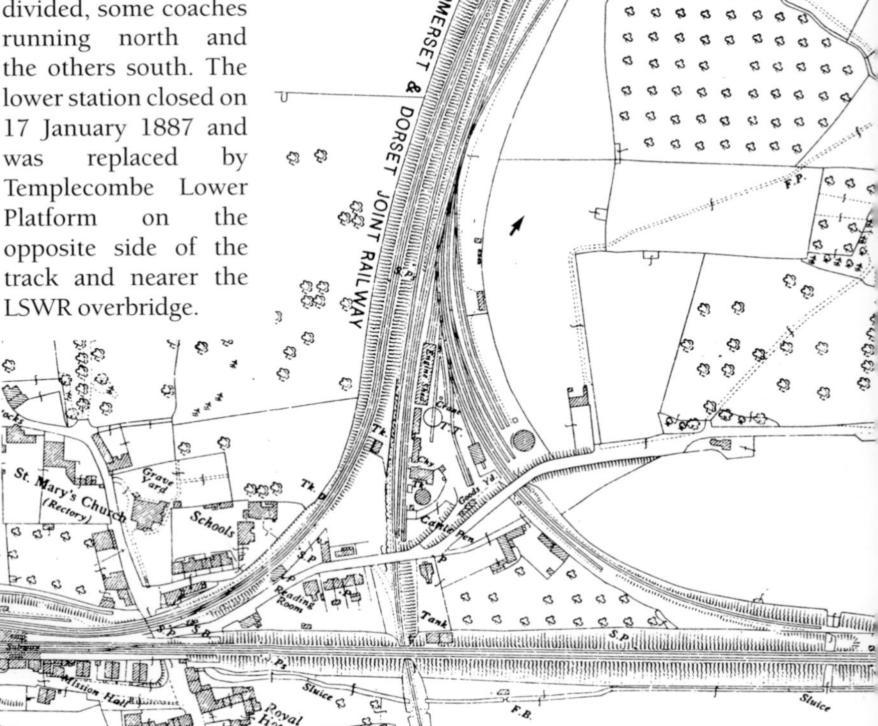

Templecombe from a 1930 survey.

On 5 August 1963 Ivatt Class 2 2-6-2T No 41296, having coupled to the rear of the 3.40pm from Bournemouth West to Bath, hauls it to Templecombe Upper station past Templecombe Junction signalbox. A 'falling man'-type tablet catcher is prominent in the right foreground. *S. P. Derek*

Templecombe Upper station, although owned by the LSWR, was largely treated as joint property. The two LSWR main platforms, 653ft long, were linked by subway. The up platform was an island, the outer face 643ft in length used by the S&D. Two S&D trains could use it at one time, thanks to a 'calling-on' arm. Templecombe was an important exchange for goods and passengers and it was not unknown for the station to deal with six trains at once. Several LSWR stopping trains ran to Templecombe and connected with fast trains. On arrival these slower trains decanted passengers who wished to change, the train then being placed in a siding and eventually following the fast train. Other traffic of consequence included pigeon specials, an example being a 22-vehicle train on 11 May 1963.

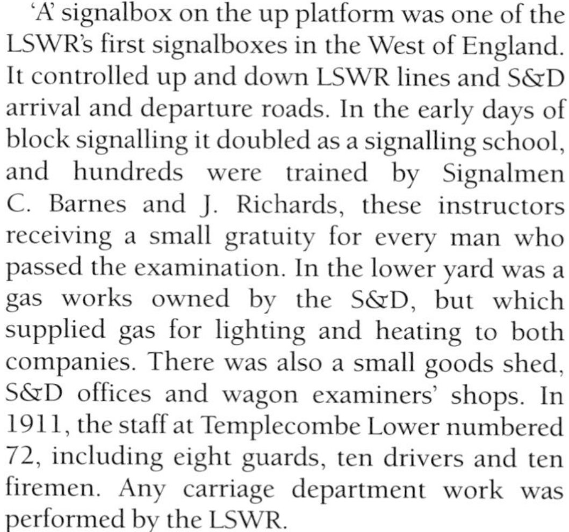

'A' signalbox on the up platform was one of the LSWR's first signalboxes in the West of England. It controlled up and down LSWR lines and S&D arrival and departure roads. In the early days of block signalling it doubled as a signalling school, and hundreds were trained by Signalmen C. Barnes and J. Richards, these instructors receiving a small gratuity for every man who passed the examination. In the lower yard was a gas works owned by the S&D, but which supplied gas for lighting and heating to both companies. There was also a small goods shed, S&D offices and wagon examiners' shops. In 1911, the staff at Templecombe Lower numbered 72, including eight guards, ten drivers and ten firemen. Any carriage department work was performed by the LSWR.

Water was a problem and had it been more freely available, more trains may have terminated there. The S&D had small wells in the Lower Yard and also took 70,000 to 80,000 gallons of water weekly in winter when the LSWR supply was plentiful, but this was not possible in times of low rainfall. Travelling tanks made from old

Having reversed out of Templecombe Upper along the road on the left, BR Standard Class 4 2-6-4T No 80085, minus shed plate and smokebox number plate, proceeds to Bournemouth Central, 28 February 1966. *Rev Alan Newman*

Upper right: 'Scottie' 0-6-0 No 35 at Templecombe Upper *c*1900. Notice the signalman's observation catwalk and the footplate crew resting against the tender, chatting. *Author's collection*

Lower right: Class 7F 2-8-0 No 53800 and Class 2 2-6-2T No 41296 at Templecombe shed. An air-smoothed Pacific heads a down train to Bournemouth West while a short freight seems to be setting off northwards. The fence posts in the foreground are economically made from old rail. *R. E. Toop*

Above: Class 4 4-6-0 No 75073 in 1965 passes Henstridge with a down goods. *P. Strong*

Right: Class 5 4-6-0 No 5440 with a down stopping train near Stalbridge, 7 July 1938. *H. C. Casserley*

'Large' 4-4-0 No 71 at Stalbridge with a down passenger train. Just 'SD' on the buffer beam was unusual – it was usually 'SDJR'. The three coaches show signs of bowing. *Author's collection*

tenders collected water from Blandford and Shepton Mallet. They were usually attached to ordinary trains, but were sometimes run as a special. They were taken to Templecombe Upper, run over a sump in the track and the water fed by gravity to a 25,000gal tank in the Lower Yard. Engines stabling at Templecombe were expected to fill at the last watering point to avoid using Templecombe water. In later years a reliable supply was piped to Templecombe from Milborne Port.

In 1931 only one booked train weekly called at Templecombe Lower (36 miles 38 chains) — the 9.35pm Saturdays-only from Bournemouth to Templecombe which arrived at 11.6pm. In the 1960s it still survived as the 10.5pm Saturdays-only (10.4pm from Central after the closure of Bournemouth West), arriving Templecombe at 11.19pm. Using Templecombe Lower simplified its termination late at night.

In 1899, Dykes said that south of Templecombe, land was being bought for doubling and that eventually the whole line would be double tracked. Time proved that because traffic was lighter, the Templecombe to Broadstone doubling was not needed.

Beyond Templecombe Lower the S&D passed below the LSWR which was carried on a brick arch with masonry abutments.

Henstridge station (38 miles 27 chains), the smallest on the line, had a platform only 145ft long surmounted with a brick and timber building. The solitary siding was worked from a ground frame, the levers being in the stationmaster's office. The Virginia Inn at Henstridge was where, reputedly, Sir Walter Raleigh's servant, seeing him smoke, emptied a pot of beer over him, believing him to be on fire. Half a mile south of the station the line crossed from Somerset into Dorset.

Stalbridge (39 miles 66 chains) had a standard DCR station in red brick which, like most of those on the DCR, lacked a canopy over the platform. The stationmaster's house adjoined. A crossing loop was provided here and also at Sturminster Newton and Shillingstone. Down trains had a curved line and up trains the straight. The layouts were never remodelled to offer a non-stop train a straight line and so avoid the speed restriction of 30mph. During the Second World War the goods shed siding was extended across a road to a Ministry of Food depot.

Sturminster Newton (43 miles 63 chains) dealt with considerable dairy and cattle traffic in addition to general goods. The water column was fed from a public supply. The platforms were staggered, so to ease access from the station offices on the up platform to the down, as no footbridge was provided, a dip in the up platform gave access to a foot crossing.

An excess fare ticket issued at Sturminster Newton for a journey to Templecombe. As it was towards the end of passenger train working, the station had not ordered any more printed stock. *Author*

BRITISH RAILWAYS BOARD (W)

STURMINSTER NEWTON 92453

ISSUED AT........

AVAILABLE FOR ONE PERSON ONLY

DATE 1 Jan 1966 VALID FOR day

FROM STURMINSTER - NEWTON

TO Templecombe.

VIA........

For alternative routes, see Book of Routes

Description of Ticket	Class	Fare £	s.	d.
ORDINARY SINGLE				
FORCES LEAVE SINGLE				
OTHERS (insert details) PRIV SINGLE	2nd			8
ORDINARY RETURN				
DAY RETURN				
CHEAP DAY				
FORCES LEAVE RETURN				
EARLY MORNING RETURN				
OTHERS (insert details) RETURN				

Issued by........

NOT TRANSFERABLE

Issued subject to the Conditions and Regulations in the Publications and Notices applicable to British Railways.

B.R. 4467

Shillingstone (46 miles 67 chains) was given a platform canopy as King Edward VII used this station when visiting Iwerne Minster House. Stourpaine Loop signalbox (49 miles 13 chains) opened in the 1900s, was manned ten hours daily, but latterly only switched in for heavy holiday traffic and closed entirely 18 December 1951.

Stourpaine & Durweston Halt (49 miles 52 ch) opened on 9 July 1928, its components originating from the Exmouth Junction concrete works. Half a mile north of Blandford was Milldown Crossing which retained its disc and crossbar signal until the crossing was replaced by a bridge on 8 August 1902. The trailing Milldown siding 175yd beyond was opened during World War 1 to serve a prisoner-of-war camp.

Above: Shillingstone: the view up, *c*1966. The goods shed can be seen beyond the signalbox. *Christopher Steane*

Right: Class 9F No 92220 *Evening Star* leaves Shillingstone with an up train on 30 September 1963. The single-line tablet has just been collected and is yet to be retrieved by the fireman. The signalbox coal supply is stored within the breeze block walls conveniently near the entrance door. *Rev Alan Newman*

Below: Stourpaine & Durweston Halt: the view up on 4 May 1963. Its components were cast at the SR's Exmouth Junction concrete works. *Author*

Blandford (52 miles 24 chains), with 'Forum' added to its name on 21 September 1953, possessed a splendid station building, subway and tall signalbox. The latter was struck by lightning on 23 June 1906 and ignited without harming the signalman. Livestock was important, sometimes 50 wagons of sheep leaving in a single day.

South of the station the line to Blandford Army Camp curved eastwards; the junction, which was double track, soon became single. Opened on 12 January 1919, it was disused two years later and the track lifted on 18 December 1928. Trains on the branch were restricted to 10mph and were required to stop before level crossings.

Left: Class 9F 2-10-0 No 92220 *Evening Star* heads an up train at Blandford Forum on 30 September 1963. *Rev Alan Newman*

Lower left: The interior of Blandford Forum goods shed *c*1965. The platform appears to have been raised. *Christopher Steane*

Above: Blandford Forum goods yard *c*1965. The Austin articulated lorry is registered VYT 816. *Christopher Steane*

A maximum of 12 loaded, or 15 empties, was imposed plus one 10 ton brake van. In 1919, the 8.45am passenger train from Wareham ran to the Quarter Master's siding and the coaches were stabled there until the train returned at 5.45pm, or 1.45pm on Saturdays. 20 minutes was allowed for a train to travel between Blandford station and the Camp and 31 minutes in the reverse direction. The Blandford shunting engine worked wagons to and from the Camp sidings.

South of Blandford station the S&D crossed the River Stour and just beyond was the site of Blandford St Mary, the original station which was open only from 1 November 1860 until 31 August 1863 when the river bridge had been completed thus allowing access to the permanent station. Water was pumped from the Stour for locomotive purposes and by 1913 there were two pumps, one condensing and one non-condensing, which fed a 20,000 gallon tank.

Charlton Marshall Halt (54 miles 0 chains) opened on 9 July 1928 and although closed to the general public 17 September 1956, continued to be used at the beginning and end of term by Clayesmore School until 1 December 1963.

Spetisbury (55 miles 47 chains) was reduced to halt status on 13 August 1934. Unusually for a station, it lacked a goods siding. In single-line days it was not a block post and until 16 April 1901, a fortnight before the line was doubled, the disc and crossbar signal was operated only when a train was required to call. Spetisbury box was opened only when traffic was heavy. It closed on 18 December 1951.

Top: Widening an overbridge at Blandford St Mary, 5 March 1900. *Courtesy BRB(R)*

Above: Charlton Marshall, the view down *c*1966. Its parts were supplied by Exmouth Junction concrete depot. *Christopher Steane*

Right: Spetisbury station: view up *c*1905. The small, low signalbox can be seen at the end of the platform ramp. The platform seat is set at an angle – perhaps the photographer had previously taken a shot of the station staff sitting on it? Pears' soap adverts appear on the station fencing and one poster board on the station building is labelled 'Midland'. *Author's collection*

Bailey Gate (58 miles 33 chains) had important United Dairies sidings. Initially milk travelled to London via Wimborne, but following closure of the direct line on 17 June 1933, it was sent via Templecombe. A large corn store was provided in the yard, but only a small lineside goods shed. Until 16 April 1905, what appeared to be double track to the south was actually two parallel single lines: one to Wimborne and one to Broadstone, but on that date double track was extended to Corfe Mullen Junction and the lines diverged there. The Corfe Mullen cut-off, opened to goods on 14 December 1885 and passengers on 1 November 1886, obviated a reversal at Wimborne. The Admiralty Pumping Station sidings were passed before reaching Corfe Mullen signalbox (60 miles 18 chains). Although the branch from Corfe Mullen Junction to Wimborne closed on 17 June 1933, the line as far as Carter's Siding was retained and not lifted until 1969/70. Carter's Siding, a mile up the erstwhile branch held four or five clay wagons and although closed on 19 September 1959, was kept for wagon storage.

A few chains beyond Wimborne Junction (63 miles 19 chains) was the end of the S&D, and before reaching the station using running powers, the line crossed by an ornamental bridge, the drive through Canford Park, the seat of Lord Wimborne. The station was manned by the LSWR. Wimborne was important in the early days when all S&D trains had to reverse there. A resident steward supervised the lodging house for train crews and when it closed he became a steam raiser at Branksome. The model rest house, built in February 1902 at a cost of £1,200, was sited conveniently near the Willet Arms public house. Whitaker had seen the difficulties men had in obtaining lodgings and repeatedly pressed his directors to grant funds. Of red brick, 48ft by 27ft, it was designed and built by H. G. Edwards, chief engineer, LSWR, Exeter. The steward and his wife lived in an adjoining cottage. The house had parquet floors.

In the hall on the ground floor were lockers and a lock-up meat safe for each man to place his belongings and food. Leading from the hall were lavatories with wash basin and bathrooms with hot and cold water — probably many did not have this facility at home. The well-lit dining room measured 24ft by 13ft. Its table was covered with American cloth and Windsor chairs were provided. At the good cooking range, utensils were provided free for cooking in addition to cups and saucers, plates, knives and forks.

Bailey Gate: the view east to the rail-served United Dairies factory *c*1966. *Christopher Steane*

A wash trough with hot and cold water was at one end of the room which had a lino floor. The smoking room, 24ft by 13ft, had a long table, Windsor arm chairs and deck chairs. On the wall was an S&D gradient diagram and a model of locomotive valve gear. Upstairs, 12 private sleeping cubicles were entered from a corridor. Each had a bed, lamp stand 'and other requirements', which the reader is required to guess. A rug lay on the floor of each cubicle. When the lodging house closed, the furniture, made at Highbridge Works, was sent to Bath. A large table arrived and eight to ten armchairs with 'S&DJR' carved on them. The table was eventually placed in Green Park booking office and the chairs distributed to Bath and Bristol Barrow Road MPDs (Motive Power Depot). When they were sent to Derby, Eastleigh and Swindon for repair, they were never returned. The lodging house closed on 1 December 1922, Wimborne locomotive shed on 22 January 1923, and the turntable was last used on 6 July 1931. Charles Osman, born on 29 May 1854 and employed at Wimborne as a pumper on 15 April 1877, due to shortness of work was discharged on 19 August 1922.

Corfe Mullen Halt (61 miles 39 chains) opened on 5 July 1928, and the S&D joined the LSWR's Southampton & Dorchester line at Broadstone Junction (63 miles 6 chains), which was literally the end of the S&D. Broadstone station (63 miles 12 chains) had four platform faces: Nos 1 and 2 for trains to Holes Bay Junction and Nos 3 and 4 to Hamworthy Junction. The squat station buildings

Above left: Corfe Mullen Halt, the view down on 4 May 1963. It had closed on 17 September 1956 which explains why the nameboard is lying on the platform. The formation here was built to allow for double track. *Author*

Above right: On 6 March 1966 an up train passes Platform 2 at Broadstone Junction and curves left to the S&D line. *Christopher Steane*

Right: Poole: the view west *c*1880. The crossing gates overlap because the road was wider than the railway. Spare level crossing gates lie beside the track. *Author's collection*

had tall chimney stacks. LSWR charges for running powers from Broadstone to Bournemouth in 1910 were 11½d per mile for goods trains and 9d a mile for passenger trains. From Broadstone the line fell at 1 in 75 for two miles. Beyond Creekmore Halt (64 miles 40 chains), opened on 19 June 1931 and closed on 7 March 1966, were sidings to Sykes's Pottery and the Ministry of Supply. At Holes Bay Junction the line from Hamworthy joined.

Poole (66 miles 50 chains) was situated on a sharp curve. When the line was planned through Poole, two streets required to be crossed, one on each side of the station. In order to obviate the expense of building two bridges, an arrangement was made with Poole Corporation that in return for being allowed to cross two roads on the level, all passenger trains would call at the station. *Circa* 1899 the LSWR introduced an express which ran through Poole non-stop. The Corporation disapproved of this slight and insisted that all trains, including those of the S&D, were required to uphold the agreement.

Beyond the station rose the mile-long Parkstone Bank at 1 in 60 which prevented a fireman from letting his fire become low before the terminus.

A 'Small' 4-4-0 heads a down train at Poole *c*1900.
Author's collection

Parkstone (68 miles 34 chains) had a pottery siding. The pottery opened in 1856 and a standard gauge line about ¼ mile long was opened to the station, and between 1874 and *c*1925 also gave access to Salterns Pier. Latterly, the line was worked by a Peckett 0-4-0ST, *George Jennings*. A 2ft gauge line worked by internal combustion-engined locomotives linked the clay pits with the pottery. The pottery's principal product was drainpipes, but due to the falling demand as those of the plastic pattern rose, the pottery closed *c*1963.

Branksome (69 miles 59 chains) was at the head of the incline and immediately beyond the station was the south-west apex of the Branksome triangle, S&D passenger trains keeping south past the S&D engine shed.

Class 4F 0-6-0s Nos 44100 (17B, Burton) with 'British Railways' on the tender, and 43875, head a Bath to Bournemouth West stopping train at Parkstone on 5 August 1950.
S. W. Baker

Right: Class 4F 0-6-0 No 4561 (22C, Bath) ex-S&D No 61, at Bournemouth West heading the 6.40pm to Bath on 18 April 1949. The coach set is No 421. On the right, 'M7' 0-4-4T No 30106 has propelled a local from Brockenhurst. *M. F. Yarwood, Colin Roberts collection*

Right: Class 5 4-6-0 No 5029 (22C, Bath) at Bournemouth West working coach set No 418 to Bath *c*1939. On the far right is auto set No 23. *Author's collection*

Below: 'Small' 4-4-0 No 15 at Bournemouth West with a train to Bath *c*1910. On its cab is the classification '2P 1G'. *Author's collection*

Bournemouth West (70 miles 77 chains) opened in 1874 and was enlarged in 1888. It had six terminal platforms:

Platforms 1+2	220yd long, umbrella roof provided cover for 160yd.
Platform 3	230yd long, umbrella roof provided cover for 160yd.
Platform 4	170yd long, umbrella roof provided cover for 160yd.
Platforms 5+6	180yd long, uncovered.

Platforms 1 to 3 accommodated two four-coach sets and Nos 4 to 6 one four-coach set. Station offices were on the south side of Platform 3. Passenger station staff in 1910 consisted of the stationmaster, seven clerks, two inspectors and five ticket collectors plus porters, shunters, carriage cleaners etc, making a total of 88. In addition, the goods staff comprised of two yard foremen and 23 hands.

– 3 –

Construction of the line between Evercreech Junction and Bath

AN Act of 21 August 1871 allowed the S&D to construct a line from its existing Evercreech station (which became Evercreech Junction) across the Mendip Hills to join the MR's Mangotsfield to Bath branch at Bath Junction. This Act allowed the company to raise the necessary £400,000 by issuing Bath Extension 4% Guaranteed Stock which formed the first charge on the undertaking.

The line was neither easy to build, requiring tunnels, viaducts and substantial earthworks, nor were the long gradients of 1 in 50 easy to work. The Somerset Coal Canal tramway between Radstock and Midford was sold to the S&D for £15,000 cash and £5,000 in paid-up S&D shares. The tramway extensions to Welton and Clandown were included in the sale, but private colliery tramways were unaffected, such as that carried by the 'Marble Arch'. This arch originally spanned the canal tramway.

Messrs Thomas & Charles Walker secured the contract for building the line at a cost of £352,000. Their chief engineer was A. Priestly and the resident engineer in charge of the office was Mr Branfill. The *Bath Chronicle* for 1 February 1872 reported that engineers had surveyed the route during the previous week and also quoted an unnamed Plymouth contemporary: '. . . the works will be commenced next month. It is confidently expected that before Christmas 1873, the North mail will be able to run from Plymouth to Carlisle without change of carriage and that cases of fruit, fish or perishable goods will be in the Midland markets within a few hours of their being landed on our quays, and this without the injury caused by break of gauge at Bristol.'

Messrs Walker probably began work in March 1872. The exact date does not seem to have been recorded, but the *Bath & Cheltenham Gazette* of 20 March 1872 announced that work had commenced 'and it is intended that the works should be pushed on in such a vigorous manner as will effect its completion in two years. The work has been commenced at the heaviest part, viz. the two tunnels which will pierce the eminences upon which Devonshire Buildings and Combe Down stand . . . Messrs Walker, of Westminster, are the contractors for the construction of the line and the erection of the necessary buildings.'

A month later, on 24 April, it enthusiastically recorded that the Walkers were '. . . pushing on the work with great vigour. The setting out of the line has been finished, and in many instances the land required has been purchased.' It said of Combe Down Tunnel: 'The most progress has been made at the Midford end of the tunnel, the mouth of which will be 50 feet from the surface . . . About 50 men are engaged on this end of the tunnel.'

For obvious reasons, men who took up navvying were tough and sometimes pugnacious. On 23 May 1872 five quarrelled over some matter near St Luke's Church, Bath, a building only about 100yd south of land covering Devonshire Tunnel, and a fight commenced. 'One combatant was knocked down, upon which he was seized by the legs by his antagonist and tugged about the road. Two more were writhing on the ground, and while thus prostrate a third came forward and deliberately kicked one of them with his heavy boot in the head, inflicting a dreadful gash from which the blood flowed freely. With the assistance of a comrade the two were separated, and with blood-smeared faces they regained their feet. Meanwhile a third had been knocked down and kicked in the eye, and thus bruised and battered the fight continued to the alarm of the passers by. At length some expostulation produced a truce, and the condition of the man who received a wound in the head, alarming one of his friends, he was led away, and the others took an opposite direction.' — *Bath & Cheltenham Gazette* 29 May 1872. Quoting from an unnamed contemporary it continued: 'Looking at the classes from which these 'navvies' are recruited, the Watch Committee would certainly be conferring a boon on the neighbourhood as well as on the men themselves by placing an extra officer in the district, or restricting the beat so as to enable the constable on duty to traverse it more frequently.'

However, it was not all rough and tumble, for on the evening of Friday, 8 November 1872, 110 navvies who had been engaged in making the cutting at the north end of Devonshire Tunnel, crowded into St Mark's School, Widcombe, Bath, 'to partake of some substantial fare' the cost of which had been defrayed by subscription. Each man was provided with a plate of beef and potatoes 'of the most satisfying appearance', and as much tea, bread and plum pudding as they could eat. After tea some hymns were sung and many of the navvies joined in. The meal was organised by 'good-natured ladies whose sympathies the navvies had enlisted'.

A similar type of gathering was held at Shepton Mallet on Saturday, 20 September 1873 when 250 labourers were entertained at the Music Hall. 'After supper religious addresses were given by the Rev. E. H. F. Cosens, Stiles and Thwaits. The men, who were very attentive, were each presented with a small Testament.' At East Twerton, Bath, 40 or so navvies working on the S&D and completely illiterate, were taught by Miss Isabel Spence to read and write as well as having imparted to them knowledge of the Christian faith.

Around Christmas 1872 a Shepton Mallet landlord let a house to an S&D navvy and family. After several weeks when no rent was forthcoming, he sacrificed what was his due and turned them out into the street. After they had left, the landlord found to his dismay that floorboards had been pulled up and used as firewood — poor recompense for free lodgings.

The *Bath & Cheltenham Gazette* reported on 17 July 1872: 'The progress which has been made is surprising. The arches for the accommodation of the foot and vehicular traffic in the fields in the rear of Oldfield Road have been built, and the embankment that will carry the line from the mouth of the first tunnel [Devonshire] across the dip in the land, and into the cutting to the Twerton meadows, has been carried a considerable distance on the other side of the arches. On the Wells Road side very considerable progress has been made with the deep cutting that will lead up to the first tunnel.'

Not all welcomed the S&D. A letter written to the *Bath & Cheltenham Gazette* by *Eheu Fugaces* on 19 April 1876 said that Greenway Lane was becoming a misnomer: 'The prospect from the lane has been certainly altered — I will not say improved.'

The *Bath Chronicle* of 25 July 1872 encouragingly reported that the line was likely to be completed by December 1873. 'The readiness with which the shares of the Company were taken up in this neighbourhood showed no want of interest in the undertaking amongst those most capable of judging its utility.' The reporter commented that the broad gauge line serving the Radstock coalfield was 'practically useless' regarding supplying Bath with coal and that a stranger whose feelings were 'in sympathy with those of the Society for the Prevention of Cruelty to Animals would, in the course of a ten mile drive southward of the city, find many an object for pity in overloaded horses and donkeys toiling uphill, suffering under the additional disadvantage in many cases of raw wounds under the collar and saddle pad'.

'That Messrs Walker are taking the work in hand in earnest is shown by the fact that along the whole line, which is twenty-six and a half miles in length, about a thousand men are engaged, working in night and day gangs. The line has been divided into three sections [No 1 district Evercreech Junction–Nettlebridge Viaduct; No 2 Nettlebridge Viaduct–Midford; No 3 Midford–Bath Junction] in each of which the work is being rapidly pushed forward.'

The portion between the bridge over the GWR and Bath Junction had yet to be commenced and the *Bath Chronicle* advised its readers: 'If we wish to see active operations we must go some distance along the line marked out to Englishcombe fields. The quiet pastoral aspect of the

An up train about to enter Combe Down Tunnel c1966. In the foreground is Tucking Mill Viaduct. *Christopher Steane*

meadows here suffers to a large extent from the presence of a high embankment which is being raised. The pathway which leads from the back of Oldfield-road across the fields is crossed by a stone archway, with an embankment on either side. The embankment is growing gradually, being steadily added to by the deposits of trolley-loads of earth brought along a narrow gauge tramway which is laid down upon it, and which of course is lengthened as the embankment extends. On the Twerton side of the archway the embankment has reached a height of fully thirty feet and this will be exceeded as the work progresses in the direction of the junction.

'Walking now in the direction of Wells-road we find that the embankment gradually becomes lower in consequence of the rising of the ground — though of course the same level is maintained — and at about fifty yards from the archway it is followed by a cutting into the hill which slopes down from the direction of Bloomfield-road. The cutting as it proceeds gradually becomes deeper and deeper, revealing deposits of soft, fine gravel, distributed in a strangely irregular manner, and lying above a thick stratum of inferior lias, or blue clay.'

About this time, one Bath schoolmaster got his pupils interested in geology by taking them to these excavations to observe the different rocks and to note the varying botanical growth when removed into the open. The boys were particularly fascinated by 'stink stone', a pungent rock with sulphur content found by the navvies in Combe Down Tunnel.

At the Bath end of the line the contractor used four locomotives, three traction engines, six portable engines, 350 tip wagons and 400ft of temporary rails.

'Cuttings were made in a similar manner to tunnels. 'The mode of "cutting" is not done, as some might suppose, by digging straight ahead into the slope. First of all what is called a "heading" is cut some hundred yards or more into the hill at a level with the horizontal line the rail will follow. A "heading" is a rather narrow tunnel cut into the hill with spade and pickaxe, the roof being supported by a rough ceiling resting upon wooden supports. As the heading progresses a narrow gauge line of rails is provided in continuation of that running along the embankment and other parts of the work. A train of trucks, propelled by a small steam engine, is brought into the heading, and now the process which in time converts the heading into an open cutting begins.

'Immediately over the heading and at intervals agreed upon, what are technically termed 'shoot holes' are dug as far as the wooden roof of the heading, and a small portion of this being removed, the trucks in readiness below are filled with earth from above, and when loaded are run out to the end of the embankment where they are overturned, the material brought out being so much more added to the structure. Of course the shaft holes disappear in time, when the excavation assumes something more of the form of a cutting, and then the earth is thrown from each side into the trucks standing in readiness below.

'Within 100 yards of Bloomfield-road where its depth is no less than 40 feet, at this spot the [Devonshire] tunnel will commence and a shaft has been opened for the purpose of letting down stone and other materials used in the work.

The cutting in Lyncombe Vale, *c*1966. The north portal of Combe Down Tunnel is behind the photographer. *Christopher Steane*

Already the tunnel has penetrated the ground as far as Bloomfield-road. It will emerge from the ground in Mr [James] Kirtley's [nurseryman] garden, the spot being indicated by a heap or two of earth thrown up in making the necessary trial borings.' — *Bath Chronicle* 25 July1872.

Devonshire Tunnel was bored in the same way that a cutting was made, and the *Bath Chronicle* reporter found that navvies had excavated nearly as far as below Devonshire Buildings. 'A prolific stream of water has been met with in the boring of the preliminary tunnel, which gives the men considerable trouble to contend with. Several beds of good gravel have been found.'

After crossing Lyncombe Vale, the line entered a deep cutting about 200 yards long 'which is being made in the manner we have described, the material taken from the hill being used in the construction of an embankment across the valley. The cutting ends at the back of Lyncombe House, not 200 yards from the premises, and here there is a pronounced dip in the contour of the fields. An embankment at this spot, though by no means impracticable, would very much detract from the beauty of the landscape so that the best that could be devised under the circumstances is being done in the erection of a light and not inelegant stone viaduct, carried on four piers. The stone used in the construction of the viaduct is brought from the quarries at the back of Bloomfield-crescent, the tunnelling having as yet yielded none which will be of any service in building. The only material obtained in boring under Combe Down has so far been a soft sandstone, of little more consistency than clay, which does good service in making embankments, but the hopes indulged in by many — perhaps however not the best competent to judge — that Combe Down would yield stone which would largely remunerate the contractor, have not at present been realised. In fact the stone which will be used in the masonry of the tunnel is being procured from quarries in the neighbourhood.

The Combe Down tunnel enters Fox-hill at a short distance from the viaduct. From the Midford end it has been bored more than 200 yards in the direction of Bath. Blasting has, to some extent, been employed, but, owing to the soft nature of the ground, it has not so far been very effectual.'

The *Bath Chronicle* for 8 August 1872 reported that the whole length of the extension had been surveyed and plans and notices served to three-quarters of the landowners. More than half the land required had been purchased and a large proportion of this already fenced, while fencing materials were provided for the remainder.

Prestleigh Viaduct was well advanced and one near Shepton Mallet commenced. Works south of Winsor Hill Tunnel had begun and work on the tunnel itself would soon start. Nettlebridge Viaduct and work on a nearby cutting were under way.

No 3 district 'is one uninterrupted series of heavy work . . . A commencement is made of Combe Down tunnel at both ends and a heading driven for the tunnel for 270 yards — two thirds of which is excavated to nearly the required size.' Tucking Mill Viaduct was in a forward state — both abutments and two piers ready for arches and three-quarters of the other five piers finished. In Lyncombe Vale the three-span Watery Bottom underbridge was ready for the arches and the three-span Moger's bridge near the north portal of Combe Down Tunnel complete, but for the parapet walls.

In the evening of 26 September 1872 two inquests were held at the Bear Inn, Bear Flat, Bath, on the bodies of Frederick Viney, otherwise Joseph Pabst, and Joseph Bayliss, otherwise Williams, who were killed by a fall of earth in a cutting being made near Bloomfield Place. Viney, aged 30, was from Weston, Bath, and Bayliss, 24, from Combe Down.

Viney had gone to work that morning for the very first time. Foreman George Barnes stated that between 7am and 8am the deceased men were in the cutting filling a wagon from the 'benching' and while they were working, a portion of earth forming the wall of the cutting gave way. The slip occurred about 10ft above the heads of the men. The quantity of earth which fell on them weighed 3-4 tons. Barnes was unable to say the cause of the slip which was composed of blue lias clay which was generally not prone to slipping, but was ledged on a bed of stone left partially uncovered after the accident. He made all the haste he could to get them out, but ten minutes elapsed before this could be done and by this time they were quite dead. Barnes said: 'In the construction of lines we are always liable to such accidents, and nothing can be done to prevent them.'

Dr Joseph Lawrence, 31 Claverton Street, reported that Viney had a compound fracture of the skull and knee. Bayliss's head was 'beaten in' as were several of his ribs. The jury returned a verdict in both cases of 'Accidental death'. Another man, James Bush of Odd Down, had his leg broken in the same accident and his limb was amputated at the Royal United Hospital (RUH).

Unfortunately, the line's construction was marred by other serious accidents, the most severe being on 18 August 1873. Navvies were at work near Winsor Hill Tunnel when a rock weighing several tons fell, killing four men and injuring another. Navvies at work nearby rushed to extricate them which they succeeded in doing after two hours, but all was to no avail for 'when found the bodies of the deceased men were in a fearfully mangled state' — *Bath Chronicle* 21 August 1873. And what of the stone which caused the fatality? It was made into a memorial marking the grave in Shepton Mallet cemetery and this gruesome reminder can be seen today.

The rock which killed four navvies boring Winsor Hill Tunnel, now forming their tombstone in Shepton Mallet cemetery. *Author*

Four months later another tragedy occurred. At 2pm on 16 December 1873 three men were standing on the particular arch of Midford Viaduct which spanned the Somerset Coal Canal. 'One of them observing an opening in the bricks, put his foot to it.' Just as he did so, the entire arch fell. Masons George Kempton and Hubert Sheppard tumbled through the hole and were buried by bricks falling on them. The third mason, named Cann, had the foresight to jump into the canal as the brickwork collapsed and this act saved his life. He was injured, but not sufficiently to prevent him walking four miles to his lodging in Snow Hill, Bath. The accident was attributed to the action of frost on the new work, but F. G. Slessor, resident engineer, said at the inquest that the arch was constructed in a proper manner. Albert Patch was the sub-contractor for the viaduct.

Neither was it only fully grown men who received fatal injuries. About 4.30pm on 6 August 1873 William Rawlings, a horse driver for Messrs Walker, said that he was driving his cart along the railway formation at Midford when William Nott, aged 14, employed as a tool worker, came up to him and offered to show him where to take the load. Rawlings accepted and the lad climbed up to have a ride on the cart. Just as it reached a temporary bridge, the horse turned right and fell over, the cart falling on William Nott's neck. William Hunt, foreman of works, and William Rawlings removed the cart from Nott who, after giving one or two gasps, died.

It was not only humans who suffered fatalities. On 30 September 1872 a horse belonging to Messrs Walker and valued at 50 guineas was allowed by the man in charge of it to stray. It fell from a considerable height into the cutting near the north end of Combe Down Tunnel and broke its back. Perhaps it is not surprising to read that 'the negligent servant decamped'.

Some human injuries were less serious. On 21 November 1872 Henry Gould and another man were in Combe Down Tunnel driving in a wedge with sledge hammers. The second man's hammer slipped off and struck Gould in the eye. He was taken to the RUH where the wound was serious enough for him to be detained.

On the night of 30 July 1873 Gideon Morris of Trowbridge was taken to the RUH suffering from a serious cut on the head caused by falling scaffolding. On St George's Day 1874 a man called Fletcher was at work on the line near Bath when a quantity of earth fell on him. He was taken to the RUH but fortunately no bones were found to be broken.

The *Bath Chronicle* for 10 October 1872 reported that Messrs Walker had been summonsed for using a five to six months old Aveling & Porter traction engine on the highway on 2 September at Dunkerton which 'did not consume its own smoke' and whose wheels were not cylindrical. J. H. Simpson, engineer in charge of the engine, told magistrates that when he was near Red Post gate, Peasedown, he was stopped by PC Chapman who said: 'You have not got the weight of the engine' so he replied: 'If you look, you will see.' Chapman continued, 'Well, you have not got the name on' and was told, 'If you look you will see that also,' to which Chapman replied: 'Well then, you are not consuming your own smoke.' Simpson told him that it was impossible to make any smoke because he had only coke to burn and invited Chapman to look, but he declined. W. Topham, Walker's agent for the Shepton Mallet district, confirmed that the engine had been loaded with coke at Shepton.

Messrs Walker were also charged for a smoke nuisance on 1 September, PC Chapman and W. Daniels, a Wellow farmer saying that the engine smoked for a mile going uphill. The engine's cylindrical wheels had shoes attached and these were allowed by Act of Parliament. The Bench discharged the case against the wheels, but as the other charges had been sworn by witnesses, it inflicted a fine of £2 plus costs in both instances.

It is very likely that the contractor suffered an injustice because the witnesses were never asked to define 'smoke'. That was a grave omission as 'smoke' from a bonfire can look very like condensing steam from an engine and it was probably condensing steam that the witnesses saw.

In the same court a navvy, Mallett, employed by Walkers, was summonsed for assaulting Robert Charles Walker, nephew of the contractors. In consequence of a remark made about the way

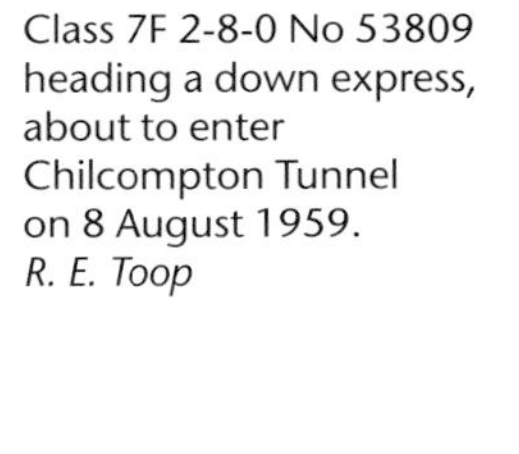

Class 7F 2-8-0 No 53809 heading a down express, about to enter Chilcompton Tunnel on 8 August 1959. *R. E. Toop*

Mallett was working, the defendant struck and subsequently threatened him. He was fined 10s and bound over to keep the peace for six months.

The wet weather experienced in November and December 1872 caused some delay in carrying out the works. Devonshire Tunnel was pierced late in February 1873 and that month shareholders approved the substitution of a bridge at Radstock by a level crossing. Nearly all the share capital had been issued and all instalments had been paid except for one arrears of £800, while £1,532,345 had been expended.

By the beginning of March 1873 shareholders were told that practically half the line was finished, while the Bath end was almost complete. By August, Winsor Hill Tunnel through limestone was over a third finished and work on it continued night and day from both ends, while Combe Down Tunnel was in 'a very forward state' because the workings from both ends had met and the north portal constructed. To be completed it needed only a south portal and widening of parts of the interior 'which was being rapidly carried on'. Devonshire Tunnel was being lined throughout and would, except for the portals, be finished before the end of August. Steady progress was being made in heavy cuttings at Shepton Mallet, Masbury and Chilcompton. Walkers had six locomotives and 150 horses at work on the whole line.

On 12 June 1873 Combe Down Tunnel was pierced when the two gangs who had commenced working over a mile apart, 15 months previously, met 'and such was the accuracy of the workings that metals were enabled to be laid down at once, and it was impossible to discover from any different level where the meeting actually took place. This could only be discovered by observing the direction of the marks of the "pick" upon the sides of the tunnel.'

On Friday [13 June] several of the directors and gentlemen connected with the line passed through the tunnel from end to end, and on Saturday, the workmen who had been engaged in boring the tunnel were entertained to a cold collation at the William the Fourth [Combe Road, Combe Down] under the presidency of Mr James Burroughs and Mr George Rose the two foremen of works . . . It is a matter of much congratulation, that during the piercing of the Combe Down Hill, no life has been lost and little or no bodily injury sustained by the workmen engaged.' – *Bath & Cheltenham Gazette* 18 June 1873.

It was cut in the remarkable time of 15 months. 'A headway was first driven through in the bottom — which took twelve months — and then, by what is known in Cornwall as overhand stopping, the stuff that is required to be excavated was removed both quickly and by comparison, cheaply, three months sufficing.' – *Bath & Cheltenham Gazette* 17 June 1874.

The same newspaper of 6 May 1874 announced that subject to Board of Trade approval, the extension would open on 1 June: 'The beautifully fine weather of the past few days has been fully taken advantage of by Messrs Walker, contractors, whose officers and large gangs of men are working long hours . . . The work is now so far advanced at Radstock that the level crossing has been constructed . . . Last week a full-sized engine was driven to and fro between Radstock and Bath, Mr Walker, one of the contractors, being a passenger.'

The next week's issue said that during the past week, E. M. Needham, Superintendent of the MR, accompanied by Mr Brince, chief of the signalling department, and Inspectors Loveday and Allard, met F. G. Slessor, S&D engineer, and other S&D officers to arrange a junction at Twerton. 'The Somerset & Dorset Company and the contractor are using strenuous efforts to bring about the opening of the line on June 1st and although considerable work remains to be accomplished, yet as constant relays of men are employed and fine weather continues, there is every probability that they will accomplish their end by the day specified.' Time proved this statement optimistic.

The S&D and Messrs T. & C. Walker, aware of the value of publicity, made a horse-drawn trolley available on 11 June in order that reporters could see the line before it was opened to the public.

The *Bath & Cheltenham Gazette* reporter commented in the issue of 17 June 1874: 'The line has been referred to as the missing link, which alone was wanting to complete the direct narrow gauge communication between the northern and midland districts of England and the west, and the importance of it was fully recognised in the opposition offered to the Bill, which was of a very persistent character, but the powers sought were granted . . . The permanent way, or all but a fractional part of it, has been laid, and the ballasting near completion on each section . . . Gangs of men are being worked night and day, and every endeavour possible is being made to accomplish the task by the allotted time. Notwithstanding this great pressure of work, and that on Thursday last [11 June] visitors could not pass along the line without great inconvenience, the officials who had the overlooking of each section, and every one of those under them, willingly did all in their power to enable the writer and his companions to give an accurate description of the different works (some of which are of a very heavy character) on the line, and of the beautiful tracts of country through which it passes.'

On the 26-mile-long line there were nine stations. 'This may appear a great number of stations on so short a line, but they serve a double purpose, not only of accommodating a numerous, though scattered, population, but the line being only a single one, greater facilities are thereby offered for working it. It is worked on the block system, the apparatus for which has been supplied by that well-known firm of Saxby & Farmer, who possess the patent for the system, and who must be driving a tremendous trade in this respect. Throughout the whole district their men are busily engaged in fixing the signals and the necessary appliances for their proper working.

'Along the entire route there are several tunnels, still more viaducts (all built of stone and brick), some heavy cuttings, and numerous embankments. The occupation and cattle bridges, and work of that character, have also been numerous and heavy, and taking everything into consideration, especially the question of labour, it is a matter of surprise that the works have progressed so far. Messrs Walker, however, have been constantly pushing forward, and have sometimes had as many as 3,000 hands employed throughout the works.

'The stations are very nearly completed, and the telegraph posts, and posts showing the different gradients, were being put up on Thursday. The fencing of the whole distance is different from that generally adopted, being made of galvanized wire, running through wooden posts. The metals of the line are of wrought iron, and instead of being fastened in the usual way by chairs, are secured to the sleepers by bolts, which screw into a diamond-shaped piece of iron, with teeth at each corner under the sleeper, and which is said to be much more safe plan, and also a less costly one.

'By arrangement, we were met at the point which the line joins the Midland branch at Twerton, where it should be said a large signalbox had been erected, with a view to the efficient working of the line at that spot. Here, through the kindness of Mr Lean [contractor's agent for that section], we found a small "trolly" usually used by the men whilst repairing the line, had been nicely and conveniently fitted up to convey us as far as Wellow, the end of Mr Lean's section. The time was fixed for 11 o'clock, but from unavoidable circumstances, Mr Lean did not meet us for some short time afterwards, so that the arrangements for our reception at the different points were somewhat thrown out, and a few little inconveniences which were not anticipated, had to be put up with through our journey. However, taking the trip as a whole, it was a very novel and a very pleasurable one. One of the fine horses generally in use by the contractors, was attached to our "trolly".' Regarding Combe Down Tunnel the reporter stated that 'Signals are erected about 600 yards in at either end to ensure its safe working' — this was when the contractor worked the line, and they were not kept in the S&D era.

Looking after the inner man, Mr Lean provided refreshments at Midford. Wellow was the end of Lean's section. The horse drew the trolley for about a mile beyond Wellow to a spot where they were picked up by an engine under the charge of Walker's nephew and proceeded to Radstock. 'The new station adjoins that of the Great Western Railway, the line of which is now broad, but about to be changed to narrow gauge, of which the company has given notice this past week.'

At Radstock in the centre of his district, they were met by Mr F. Caulton; Mr Hawkins, section agent; and Mr Colson, resident engineer. Caulton entertained the party to luncheon at the Bell Inn. The bridge across the BNSR still needed some time before it was thoroughly completed, so near the Five Arches the party walked a mile because the temporary way was being removed for the laying of the permanent way. This was the only place where it had not been laid. Before they reached Midsomer Norton station, they were picked up by a locomotive.

At Binegar the party was handed over to Mr Kenway, assistant to T. Topham, contractor's engineer for the last section of the line and shortly after, the group was handed to A. Priestly, chief engineer of the line who procured an engine for their transport.

Shepton Mallet was Topham's headquarters. The journey through Cannard's Grave cutting

A bridge in Cannard's Grave cutting *c*1886 rebuilt during track doubling.
BRB(R)

had to be made on foot as every available locomotive was employed, and being a single line, it was blocked with wagons loaded with ballast. 'At Evercreech village there is a small station, and the junction is just a mile beyond. The old Evercreech station on the main line will now be made the junction station, and is being rebuilt (the old structure will be used as the stationmaster's residence), and extensively enlarged for that purpose. There are three lines of rail, several sidings, a large goods shed, and everything that can be required for carrying on a large amount of traffic. In fact, it is quite clear not only that a large traffic is anticipated, but that the company are determined that nothing shall be left undone, both to facilitate and encourage it. Evercreech Junction is destined to become a place of importance.'

Colonel Rich on behalf of the Board of Trade, started his inspection of the S&D Extension on Thursday, 18 June 1874 and completed it on Saturday the 20th. The S&D was represented at the inspection by Robert A. Read, managing director; James Clark, director; A. Difford, traffic superintendent; F. G. Slessor, engineer; B. S. Fisher, locomotive superintendent; and Inspector Wood. Thomas Walker, contractor, together with W. Lean, one of his engineers, was also present.

The train used for the inspection consisted of 'five of the company's large carriages and a break van, fitted with Clark's patent continuous breaks, the whole being drawn by two powerful locomotives — one being a heavy goods engine'.

The inspecting party left Bath shortly after 9am on Thursday morning and a very minute inspection was made of the skew bridge across the Lower Bristol Road at the foot of Brook Road. Devonshire and Combe Down tunnels were

Cannard's Grave Cutting, viewed from an up train on 6 December 1965.
Rev Alan Newman

closely inspected as was Midford Viaduct. The party continued a detailed inspection of the line as far as Radstock and the train returned to Bath at 7pm.

On Friday morning the party again left Bath about 9am and ran straight through to Radstock where they started the inspection. The *Bath & Cheltenham Gazette* of 24 June 1874 recorded an unusual use of the inspection train: 'In addition to the ordinary carriages, a truck with a load of bricks was also attached to the train and conveyed to Radstock. The gross weight which passed over the line was between 150 and 200 tons.' That day the train continued as far as Shepton Mallet, the examination being completed through to Evercreech Junction on the Saturday. The line was announced to be opened for local traffic on Monday 22 June, '. . . but this was found impossible to do, much to the disappointment of many persons who had made up their mind for a trip over the new line. Strenuous exertions, we believe, will be made to open it by the 1st July'. The reason for the delay in opening was the fact that Rich was unable to inspect the stations as they were still incomplete. Several other features caused him disquiet: for example, some distant signals were not distant enough.

The same day the *Gazette* also divulged that 'A new shed is being erected at the Midland terminus, for the accommodation of locomotives of the company. It is proposed to run six trains each way daily, all of which will run into the Midland Railway terminus. A ticket office has been built a short distance beyond the junction with the Midland line.' This was actually a ticket platform, not an office.

Rich's requirements were carried out and as the line was considered safe several days before he could make his re-inspection, one freight train was run daily, the *Bath & Cheltenham Gazette* of 22 July revealing: 'Great quantities of goods have already found their way over the line.' The arrival of the first barrel of beer by rail, at Wellow, supplied by Garton, Russell & Co to Mr E. Hill of the George Inn, 'was made the occasion of spending a short time of pleasure. "Success to the new Line" was drunk and the hope expressed that by its extension to that place, the inhabitants might be greatly benefited and brought more into contact with their neighbours.'

Colonel Rich made a re-inspection on Friday, 17 July when he declared that the line could be opened. Trial trains were run on the following day, the *Bath & Cheltenham Gazette* of 22 July 1874 giving details. 'The Somerset and Dorset Railway Company authorities arranged for the running of several trains on Saturday, in order to acquaint their servants with the characteristics of the line, and to clearly ascertain a variety of circumstances in reference to the time occupied in running over the distance between Bath and Evercreech, and Bath and Templecombe. The first train left the Midland Station at 10 o'clock, amongst the passengers being Messrs Read (managing director), A. Difford (secretary), Walker (contractor), Wood (general inspector), Fisher (locomotive superintendent), Saunders (telegraphic contractor), Lean and Priestly (contractors' engineers), and a number of other gentlemen and members of the press. The train, which was drawn by a powerful engine belonging to the Somerset and Dorset Company, of which the new line is a branch, was timed as an ordinary one, and getting away in good time, Radstock was reached in exactly half-an-hour, after stopping at Midford, the time to Radstock having been punctually kept. Midsomer Norton, Chilcompton and other stations were paused at, and at Shepton Mallet water was taken in. After stopping at Evercreech, which was reached in an hour and ten minutes, Cole and Wincanton followed, and the train arrived at Templecombe, where the Somerset and Dorset joins the South Western line, in sufficient time to allow several of the passengers to take the London and South Western morning express to London, which is a very fast train.

'After a short interval, the return journey was commenced, and on this occasion the running of the train was arranged as an express; the only stoppage made was at Shepton Mallet, and the journey to Bath made in little under an hour. Combe Down Tunnel, which is nearly a mile and a quarter in length, being passed through in less than two minutes. The passengers were unanimous in praising the thorough smartness with which the line ran; a completeness of arrangements of both the telegraph and the signal apparatus being in good working order, and the excellence of the time kept. The officials were also pleased at the success of this first run, after the passing of the line; and considered that there are several gradients with which of course the engine drivers and guards cannot yet be fully acquainted, the trip must be

Class 5 4-6-0 No 44830 (22C Bath) heads the 'Pines Express' at Templecombe Junction on 30 June 1950. Its tender still bears the inscription 'LMS'. This was one of the Bath oil-burning locomotives. *Pursey Short courtesy Roger Venning*

considered highly successful. Subsequently other trains ran.'

The *Bath Chronicle* reporter in the issue of 23 July 1874 was not quite so enthusiastic. 'It has been stated that Mr Brunel, in his later years, considered railways with many curves were safer for travelling than those which were straight. If so, the new line may be considered as one of the safest in the kingdom . . . in fact, it is almost a succession of curves, resembling somewhat the South Devon line, which resemblance is also strengthened by the steep gradients. With the exception of that at Midford, which is a small structure of wood, the stations are neat buildings of rough stone with freestone dressings, varying somewhat in size, and having veranda fronts over the platforms, which are not covered.' As the stations had only one platform 'There is no positive necessity for crossing the rails, but as there are generally two lines at the stations, it would be desirable at some time to carry over at least the platforms of the more important stations, and to start trains from opposite sides. This would of course necessitate bridges, or should do so. No provision, however, appears to have been made for doubling the line throughout, so that it may be presumed the traffic is not expected to be enormous. The platforms are gravelled and edged with rounded vitrified bricks. The signalling is effected by Saxby & Farmer's patent levers with locking apparatus attached . . . The levers are in covered boxes on the platform, and therefore, like the pointsman, are easy of access. Close to each box is a clock with chocolate covered face and white figures. Unfortunately all the clocks were more or less behind hand on Monday last.'

The first train left Bath at 7.25am on 20 July. The *Bath Journal* revealed: 'There was a little amiable diplomacy at the booking office to obtain the first ticket and judging from his appearance the individual who secured the honour was well pleased . . . About thirty passengers booked to different stations on the line, the greatest booked being to Evercreech, although the next contained several passengers for more distant places. Mr Difford, the secretary of the Somerset and Dorset Company, was amongst the passengers in the first train, whilst on the engine drawing it was Mr Fisher, the locomotive superintendent.' A considerable number of spectators watched the first train as it left the departure platform of the Midland terminus, 'which arrangement caused some little confusion, as passengers for Bristol and the north had, in consequence, to start from the arrival side'.

The first train was welcomed to Wellow by church bells. The station had been decorated by the stationmaster assisted by some of the villagers including a rose fancier who contributed several baskets. 'One enthusiastic resident had lavishly decorated himself. His head, which a countryman irreverently termed a "top-not", was bedecked with numerous large hollyhocks and other flowers, and as he strolled about alone in his glory, he protested again and again that he never expected to have lived to see a railway at Wellow.

'In the evening nearly all the inhabitants of the village assembled at the station and one elderly man said to be quite an infant in regard to the railway travelling, was unmercifully chaffed about a little mishap that occurred to him in returning from his primal trip to Bath and back. In his inexperience he had imagined that somebody would ask him to leave the carriage and when the train moved on without this mark of deference being paid him he practically shouted "Stop the train, stop the train." This request was not complied with, and the traveller had to go to Radstock and return by the next train. On arriving at Wellow he calmly assured his friends that he had been to Radstock "on business".'

A flag flew at Binegar and in an adjacent field a large red banner bore the words: "Success to the Railway". A large number of persons in addition to intending travellers were at Evercreech Junction to see the first down train from Bath and also there was a crowd at Wincanton. Delays at Evercreech Junction and Wincanton caused passengers to miss the down train from Templecombe to Exeter and so instead of arriving at Exeter at 11.53am they had to wait for the next. As things turned out this was very late and instead of arriving at Exeter at 1.20pm did not reach there until 1.55pm. The anti-S&D *Bath Chronicle* commented: 'This is a bad beginning. May the Somerset and Dorset managers speedily "mend their ways" in the matter of punctuality, or they will only too quickly find that would-be travellers will go by their longer yet fairly punctual competitors, rather than by a route where times of arrival are uncertain and delays not improbable, albeit the mileage may be considerably less.'

Messrs Fuller, Horsey, Son & Co of 11 Billeter Square, London, were instructed by Messrs T. & C. Walker to sell on 11 August 1874 and subsequent days at all stations on the Bath Extension, contractors' plant, while on 17 August, horses, vehicles, harness and stable fittings were sold at Shepton Mallet.

In December 1874 the S&D became involved in a case at Bath City Police Court: Kelson versus the S&D. The summons set out that 'in or about the month of September last a difference arose between one James Kelson and the S&D respecting the sufficiency of the accommodation works' which the company was required to make to Kelson as owner and occupier of lands adjoining the railway in the Oldfield Park area. Kelson, landlord of the Windsor Castle Inn, Upper Bristol Road, also owned 28 acres of land which he used for market gardening and a dairy farm. Near its ticket platform, the S&D had cut through Kelson's land when making its Bath Extension. Prior to the railway's construction, Kelson had a roadway from one end of his property to the other, but the S&D bisected this road and blocked it.

Kelson made an application to the company and at first it consented to make a level crossing a short distance from where the former road had passed. Instead of carrying out the promised work, a ticket platform was erected at the spot and no crossing made. In the court case Kelson contended an accommodation bridge or level crossing to be made and a bridge already erected by the company on Kelson's land should be made larger and wider; that a certain ditch should be made large enough to carry water into a culvert, and finally that a watering place for Kelson's cattle be made in one of the fields to replace one that had been cut off.

To enable the magistrates better to understand the situation of the ground and the requirements asked for, the S&D provided a special train which

Circa 1938 two Class 2P 4-4-0s head a local passenger train at Binegar. The pilot engine is No 633 and the Dabeg water heater can just be seen on the far side of the smokebox. *Author's collection*

conveyed the magistrates and interested parties to the location.

The S&D consented to construct a drain on each side of the railway to carry off water and also to create a culvert; the only question the Bench needed to decide was whether the S&D was required to make either a bridge or a level crossing. Had the bridge been built in the position proposed by the S&D it would have caused Kelson to travel an additional 220yd on each journey, and furthermore his carts would have to pass under a building with an archway of only 6ft 6in in height, insufficient to allow a cart laden with baskets to negotiate.

The S&D contended that Mr Kelson had been a difficult gentleman to satisfy from the first, in matters of price and otherwise. Of his estate of approximately 28 acres, the S&D had taken 1 acre 3 rood and 30 perches for which he had first demanded £2,300. In order to save the expense of arbitration, the company had offered him £700 and also undertook to make a level crossing, but as that offer was rejected and instead he had opted for arbitration, therefore the S&D's liabilities to make the crossing no longer held.

The S&D had settled three of Kelson's complaints, but regarding the fourth, Henry Spackman, a Bath surveyor whose offices were at 6 Terrace Walks, said that the route through the archway could easily be avoided by removing a bank and erecting a gate and he believed the S&D would be willing to do this.

Mr Swayne of Glastonbury, solicitor for the S&D, submitted that Kelson had been paid ample compensation for all severance, for the value of the land and for inconvenience. The accommodation given by the S&D was quite as much as was usually given on so short a distance of line. A railway could not be built if a level crossing or a bridge had to be made for almost every field severed.

G. C. Ashmead of Bristol, a surveyor with large railway experience, considered the accommodation provided by the S&D sufficient, taking into consideration the amount of compensation that had been paid – £926, a sum he believed double what the jury ought to have given. 'If another bridge was made it would be an unusual amount of accommodation for so small an estate.'

The Bench ordered that the points conceded be carried out and that as suggested by Spackman — better access to Kelson's market garden be offered by an entrance being made close to the archway. The Bench made no order as to costs.

— 4 —

Passenger and freight train services, and signalling

UNTIL the summer of 1880, passenger train services were mostly local in character, but that year the MR introduced through trains from the North to Bournemouth via Bath. Through coaches were carried by expresses from Bradford and Newcastle, detached at Mangotsfield and taken on to Bath. The down train left Bath at 2.30pm and arrived at Wimborne at 4.33pm calling at three intermediate stations. The average speed of 31.75mph was very good considering the single line and gradients; these fast trains were headed by an 0-4-4T. It arrived at Bournemouth West 35 minutes after leaving Wimborne. The corresponding up train left Wimborne at 11.50am and took two hours to Bath, giving an average speed of 32mph.

In July 1891, responding to the opening of the Severn Tunnel forming a rival route, a through coach was run from Bradford to Plymouth Friary via Templecombe and the LSWR. Patronage must have been poor because it was withdrawn after running the following year. In 1891 the best up train left Bournemouth at 9.40am and arrived in Bath at 11.50am, the section over the Mendips from Shepton Mallet to Bath being booked to take 35 minutes, that is an average speed of 37.3mph.

In the summer of 1907 the S&D introduced an additional train which left Bournemouth at 10.50am and called at Poole and Broadstone from where it ran non-stop to Bath, arriving at 12.40pm to connect with the 12.55 from Bath, which connected with a train to the North.

Between 1910 and 1914 four fast or semi-fast trains ran from Bath to Bournemouth and back. In 1910 and 1911 the

South Western and Midland Railway Companies'

SOMERSET AND DORSET JOINT LINE.

EVERY MONDAY,

During June, July, August and September,

(Except Bank-Holiday, Monday, August 2nd)

EXCURSIONS TO

BOURNEMOUTH

(WEST)

For 1, 2, 3, 4, 5, 6, 8, or 15 Days,

WILL RUN AS UNDER:—

LEAVING	TRAIN.	Fares—Third Class.		
	a.m.	Day Trip	2, 3 or 4 days.	5, 6, 8 or 15 days.
Midford - -	7 10	3/9	7/-	8/-
Wellow - -	7 17			
Chilcompton -	7 40	3/9	6/6	7/6
Binegar - -	7 47	3/6	6/6	7/6
Masbury - -	7 52			
Evercreech New -	8 9	3/3	6/-	7/-

Passengers with Day Trip Tickets return from Bournemouth (West) at 6.45 p.m.

Passengers holding Tickets at the higher Fares return on the following Tuesday, Wednesday, Thursday, Friday, Saturday, Monday, or Monday week, from Bournemouth (West) at 1.30 p.m.

NOTICE.—The Tickets are not Transferable, and will be available for returning by the Trains named, and on the date for which issued only. Passengers leaving the Trains at intermediate Stations will forfeit their Excursion Tickets, and be required to pay the full Ordinary Fares.

The Committee give notice that Tickets for these Excursions are issued subject to the condition that the Committee shall not, under any circumstances, be responsible for any loss, damage, injury or delay to passengers arising off their own Railway, and to the further condition that they shall not be liable for any loss, damage, injury, or delay to passengers arising on their own Railway except upon proof of negligence.

No luggage allowed to Passengers holding day trip Tickets; but for the longer periods Sixty pounds of luggage, labelled with the name of the passenger and of the station to which the passenger is booked, allowed free. If taken into the compartment with the passenger, or delivered to the Committee without being fully addressed and labelled, the Committee shall not be answerable for loss, injury, or delay to it, and if delivered to the Committee duly addressed and labelled they will not be liable for loss, injury, or delay on their own Railway except on proof of negligence, and will not be liable, under any circumstances, for loss, injury, or delay off their own Railway.

Children under Three years of age, Free; Three and under Twelve, Half-fares.

Note.—For particulars of Excursions on Bank-Holiday, Monday, August 2nd, see Special Bills.

GEORGE H. EYRE,
Traffic Superintendent.

Offices, Mid. Station, Bath, June, 1909. No 68 | 200 | 2000.

F. Goodall, Printer, 18 & 19, Westgate Buildings, Bath.

1909 handbill.

Left: Class 4F No 44559 (ex-S&D No 59) and 'West Country' class No 34044 *Woolacombe* leaving Bath Junction with the down 'Pines Express' on 30 July 1955. The Bulleid Pacific has the tablet catcher extended and the door of the top lamp of the 0-6-0 is open. *Rev Alan Newman*

8.37am ex-Bournemouth had two restaurant cars for Nottingham and Manchester and through coaches for Bradford and Bristol. It reached Bath in 1 hour 50 minutes calling at Poole and Evercreech Junction. At Gloucester this train was combined with a train from Bristol Temple Meads which carried through coaches to Edinburgh and Glasgow. The 9.40am Bournemouth to Leeds train called at six stations *en route* to Bath and from October 1910 included coaches for Manchester. The 10.40am from Bournemouth to York ran only between July and September. The 12.20pm semi-fast from Bournemouth included a York coach, while the 2.5pm from Bournemouth ran through to Sheffield. In the down direction, in 1910 the 2.13pm ex-Bath had restaurant cars from Nottingham and Manchester reaching Poole from Bath in 1 hour 44 minutes. It was followed by a semi-fast leaving Bath at 2.23pm and serving more stations. The 4.5pm and 6.7pm from Bath carried coaches from Bradford and York, the former also having one from Harrogate and the latter, one from Newcastle. In 1914, the fastest train from Bath to Bournemouth took 1 hour 54 minutes calling only at Poole, and the fastest up, at 1 hour 50 minutes, calling at two stations. These times remained unbeaten. Average speed from Bath to passing Masbury was 31.04mph and to passing Blandford, 46.6mph.

Following the First World War the 8.37am from Bournemouth did not reappear, the principal up train being the 10.20am with restaurant cars for Derby and through coaches for Bradford,

Below: LSWR 1914 handbill.

LONDON AND SOUTH WESTERN RAILWAY.

On BANK HOLIDAY, MONDAY, 3rd AUGUST,

CHEAP EXCURSIONS

From BOURNEMOUTH (West), POOLE, &c.,

AS UNDER:—

TO GLASTONBURY OR WELLS

STATIONS FROM WHICH PASSENGERS WILL BE BOOKED.	TIMES OF DEPARTURE.	RETURN FARE, THIRD CLASS. To GLASTONBURY or WELLS.	TIMES OF RETURN ON THE DAY OF ISSUE ONLY.
	a.m.	s. d.	
BOURNEMOUTH WEST	7 0	3 6	From Wells at 5.10 p.m. From Glastonbury at 6.14 p.m. Wells Tickets are available at Shepton Mallet or Masbury either on the forward or return journey. The return Trains call at Masbury at 5.55 p.m. and Shepton Mallet at 6.53 p.m.
BRANKSOME	7 4		
PARKSTONE	7 8		
POOLE	7 14		

TO SHEPTON MALLET & BATH

STATIONS FROM WHICH PASSENGERS WILL BE BOOKED.	TIMES OF DEPARTURE.	RETURN FARES, THIRD CLASS. To Shepton Mallet.	To Bath.	TIMES OF RETURN ON THE DAY OF ISSUE ONLY. From Shepton Mallet.	From Bath.
	a.m.	s. d.	s. d.	p.m.	p.m.
Bournemouth West (see Note A) ...	9 40	3 6	4 0	6 53	6 7
Branksome	9 * 22				
Parkstone	9 47				
Poole	9 53				

* Change at Poole.

A—Tickets to Bath may also be obtained at the Midland Rly. Co.'s Office, 234, Old Christchurch Road, Bournemouth.

ATTRACTION :—Shepton Mallet Sports.

CONDITIONS upon which EXCURSION TICKETS are issued.

The Tickets are issued at a reduced rate subject to the Special Condition (a) that each Company or person owning, working, or using any railway, vehicles, vessels or premises (whether jointly or otherwise) upon which the Tickets may be available, shall not be liable for personal injury (whether fatal or otherwise), damage, delay, detention, or misconveyance however caused, and (b) that their holders waive the ordinary passengers' right to have any luggage carried free, the price of the Tickets being for the holders' carriage alone, and that the acceptance of the Tickets is to be understood as an agreement to that effect.

The Tickets are also issued subject to the Bye-Laws, Regulations, and Conditions published in the Time Tables, Bills and Notices of each such Company or person, relating to (a) "Cheap Tickets" and (b) "Ordinary Tickets" in so far as such Regulations and Conditions are applicable thereto, and are not inconsistent herewith.

The contract and liability of each such Company and person is limited to their or his own railway, vehicles, vessels or premises.

The Tickets are not transferable and may be used only on the days and by the trains advertised and for the Stations named on the Tickets, except where otherwise specified in the Company's Time Tables, Bills or Notices.

If a Passenger travels by an Excursion Train without having taken a Ticket the full ordinary fare will be charged.

Passengers will be conveyed by Excursion Trains subject to the ordinary liability of a Railway Company in case of injury or otherwise upon payment of the full ordinary fares.

Children not exceeding three years of age are conveyed free. Children over three and under twelve at half-fares; minimum fare one penny.

No luggage is allowed free to passengers holding Day or Half-day Cheap Tickets in any case, but each adult passenger holding a Cheap Ticket available for more than one day may bring 60 lbs. of personal luggage under his own care for which the Company will not charge and will not be responsible.

Bicycles, perambulators and mail carts will be conveyed at the rates shown in the Company's Time Tables.

H. A. WALKER, General Manager.

THE ... COMPANY'S OFFICIAL ILLUSTRATED GUIDE and LIST OF HOTELS, BOARDING HOUSES, APARTMENTS, ETC. For 1914 is now published, and can be obtained FREE at any of the Company's Offices or stations, from Mr. S. W. Milford, Central District Superintendent, West Station, Southampton, Hants, or from Mr. Henry Holmes, Superintendent of the Line, Waterloo Station, S.E.

Advertisements intended for the Guide to be issued early in May, 1915, must be forwarded before 1st March, 1915, to the Editor & Manager, 146, Kingshall Road, Beckenham.

2410/ 3,000/4217.

Waterlow & Sons Limited, Printers, Dunstable and London.

Right: Class 2P 4-4-0 No 40563 and Class 7F 2-8-0 No 53801 with a train of ex-LNER coaches from Cleethorpes to Exmouth on 16 July 1960. Ex-GWR '57xx' class 0-6-0PT No 3742 stands on the right with a van. *Colin Roberts*

Below: Extracts from the working timetable 14 September 1931.

18

INSTRUCTIONS TO STAFF.

Several Trains in the Public Time Tables are advertised to leave stations a little earlier than shown in the Working Time Book, and such timings must be adopted when possible All concerned in giving information o the Public must do so in accordance with the times shown in the Public Time Tables.

Errors or inaccuracies must be reported to the District Controller without delay.

SMALL figures denote Staff or Tablet purposes only.

Trains shown thus arr. 1 | 10 dep. denote the time at which Trains should **PASS** the Stations or Junctions, not stopping.

Guards must shew on the Journals of all Ordinary and Excursion Trains not booked to stop at Midford, Radstock, Binegar, Evercreech Junction, and Templecombe No 2 Junction in the case of Down Trains, and those not booked to stop at Templecombe No 2 Junct., Evercreech Junction, Binegar, Radstock and Midford in the case of Up Trains, the times such Trains pass the Stations named.

Trains will be Banked out of Bath as far as the North end of Combe Down Tunnel when required. The Regulations for working the Bath Bank Engine, as shown in Appendix No. 16 must in all cases be strictly carried out.

Engines Assisting Up Trains from Evercreech Junction to Binegar, or Down Trains from Radstock to Masbury Station must, in all cases be coupled to the Train Engine, and must not be detached until the Train has been brought to a stand at Masbury Station in the case of Down Trains, or Binegar in the case of Up Trains. Should a Train be Assisted which is not marked to stop at Binegar or Masbury Stations, as the case may be, the Train Driver of such Train must stop in order that the Assisting Engine may be detached. Should however the load of any train exceed 450 tons the Assisting Engine must be coupled at the rear of the train.

No Engine or Train, or portion of a Train shall be permitted to stand on or to shunt over the level crossing of the turnpike road at Evercreech Junction, so as to prevent the gates from being closed across the Railway, and no persons travelling along the road shall be detained for a longer interval of time than five minutes, by the gates remaining closed against them

The Line over the Southern Co's. system as between Wimborne or Broadstone and Bournemouth West must be understood to be the "Up Line," and the Line between Bournemouth West and Broadstone or Wimborne must be understood to be the "Down Line." All concerned to note.

Appendix to Working Time Book No. 16, and the Supplements Nos. 3, 4, 5 and 6 thereto will continue in force.

PASSENGER ENGINE CLASSIFICATION.

Passenger and Goods Engines are classified, and bear a classification plate on the cabside.

The division into classes will be as follows :—

Passenger Train Loading.

CLASS OF ENGINE.	LOADED COACHES BETWEEN		
	Bath & Evercreech Jn.	E'creech Jn. & Bailey Gate including T'Combe Upper.	Bailey Gate & B'mouth.
No. 1 Class	130 tons	200 tons	175 tons
No. 2 Class	190 tons	290 tons	260 tons
No. 4 Class Freight ..	230 tons	350 tons	310 tons
No. 7 Class ditto ..	310 tons	450 tons	415 tons
Engines Nos. 301, 302 303, 320 and 321 ..	160 tons	245 tons	215 tons

In case of Empty Coaches or Pigeon Specials 20 tons may be added to the above figures. Bank or Assisting Engines must not be taken with these loads unless through very bad weather or other exceptional causes.

Loaded Passenger Trains, Empty Coaches or Pigeon Specials, should not exceed 450 tons.

When working Passenger and Milk Trains between Highbridge and Templecombe the full load of a No. 1 Class Engine is 250 tons.

The loadings of the Bogie Side-tank Passenger Engine working Goods Trains between Wells and Glastonbury may be made equal to the loading of No 1 Class Goods Engine. (B.G.90411).

19

SPECIAL INSTRUCTIONS.

Enginemen are instructed to exercise proper care and caution in order to ensure a steady and safe passage for Trains when running over curves, especially reverse curves, or in crossing from one line to another, whether or not a specific instruction or special instruction is laid down. (C.G.7656).

In the case of Passenger Trains which are behind time and lightly Loaded, running time in sections should be recovered, particularly on the up gradients.

In every case, however, due attention must be given to the safe running of the Train, and time must not be made up in running on down gradients. (O.G.12948

The instructions shown on pages 58 and 59 of Appendix No. 16, with amendments and additions as per Supplement No. 6, are hereby cancelled and substituted by the following.

The note on page 59 limiting speed through Junctions to 15 miles per hour will continue to apply in all cases (including the Branch) except as shown below :—

Speed Restrictions.

Down Main Line. Situation.	Miles from Bath.	Reason for Restriction.	Limit of Speed.
Bath Junction ..	½	Junction Facing Points	20 m.p.h.
Radstock	10½	Curve on Level Crossing	25 ,,
Winsor Hill ..	20	Crossing and Curve	40 ,,
Evercreech Jct.	26—26¾	Junction	25 ,,
Wyke Curve ..	29	"S" Curve	25 ,,
Templecombe No. 3	36¼	Junction Facing Points	20 ,,
Templecombe No. 2	36¾	Junction Facing Points	20 ,,
Stalbridge ..	40¼	Loop Facing Points	20 ,,
Sturminster ..	44½	Loop Facing Points	30 ,,
Shillingstone ..	47¼	Loop Facing Points	20 ,,
Stourpaine ..	49¾	Loop Facing Points (when Stourpaine Signal Box is open)	20 ,,
Blandford ..	52¾	Loop Facing Points	40 ,,
Corfe Mullen ..	60½	Junction Facing Points	25 ,,
Broadstone ..	63¾	Junction and Curve..	20 ,,
Holes Bay Junction	66½	Junction and Curve..	30 ,,
Branksome ..	70¼	Junction Facing Points	30 ,,

Up Main Line. Situation.	Miles from Bournemouth.	Reason for Restriction.	Limit of Speed.
Holes Bay Junction	5	Junction and Curve..	30 m.p.h.
Broadstone ..	7¼	Junction and Curve..	30 ,,
Blandford ..	18¾	Loop Trailing Points	40 ,,
Templecombe ..	34½	Junction	20 ,,
Wyke Curve ..	42½	"S" Curve	25 ,,
Evercreech Junction	45½	Junction Facing Points	25 ,,
Midsomer Norton	59	Slip	20 ,,
Radstock ..	60¾	Curve on Level Crossing	25 ,,
Midford	67	Loop Trailing Points	20 ,,
Bath Junction ..	71	Junction Trailing Points	20 ,,

EVERCREECH JUNCTION AND BURNHAM LINE AND BRANCHES.

The table below indicates over which Section; Engines may run and the speed limits imposed:—

ENGINE. CLASS	SECTION. Evercreech Jun. to Glastonbury	Glastonbury to Edington Jun.	Edington Jun. to Highbridge	Highbridge to Burnham	Wells and Bridgwater Branches.
2 Passenger Tender Suprheat.	Light 40	Light 40	Light 30	No 30	No 30
2 Passenger Tender Saturated	40	40	40	40	40
1 Passenger Tank	40	40	30	30	39
3 Freight Tender	40	40	15	No	No
3 Freight Tank	40	40	Light 15	No	No
4 Freight Tender	Light 15	Light 15	Light 15	No	No
7 Freight Tender	Light 15	Light 15			

Tablet Exchanging by Hand.

The paragraph in reference to speed of Trains through Tablet Stations still operates.

SOMERSET AND DORSET RAILWAY

(JOINT COMMITTEE.)

THIS TIME TABLE IS STRICTLY PRIVATE AND MUST NOT BE GIVEN TO THE PUBLIC.

Working Time Table

OF

PASSENGER AND MILK TRAINS

COMMENCING

Monday, January 1st, 1940

until further notice

EXPLANATION OF GENERAL REFERENCES.

Small Figures denote passing times only.

Departure time only is shewn at several Stations and Halts, and unless otherwise stated, one minute has been allowed for necessary duties.

A—Mixed Trains.
C—For line clear only.
D—Stops daily for passengers.
G—Stops to set down passengers when required.
L—Light Engine.
SX—Saturdays excepted.
V—Engine and Van.
W—Engine for water.
Y—Collect Tickets.

Z—The **10.15 a.m. Highbridge to Templecombe** may convey passengers if the 10.0 a.m. ex Highbridge does not wait for the G.W. Co's connection. Passenger vehicle to be returned by 4.10 p.m. Templecombe to Highbridge. Parcels traffic must be forwarded to Evercreech Junction to connect with 12.38 p.m., thence to Bath.
‡—Empty Train.
*—Cross another Train.
•—Pass another Train.
⊠—Electric Tablet Stations.
¶—Staff and Ticket Stations.

BATH,
December, 1939.

HAROLD RUDGARD,
DIVISIONAL SUPT. OF OPERATION,
DERBY.

O.T. 3666 (900)

3034

2

Distances	DOWN MAIN LINE (Up Broadstone to Bournemouth).		Line	1 Passenger	2 Passenger	3 Passenger	4 Milk	5 Passenger	6 Passenger & Milk Tanks ex H'bridge	7 Passenger	8 Milk	9 Passenger	10 Perishables etc ex Highbridge	11 Passenger	12 Milk Tanks etc.	13 Milk, etc. ex Highbridge
M. C.	Reporting Nos.			a.m.	a.m.	a.m.	a.m.	a.m.	a.m.	p.m.	p.m.	p.m.	p.m.	p.m.	p.m.	p.m.
0 0	Bath Station	dep.	1	..	7 0	8 30	..	10 5	..	2 40	..	4 25	..	6 50	..	..
0 41	Bath Junction	pass	2	..	7 2	8 32	Engine and Van to leave Templecombe Lower at 10.30 a.m. due Wincanton 10.37.	10 7	..	2 42	Engine and Van to leave Templecombe Lower at 3.55 p.m. due Wincanton 4.2.	4 27	..	6 52	..	..
4 29	Midford ⊠	dep.	3	..	7 12	8 42		10 15	..	2 52		4 37	..	7 4	..	..
6 61	Wellow ⊠	,,	4	..	7 19	8 49		..	..	3 0		4 44	..	7 11	..	..
8 46	Shoscombe & S. H. Halt	,,	5	..	7 23	8 53		..	..	3 5		..	..	7 18	..	..
10 52	Radstock	arr.	6	..	7 28	8 58		10 25	..	3 10		4 51	..	7 24	..	..
		dep.	7	..	7 30	9 0		10 26	..	3 11		4 52	..	7 26	..	..
12 42	Midsomer Norton	arr.	8	..	7 37	9 7		10 33	..	3 18		4 59	..	7 33	..	..
		dep.	9	..	7 39	9 8		10 34	..	3 19		5 0	..	7 35	..	..
14 39	Chilcompton	arr.	10	..	7 46	9 15		10 41	..	3 26		5 7	..	7 42	Sundays only	Sundays only
		dep.	11	..	7 47	9 16		10 42	..	3 27		5 8	..	7 43		
17 5	Binegar	arr.	12	..	7 54	9 23		..	..	3 34		5 15	..	7 50		
		dep.	13	..	7 55	9 24		..	..	3 35		5 16	..	7 52		
18 51	Masbury Halt	arr.	14	..	7 59	9 28		..	..	3 40		..	..	7 57		
		dep.	15	..	8 0	9 29		10 52	..	3 41		5 20	..	7 58		
21 68	Shepton Mallet	arr.	16	..	8 6	9 34		10 57	..	3 47		5 25	..	8 5	..	..
		dep.	17	..	8 8	9 36		10 58	..	3 49		5 26	..	8 8	..	..
24 72	Evercreech New	arr.	18	..	8 13	9 41		..	Z	3 54		..	..	8 14	..	..
		dep.	19	..	8 14	9 42		..	..	3 55		..	..	8 15	..	..
26 34	Evercreech Jct. Station	arr	20	..	8 18	9 46		11 7	11 35	3 59		5 35	7 11	8 20	..	4 0
		dep.	21	..	8 21	9 50		11 14	11 55	4 2		5 38	7 30	8 30	..	4 5
29 16	Cole	arr.	22	..	8 27	9 56		..	..	4 8		..	7 37	8 36	..	..
		dep.	23	..	8 28	9 57		..	..	4 10		..	7 45	8 37	..	..
33 36	Wincanton	arr.	24	..	8 36	10 5	..	11 25	..	4 18	..	5 49	7 53	8 45	..	4 17
		dep.	25	..	8 38	10 10	11 0	11 27	..	4 20	4 40	5 51	8 8	8 48	..	4 33
6 79	Templecombe Lower	arr.	26	..	..	..	..	..	..	..	..	..	..	..	..	..
		dep.	27	6‡45	..	..	..	..	..	..	..	..	..	..	1V45	..
7 7	Templecombe Upper	arr.	28	6‡55	8 44	10 16	11 8	11 33	12 15	4 26	4 47	5 57	8 15	8 54	1V53	4 40
		dep.	29	7 15	9 10	10‡30	..	12 10	..	4 38	..	6 10	8L30	9 5	2 0	..
54	T'Combe No. 2 Junction ⊠	arr.	30	7 17	9 12	..	..	12 12	..	4 40	..	6 12	..	9 7	2 2	..
	Templecombe Lower	dep.	31	7 19	9 14	..	..	12 14	..	4 43	..	6 14	..	9 10	2 5	..
		arr.	32	..	..	10‡40	..	..	..	..	..	..	8L38	..	..	..
68	Henstridge	arr.	33	7 23	9 18	..	..	12 18	..	4 47	..	..	..	9 14	..	..
		dep.	34	7 25	9 19	..	..	12 19	..	4 48	..	..	..	9 15	..	..
7	Stalbridge	arr.	35	7 29	9 23	..	..	12 23	..	4 52	..	..	..	9 19	..	..
		dep.	36	7 35	9 25	..	..	12 24	..	5* 1	..	6 20	..	9 21	2 12	..
	Sturminster Newton ⊠	arr.	37	7 43	9 33	..	..	12 32	..	5 9	..	6 27	..	9 29	..	..
		dep.	38	7 51	9 36	..	..	12 33	..	5 11	..	6 28	..	9 31	2 20	..
	Shillingstone ⊠	arr.	39	7 57	9 41	..	..	12 39	..	5 17	..	6 35	..	9 37	2 26	..
		dep.	40	8* 3	9 43	..	..	12 40	..	5 19	..	6*41	..	9 38	2 31	..
	Stourpaine Loop ⊠	arr.	41	..	..	..	..	..	..	..	..	..	..	..	..	..
		dep.	42	..	..	..	..	..	..	..	..	..	..	..	..	..
	tourpaine & D. Halt ⊠	,,	43	8 9	9 50	..	..	12 48	..	5 26	..	..	..	G	..	..
	landford ⊠	arr.	44	8 14	9 56	..	..	12 54	..	5 32	..	6 51	..	9 48	..	..
		dep.	45	8 18	10 0	..	..	12 57	..	5 35	..	6 53	..	9 50	2 41	..
	arlton Marshall Halt	,,	46	8 22	10 5	..	..	1 3	..	5 41	..	..	..	G	..	..
	etisbury	,,	47	8 27	10 10	..	..	1 8	..	5 46	..	D	..	G	..	..
	iley Gate	arr.	48	8 32	10 15	..	..	1 14	..	5 51	..	..	..	10 0	2 51	..
		dep.	49	8 34	10 17	..	..	1 15	..	5 53	..	..	..	10 3	..	..
	fe Mullen Signal Box ⊠	arr.	50	..	10 21	..	..	..	..	5 57	..	..	..	..	..	..
		dep.	51	8 37	10C24	..	..	1 19	..	5*58	..	7 4	..	10 7	..	..
	e Mullen Halt	,,	52	8 41	10 29	..	..	1 24	..	6 3	..	..	..	G	..	..
56	Broadstone ⊠	arr.	53	8 44	10 33	..	..	1 28	..	6 7	..	7 10	..	10 14	..	..
		dep.	54	8 45	10 38	..	..	1 31	..	6 8	..	7 11	..	10 16	..	..
	Creekmoor Halt	,,	55	8 50	..	..	..	1 35	..	..	..	..	..	..	..	..
67 11	Poole	arr.	56	8 53	10 47	..	..	1 40	..	6 17	..	7 18	..	10 25	..	..
		dep.	57	8 55	10 50	..	..	1 43	..	6 19	..	7 20	..	10 27	..	..
68 75	Parkstone	dep.	58	9 1	10 56	..	..	1 49	..	6 25	..	..	..	10 33	..	..
70 20	Branksome	dep.	59	9 7	11 2	..	..	1 54	..	6 30	..	..	..	10 38	..	..
71 38	Bournemouth West	arr.	60	9Y11	11Y 6	..	..	1Y58	..	6Y34	..	7Y30	..	10Y42	..	..

Working timetable commencing 1 January 1940.

Manchester and Liverpool. It took 2 hours 5 minutes to Bath, calling at four intermediate stations. Its down counterpart was the 2.38pm from Bath non-stop to Poole and reaching Bournemouth in under two hours, but in the early 1920s, a stop at Templecombe was inserted adding 13 to 14 minutes. In 1927 the restaurant cars were diverted to Manchester and the train was given the name the 'Pines Express'.

In the summer of 1929 a weekend through train ran from Nottingham to Sidmouth, Budleigh Salterton and Exmouth. A new fast summer express introduced in 1933 started at Temple Meads and left Bath at 9.20am, arriving at Bournemouth at 11.22am calling only at Poole. This was the fastest train since the First World War. A day return from Bath to Bournemouth cost 7s 6d.

In 1939, the 'Pines Express' left Manchester London Road at 10.10am and at Crewe collected through coaches for Bournemouth which had left Liverpool Lime Street at 9.40am. It arrived at Birmingham New Street at 12.2pm and ran between Bath and Bournemouth in 2 hours 17 minutes despite being Class 5 hauled, making four intermediate stops and arriving in Bournemouth at 4.37pm — 6 hours 27 minutes for 252 miles. The up 'Pines' left Bournemouth at 10.35am and made 6 stops and a better time of 2 hours 5 minutes to Bath. It arrived at Manchester London Road at 4.51pm, or Liverpool Lime Street at 5.21pm. The 'Pines' was withdrawn at the outbreak of the Second World War and the name not restored until 7 October 1946 when it took 7 hours from Manchester to Bournemouth and 7¼ hours in the opposite direction.

Right: Advert in the *Bath & County Graphic*, February 1902.

Below left: An S&DJR advertisement of 1896.

Below right: An S&D advert which appeared on 29 August 1925.

SOMERSET & DORSET JOINT RAILWAY.

A SPECIAL SERVICE OF EXPRESS TRAINS is run between

PLYMOUTH, ILFRACOMBE, EXETER, PORTSMOUTH, SOUTHAMPTON, SALISBURY, BOURNEMOUTH, BATH, BRISTOL, CHELTENHAM, BIRMINGHAM, DERBY, LEEDS, YORK, BRADFORD, SHEFFIELD, LIVERPOOL, MANCHESTER, THE NORTH OF ENGLAND AND SCOTLAND.

Through Carriages are run Daily (Sundays excepted) between the principal Stations.

The Somerset and Dorset Joint Railway Company supply Saloon, Family, and Invalid Carriages of newest Pattern and replete with every modern convenience, and these can be obtained on Two Days' Notice being given to MR. R. A. DYKES, Midland Railway Station, Bath; or to any Somerset and Dorset Joint Railway Station.—For full particulars see Midland, London and South Western, and Somerset and Dorset Joint Railway TIME TABLES.

*** Full Particulars of above, also information as to

WEEK END BOOKINGS, HALF-HOLIDAY EXCURSIONS, & TOURIST BOOKINGS FOR SUMMER MONTHS

SEE PAMPHLETS, which will be forwarded on application to the Stations, or to—

ROBERT A. DYKES, Traffic Superintendent.

OFFICES, BATH; February, 1902.

Somerset & Dorset Joint Railway.

A SPECIAL SERVICE OF EXPRESS TRAINS

IS RUN BETWEEN

PLYMOUTH, ILFRACOMBE, EXETER, PORTSMOUTH, SOUTHAMPTON, SALISBURY, BOURNEMOUTH, BATH, BRISTOL, CHELTENHAM, BIRMINGHAM, DERBY, LEEDS, YORK, BRADFORD, SHEFFIELD, LIVERPOOL, MANCHESTER, THE NORTH OF ENGLAND AND SCOTLAND.

THROUGH CARRIAGES are run Daily (Sundays excepted) between the principal Stations.

THE SOMERSET AND DORSET RAILWAY COMPANY now supply Saloon, Family, and Invalid Carriages of the newest Pattern and replete with every Modern Convenience, and these can be obtained on Two Days' Notice being given to MR. R. A. DYKES, Midland Railway Station, Bath; or to any Somerset and Dorset Railway Station.

For Full Particulars see Midland, London & South Western, and Somerset & Dorset Time Tables.

During Summer Months Special Cheap Fast Excursions

Are run from BATH (Midland Station) and all Somerset and Dorset Stations to GLASTONBURY, WELLS, BOURNEMOUTH, PORTSMOUTH, and other Places of Interest.

TOURIST AND WEEK-END EXCURSION TICKETS ARE ALSO ISSUED TO VARIOUS PLACES.

*** *Full Particulars of which will be furnished on application to—*

ROBERT A. DYKES,
Traffic Superintendent.

Offices—Midland Station, Bath.

S. & D.J.R.

HALF-DAY EXCURSION TO

BURNHAM-ON-SEA

ON **SATURDAY, September 5th, HALF-DAY** Excursion will run to BURNHAM-ON-SEA

		a.m.	
Leaving Bath (L.M.S. Stn))	...	11.0	2/6
„ Radstock	...	11.23	
„ Midsomer Norton	...	11.31	
„ Chilcompton	...	11.41	

Return train leaves Burnham-on-Sea 7.20 p.m.

GEO. H. WHEELER, Traffic Superintendent.

Below: Class 3F No 47557 leaving Bath with the 6.5pm to Binegar in 1954. It was unusual to see an S&D passenger train worked by an 0-6-0T. Behind this train are ex-GWR diesel railcars Nos W35 and W36 working the 6.18pm to Bristol Temple Meads. *Rev Alan Newman*

An interesting late introduction was made in 1960 of a Cleethorpes/Lincoln/Nottingham to Sidmouth/Exmouth train, together with one in the reverse direction: up and down trains, one of Eastern Region stock and the other of Southern green-liveried coaches crossed each other in Bath. In 1962, the last year it worked over the S&D, the 'Pines' took 2 hours 11 minutes from Bournemouth to Bath, calling at five stations and taking 15 minutes more between Manchester and Bournemouth than the corresponding train did in 1910! The 'Pines' was re-routed when through trains over the S&D were withdrawn on 10 September 1962.

Local passenger trains tended to work from Bristol (St Philip's, Temple Meads, Clifton Down or Portishead) to Bournemouth, rather than originating at Bath. This was because as the MR provided stock for through trains, to balance the account S&D stock was used for local working beyond S&D territory.

The S&D ran imaginative and attractive excursions such as Bath to Bournemouth, Weymouth or Burnham-on-Sea. In 1895 the S&D offered an excursion from Bath to London

Class 1P 0-4-4T No 58088 (22E, Highbridge) passing Templecombe Junction with the 2.5pm from Burnham-on-Sea to Templecombe, 30 June 1950. *Pursey Short courtesy Roger Venning*

departing on 5 March and returning between one and four days later. Every Monday and Friday in 1900, cheap excursions were offered to London and the Thames Valley from all S&D stations. In the early 1900s an excursion ran from Bath to Bournemouth in 2 hours for 2s 6d return, while in 1906 a return ticket from Bath to Seaton Regatta cost 3s 9d. In the summer of 1907 circular tour tickets were available for a ride from Bath–Glastonbury–Highbridge, transferring to the GWR to visit Weston-super-Mare and back to Bath via Bristol. A similar trip was Bath–Glastonbury–Wells, transferring to the GWR to Cheddar, Yatton and back to Bath via Bristol. In 1911, one could opt for a Bath to Bournemouth trip for 3s 9d and even to Cherbourg and back for an extra 5s; other offers being Bath to Weymouth return for 3s 9d, Portsmouth 5s 6d, or a half day to Bournemouth for 2s 6d.

In 1932 a through half-day excursion ran from Avonmouth and other GWR Bristol district stations to Bournemouth West, joining the S&D at Highbridge. A GWR engine worked throughout and on 11 August 1932 4-4-0 No 3367 *Evan Llewellyn* was used. The S&D supplied a pilotman from Highbridge to Bournemouth. In 1933, an evening excursion was run, leaving Warmley at 3pm and calling at Bitton, Kelston, Bath and arriving in Bournemouth at 5.27pm. The return train left Bournemouth at 10.15pm. The fare was only 3s 9d. On August Bank Holiday 1933, 470 passengers travelled from Bath to Bournemouth and 49 to Wareham. On 1 July 1934 Class 4F 0-6-0 No 4558 worked a Bath to Weymouth excursion throughout as did No 4561 on 13 July 1935. At the height of summer in the Thirties, a train ran to and from the North and Bournemouth carrying a painted headboard 'Bournemouth Rapid'. As late as 16 July 1964 an 11-coach schools outing ran from Cole to Coventry, while on Whit Monday 1965 a 15s excursion ran from Temple Meads to Bournemouth, with the final one run on Bank Holiday Monday, 30 August 1965. In addition to public excursions, the S&D provided trains for outings for groups from churches, chapels and less often, collieries, to visit such places as Bristol, Weymouth and Bournemouth.

At one period in the 19th century, 17-coach trains were double-headed from Bath to Blandford where they were split into eight- and nine-coach portions each hauled by a single engine because Bournemouth West was unable to cope with longer trains. In the 1890s the 'Small' 4-4-0s, designed by Johnson, were able to haul 11 six-wheelers from Bath to Bournemouth in 2 hours 10 minutes, making seven intermediate stops. For special trains and excursions the S&D used 0-6-0s, which for most of the time were used for goods traffic. The 1920 working timetable had paths, if required, for 'Cook's Excursions', a 3.45am from Bath for the West of England and a

An LMS advertisement from 1 August 1934.

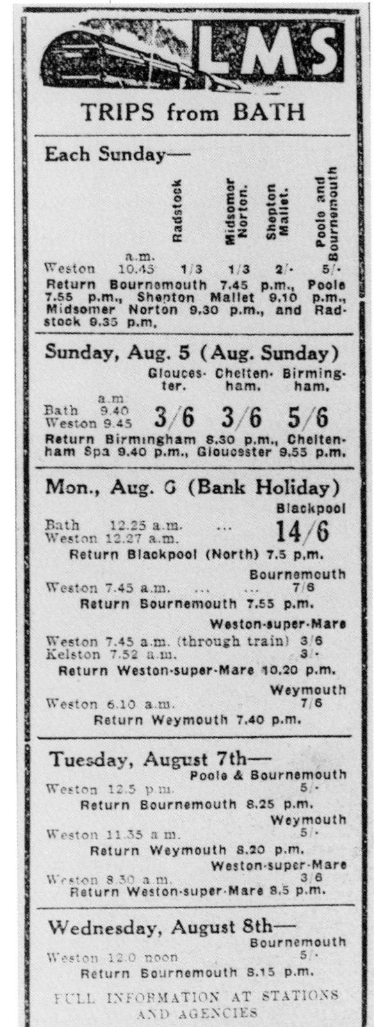
LMS

TRIPS from BATH

Each Sunday—

	a.m.	Radstock	Midsomer Norton.	Shepton Mallet.	Poole and Bournemouth
Weston	10.45	1/3	1/3	2/-	5/-

Return Bournemouth 7.45 p.m., Poole 7.55 p.m., Shepton Mallet 9.10 p.m., Midsomer Norton 9.30 p.m., and Radstock 9.35 p.m.

Sunday, Aug. 5 (Aug. Sunday)

	a.m.	Gloucester.	Cheltenham.	Birmingham.
Bath	9.40	3/6	3/6	5/6
Weston	9.45			

Return Birmingham 8.30 p.m., Cheltenham Spa 9.40 p.m., Gloucester 9.55 p.m.

Mon., Aug. 6 (Bank Holiday)

Blackpool
Bath 12.25 a.m. ... 14/6
Weston 12.27 a.m.
Return Blackpool (North) 7.5 p.m.

Bournemouth
Weston 7.45 a.m. 7/6
Return Bournemouth 7.55 p.m.

Weston-super-Mare
Weston 7.45 a.m. (through train) 3/6
Kelston 7.52 a.m. 3/-
Return Weston-super-Mare 10.20 p.m.

Weymouth
Weston 6.10 a.m. 7/6
Return Weymouth 7.40 p.m.

Tuesday, August 7th—

Poole & Bournemouth
Weston 12.5 p.m. 5/-
Return Bournemouth 8.25 p.m.

Weymouth
Weston 11.35 a.m. 5/-
Return Weymouth 8.20 p.m.

Weston-super-Mare
Weston 8.30 a.m. 3/6
Return Weston-super-Mare 8.5 p.m.

Wednesday, August 8th—

Bournemouth
Weston 12.0 noon 5/-
Return Bournemouth 8.15 p.m.

FULL INFORMATION AT STATIONS AND AGENCIES

Miles	DOWN MAIN LINE.		Line	51	52	53	54	55	56	57	58	59	60	61
	Reporting Nos.			Freight.	Light Engine.	Mail.	Freight.	Freight.	Freight.		Freight.	Light Engine.	Freight.	Light Engine.
				MX	MO			Q	MX					
				a.m.	a.m.	a.m.	a.m.	a.m.	a.m.	a.m.	a.m.	a.m.	a.m.	a.m.
0 0	Bath Station	dep.	1	..	..	2 40	..	..	..	..	..	..	..	..
0 20	Bath Yard	,,	2	12 10	2 20	2A46	3 30	5 0	..	..	5 50	..		..
0 41	Bath Junction	pass	3	12 12	..	2 47	3 32	5 2	..	..	5 52	..		..
	Bath Co-op. Siding	arr.	4	..	To Combe Down Tunnel	..	..	..	..	..	..	..		..
4 29	Midford	dep.	5	12 25		3 0	3 45	5 15	..	..	6H30	..		..
6 61	Wellow	,,	6	12 33		3 8	3 53	5 23	..	..	7H15	..		..
9 54	Writhlington Sidings	,,	7	..		..	..	..	..	..	..	..		..
10 52	Radstock	arr.	8	12 45		3 20	4 5	5 35	..	..	7 27	..		..
		dep.	9	12 48		3G25	4 8	5 38	..	..	7 40	7 5		..
12 42	Midsomer Norton	arr.	10	..		..	..	..	..	..	7 50	..		..
		dep.	11	12 58		3 35	4 18	5 48	..	..	8 5	..		..
14 39	Chilcompton	arr.	12	..		..	..	..	..	..	8 15	..		..
		dep.	13	1 8		3 45	4 28	5 58	..	..	8 35	..		..
15 56	Moorewood Sidings	,,	14	..		..	..	..	..	..	8H50	7 15		..
17 5	Binegar	,,	15	1 18		3 55	4 38	6 8	..	..	9H30	..		..
18 51	Masbury Halt	,,	16	1 25	..	4 2	4 45	6 15	..	..	9 37	..		..
20 0	Winsor Hill Siding	,,	17	..	..	..	..	..	..	..	..	..		..
20 35	Downside Siding	,,	18	..	..	..	..	..	..	..	..	..		..
21 68	Shepton Mallet	arr.	19	..	..	4 10	..	6W24	..	..	9 46	..		..
		dep.	20	1 33	..	4 16	4 54	6 45	..	..	10 45	..		..
24 72	Evercreech New	arr.	21	..	..	..	..	..	..	..	10 58	..		..
		dep.	22	1 46	..	4 29	5 7	6 58	..	..	11 25	..		..
26 10	Evercreech Jc. Nth.	arr.	23	1 50	..	4 33	5 11	7 2	..	..	11 30	..		..
		dep.	24	2D 5	..	4D35	..	..	5 25	..	12 10	..	6 35	..
26 34	Evercreech Jc. Stn.	arr.	25	2W7	..	4W37	..	..	..	..	12W12	..	6W37	..
		dep.	26	2 15	..	4 45	..	..	..	..	12 25	..	6 45	..
29 16	Cole	arr.	27	..	..	..	..	..	..	..	12 35	..	6 55	..
		dep.	28	..	..	..	..	..	..	..	1 5	..	7 5	..
33 36	Wincanton	arr.	29	..	..	5 5	..	..	5 46	..	1 20	..	7 20	..
		dep.	30	2 36	..	5 10	..	..	6 0	..	1 45	..	7 30	7 45
36 79	Templecombe Lower	arr.	31	..	..	..	..	..	6 10	..	1 55	..	..	..
		dep.	32	..	..	..	..	..	..	..	..	..	..	..
36 54	T'Combe No. 2 Junc.	arr.	33	..	..	5E20	..	..	..	..	..	..	7E40	..
		dep.	34	..	..	5 35	..	..	..	..	..	..	7 55	..
37 7	Templecombe Upper	arr.	35	2F45	..	..	..	..	..	..	..	..	..	7 53
	T'Combe No. 2 Junc.	arr.	36	3 7	..	..	..	..	..	..	..	..	..	..
		dep.	37	3K30	..	..	..	..	..	..	..	..	..	..
	Templecombe Lower	arr.	38	3L38	..	5J36	..	..	..	..	..	..	..	..
38 68	Henstridge	arr.	39	..	..	..	..	..	..	..	..	..	..	..
		dep.	40		..	..	..	..	..	..	..	..	..	..
40 27	Stalbridge	arr.	41		..	..	..	..	..	..	..	..	8 5	..
		dep.	42		..	5 46	..	..	..	..	..	..	8 15	..
44 25	Sturminster Newton	arr.	43		..	5 55	..	..	..	..	..	..	..	..
		dep.	44		..	5 56	..	..	..	..	..	..	8 26	..
47 28	Shillingstone	arr.	45		..	..	..	..	..	..	..	..	..	..
		dep.	46		..	6 3	..	..	..	..	..	..	8 35	..
49 54	Stourpaine Loop	arr.	47		..	..	..	..	..	..	..	..	..	..
		dep.	48		..	..	..	..	..	..	..	..	..	..
52 65	Blandford	arr.	49		..	6W17	..	..	..	..	..	..	8 51	..
		dep.	50		..	6 25	..	..	..	..	..	..	10 15	..
56 9	Spetisbury Halt	,,	51		..	..	..	..	..	..	..	..	..	..
58 74	Bailey Gate	arr.	52		..	..	..	..	..	..	..	..	10 30	..
		dep.	53		..	6 40	..	..	..	..	..	..	11 15	..
60 56	Corfe Mullen S.B.	,,	54		..	6 45	..	..	..	..	..	..	12N 6	..
63 56	Broadstone	arr.	55		..	6 53	..	..	..	..	..	..	12 15	..
		dep.	56		..	7 6	..	..	..	..	..	..	12 45	..
67 11	Poole	arr.	57		..	7 15	..	..	..	..	..	..	12 56	..
		dep.	58		..	7 35	..	..	..	..	..	..	..	..
68 75	Parkstone	,,	59		..	7 42	..	..	..	..	..	..		
70 20	Branksome	,,	60		..	7 46	..							
71 38	Bournemouth West	arr.	61			7 52								

F—Engine Light 3.5 a.m. to Lower Yard.
K—Change Engine.
D—Detach only.

H—Arrives Midford 6.5, Wellow 6.38, Moorewood Sidings 8.40, Binegar 8.55.

N—Arrive Corfe Mullen 11.21, Works Carter's Siding when necessary—10 minutes allowed

A—No. 53 Down arrives Bath Yard 2.41. D—No. 53 Down. Detach coupled engine MX.
G—No. 53 Down, coupled engine to bank when necessary.
J—No. 53 Down stops one minute for mails (depart 5.37)

Working timetable of freight trains 3 January 1938.

Class 1P 0-4-4T No 58072 (71J, Highbridge) climbing the 1 in 50 through Oldfield Park, Bath, with the 6.5pm stopping train from Bath to Binegar in May 1955. Normally, this train was worked at this period by an Ivatt Class 2 2-6-2T. No 58072 retains the tall brackets on the buffer beams for carrying destination boards when working suburban passenger services in the London area. *R. E. Toop*

Loading tables for engines working over the S&D.

Loading Tables for Engines working over the S&D Railway.
Loaded coaches.

Ex L.M. & B.R. Std Freight Engines

Class of Engines	3 Ex Midland 0-6-0	4 Ex Midland 0-6-0	5 Horwich † 2-6-0	7 Ex S&D 2-8-0	8 Ex L.M.S. 2-8-0	9 B.R. 2-10-0
	Tons	Tons	Tons	Tons	Tons	Tons
Bath to Masbury	190	240	240	310	310	410
Masbury to Corfe Mullen N	290	365	365	450	450	410
Corfe Mullen to Bournemouth West	260	320	320	415	415	410
Bournemouth West to Corfe Mullen	260	320	320	415	415	410
Corfe Mullen to Evercreech Junction N	290	365	365	450	450	410
Evercreech Junction to Binegar	190	240	240	310	310	410
Binegar to Bath	260	320	320	415	415	410

Ex L.M. & B.R. Std Passenger & Mixed Traffic Engines.

Class of Engines	1 Ex Midland 0-4-4T	2 Ex Midland 4-4-0	2 Ex L.M.S. 4-4-0	3 2-6-2T	4 Compound 4-4-0	4 B.R. 2 6 4T 2-6-0 4-6-0	5 L.M.&B.R 4-6-0s	6 B.R. Clan * 4-6-2
	Tons	Tons	Tons	Tons	Tons	Tons	Tons	Tons
Bath to Masbury	130	190	200	220	225	240	270	290
Masbury to Corfe Mullen N	200	290	310	335	340	365	405	425 (a)
Corfe Mutten to Bournemouth West	175	260	275	300	310	300	380	..
Bournemouth West to Corfe Mullen	175	260	275	300	310	300	380	..
Corfe Mullen to Evercreech Junction N	200	290	310	335	340	365	405	425 (b)
Evercreech Junction to Binegar	130	190	200	220	225	240	270	290
Binegar to Bath	175	260	275	300	310	320	380	400

NOTES:

N .. Including Templecombe Upper.
(a) .. Masbury to Templecombe Upper only.
(b) .. Templecombe Upper to Evercreech Junction only.
* .. This class never actually worked on the line.
† .. Strictly speaking, the Horwich 2-6-0 ought to come under the heading "Passenger and Mixed Traffic Engines".,
but in the Loading Tables contained in the various appendices to the S&D working timetables

INSTRUCTIONS RESPECTING THE WORKING OF TRAINS

Page 62—*Add*— SNOW CLEARANCE ARRANGEMENTS.

(1) When snow is probable, there must be close contact between Station Masters, Signalmen, Permanent Way Inspectors and Gangers to ensure that the District Control Office (or Divisional Control Office in the Central Division where applicable) is promptly advised and kept informed of the conditions and requirements, either by the Station Masters or Signalmen as is most convenient. Drivers who observe snow accumulating when passing through sections must stop and report the circumstances at the next station or signal box open, unless they are aware that snow clearance arrangements are in operation.

(2) Where special instructions are issued regarding the use of Snow Ploughs on certain sections of the line, they must be carefully observed, as the prompt use of the ploughs when heavy snow seems probable is the most effective means of keeping the lines open for traffic.

(3) On the other sections of the line not covered by paragraph 2, where drifts speedily accumulate, and there may be long intervals between trains, Station Masters must arrange for light engines to run as necessary to keep the lines clear, and also for signal boxes to be kept open as required. When asking for engines for this purpose, Station Masters must make the position clear so that the best types of engines for the work can be sent.

(4) When bad conditions seem probable, District Control Offices, Station Masters, Yard Masters and other supervisors concerned, must arrange immediately for **all** train loads to be reduced as circumstances require, if necessary, to 50 per cent of the regular load for the class of engine or engines. Where preferable and possible, engines of higher power may be substituted for the engines working the trains or the trains may be double headed, but any increased power provided must be subject to the above instruction and the load reduced as required, if necessary to 50 per cent of the regular load for the class of engine or engines working the train forward. It is important to note that many trains have stuck in small drifts owing to loss of speed due to the loads being too heavy for the engine to maintain speed on gradients.

It must be borne in mind that when the load and weather conditions combined overpower the engines, there is a grave risk of snow drifts accumulating under the wheels which may either cause derailment when the vehicles are moved, or make release difficult. Such stoppages delay the use of the snow ploughs and may even immobilise them owing to the ploughs being unable to pass over important sections of single line, or travel through the section in the right direction for the purpose of returning and ploughing the opposite line. Thus, stoppages of this kind on one line may quickly lead to both lines being blocked by drifts.

Freight trains running slowly or freight trains whose engines are running short of water and are likely to become " dead " must be shunted into sidings as soon as possible or they may cause the lines to be blocked or delay the use of snow ploughs.

After a train has been disposed of as above, the engine must be taken to the nearest Motive Power Depot and may be used as a light engine to clear the lines as referred to in paragraph 3. This will only apply if a supply of water is obtainable, but if the engine is unable to work to the nearest Motive Power Depot, the fire must be dropped and the usual disposal precautions taken.

(5) Train staffs must carefully note paragraph (4) and take care to guard against trains sticking in sections; if a train fails, special action must be taken to clear it quickly and if it is a loose coupled train, it should be divided and cleared in accordance with Clauses (b) and (f) of Rule 183, or assistance provided from the signal box in advance in accordance with Clause (g) of Rule 183, unless the train can be cleared much earlier by providing assistance at the rear.

22

INSTRUCTIONS RESPECTING THE WORKING OF TRAINS

SNOW CLEARANCE ARRANGEMENTS—*continued*

The object of this arrangement is to prevent where possible, loose coupled wagons being propelled through drifts, as derailments may result even though drifts are slight.

Enginemen should be specially careful to see the tanks are full when approaching areas affected by snow, particularly where the gradients are sharp, and special stops may be made for this purpose.

(6) At signal boxes which control the outlet from and/or the inlet to Locomotive Sheds, Station Masters, Signalmen, Gangers and Shed staff should make special efforts to keep the points free so that breakdown trains, snow ploughs and engines may leave or arrive without delay.

(7) **Special care is necessary at week-ends or during other times when any section of the line is closed, and any member of the staff in the departments of the Chief Operating Manager or Chief Civil Engineer becoming aware during the night that snow is imminent or falling and who cannot quickly contact the Station Master, should advise the nearest Control Office by using the Post Office telephone and seek instructions.**

Station Masters must also arrange for Signal Boxes and Level Crossings which are closed to be opened an hour or more earlier and for men to be provided to clear points.

(8) All concerned must carefully observe Rule 95, and whenever there is an indication of a heavy fall of snow, no time must be lost in calling out the Engineer's lengthmen and the Signal and Telegraph linemen to keep the lines, points and signals, etc., clear.

(9) A snow plough must be signalled by the bell signal 4 consecutive beats when going to clear the line and 3—1 beats when not going to clear the line.

Left: Supplement dated 11 July 1949 to Appendix to the working timetable, giving instructions regarding snow clearing etc.

10.43am to Bournemouth that had originated from Birmingham.

Following the end of the First World War, the S&D was the first of the three railways serving Bath to reintroduce cheap day tickets. Its newly appointed traffic superintendent, Lt-Col A. S. Redman, arranged an excursion from Bath to Bournemouth on 19 August 1920 for 10s 6d return, a sum which only slightly exceeded the normal single fare of 10s 5½d. It left at 8am and arrived at Bournemouth at 10.20am, departure for Bath being at 7.30pm and arrival at 10pm. To avoid the risk of any last-minute queues, overcrowding or disappointment, the issue of tickets ceased on or before 6pm the previous day. After the event, the *Bath Chronicle* reported that 'comfortable and up-to-date coaches' were used and included one saloon 'which enabled the passengers to obtain a good view of the scenery on each side of the line'.

The 'Sunshine' was a regular summer Sunday working in the Thirties. It left Bristol at 10.10am, arrived in Bath at 10.53, left at 11.00 and reached Bournemouth at 1.15pm. After the coaches had been stabled and the engine taken to Branksome shed with the boiler filled and left so that she would hold steam, but not make any more, the crew was free until it was time to prepare the engine to work the train home. It was termed a 'continuous duty' and they were paid for the afternoon when they were not actually working.

On one occasion, Bob Ford was firing on a double-headed train of 12 coaches. After a meal following their arrival at Bournemouth, the four footplate crew members went to a pub. Bob had a shandy and made it last, his driver had a couple of pints, but the pilot engine driver had far too many. About 3pm they managed to get him to a permanent way lengthsman's cabin and let him have a snooze.

When they woke him at 6pm they were worried because he was in no fit state to

Obstructions on the L M S Company's System necessitating Diversions over G.W. Lines. Bristol Division—*continued.*

Blocked Line	Routes to which trains may be diverted	Working Arrangements	Officers to be advised	Engine and Rolling Stock Permissions and Restrictions
Yate S. Junction and Bristol East (exclusive) (L M S)	L M S trains may run over G.W. Line via Yate S. Junction, Stoke Gifford and Bristol East (or vice versa).	L M S engines and men to work through. G.W. Divisional and Locomotive Superintendents, Bristol, to provide pilot drivers and guards if necessary.	District Controller, Gloucester, to advise G.W. Divisional Superintendent, Bristol, District Controller, Bath, and Divisional Control, Derby.	**Permitted between Yate South Jct. and Stoke Gifford:** *Class 5XP 4-6-0 (Std.) *Class 5P 5F 4-6-0 (Mixed Tfc.) * 4P 4-4-0 (Std. Compound) * 3P 4-4-0 (Midland) * 2P 4-4-0 (Std.) * 5P 4F 2-6-0 (Par. or Taper Boiler) 4F 0-6-0 (Std.) 8F 2-8-0 (Std.) 7F 0-8-0 (Std.) 3F 0-6-0 (Mid.) * Subject to special restriction of 20 m.p.h. between Yate S. Jct. and Westerleigh Jct.
	NOTE. If the obstruction is between Yate S. Junction and Mangotsfield N. Junction trains between Gloucester and Bath will be diverted to Bristol via Stoke Gifford, and then run to Bath via Fish Ponds.			
Avonmouth and Kingswood Junction (L M S and G.W. Joint)	L M S freight trains may run over G.W. Line to and from Avonmouth via Henbury and Yate S. Junction (or vice versa).	L M S engines and men to work through. G.W. Divisional and Locomotive Superintendents, Bristol, to provide pilot drivers and guards between Avonmouth and Yate, if necessary.	District Controller, Gloucester, to advise G.W. Divisional Superintendent, Bristol, and Divisional Control, Derby.	**Permitted between Avonmouth, Henbury and Yate South Junction:** Engines as above.
Mangotsfield and Bath (L M S) Bath and Templecombe No. 2 (S. and D. Joint)	Through trains between the L M S Line and Bournemouth (West) may run over the G.W. Line via Yate S. Junction, Dr. Day's Bridge Junction, Bathampton and Salisbury, and thence over the S.R. to Broadstone (or vice versa).	L M S engines and men to work through. G.W. Divisional and Locomotive Superintendents, Bristol, to provide pilot drivers and guards between Yate and Salisbury. S.R. Divisional Superintendent, Southampton, to provide pilot drivers and guards between Salisbury and Broadstone or Bournemouth. Trains will call at Bath G.W. Station.	District Controller, Bath, to advise G.W. Divisional Superintendent, Bristol, S.R. Divisional Superintendent, Southampton, District Controller, Gloucester, and Divisional Control, Derby.	**Permitted between Yate South Junction, Dr. Day's Bridge Junction, Bathampton and Salisbury:** ‡Class 5P 5F 4-6-0 (Mixed Tfc.) ‡ 5P 4F 2-6-0 (Par. Boiler) ‡ 4P 4-4-0 (Std. Compound) ‡ 4F 0-6-0 (Std.) ‡ 2P 4-4-0 (Std.) ‡—Subject to special restriction of 20 m.p.h. between Yate South Junction and Westerleigh Junction.

SPECIMEN DAY FARES

Available By Any Train Weekdays and Sundays (where train service permits) for return by any train the same day affording a service through to destination.

For full details see separate pamphlet.

(Where First Class accommodation is available, First Class tickets are issued at approximately 50% above the Second Class Fare).

	Return Fares Second Class s.	d.
From BATH (Green Park)		
To Bitton	2	0
Bristol T.M.	3	0
Cheltenham Spa ...	11	0
Cole	7	6
Evercreech Junction ...	6	9
Gloucester	10	0
Mangotsfield	2	9
Midsomer Norton South ...	3	3
Radstock North	2	9
Warmley	2	6
Weston-Super-Mare ...	8	0
From CHILCOMPTON		
To Bath (Green Park)	3	9
Shepton Mallet (C. Rd.) ...	2	9
From COLE		
To Bath (Green Park) ...	7	6
Shepton Mallet (C. Rd.) ...	2	9
Wincanton	1	9
From EVERCREECH JUNC.		
To Bath (Green Park)	6	9
Glastonbury and Street ...	2	9
Shepton Mallet (C. Rd.) ...	1	9
Wincanton	2	9
From EVERCREECH NEW		
To Bath (Green Park)	6	3
Glastonbury and Street ...	3	0
Wincanton	3	0

	Return Fares Second Class s.	d.
From MIDFORD		
To Bath (Green Park)	1	6
From MIDSOMER NORTON SOUTH		
To Bath (Green Park)	3	3
Shepton Mallet (C. Rd.) ...	3	3
From RADSTOCK NORTH		
To Bath (Green Park)	2	9
Shepton Mallet (C. Rd.) ...	3	6
From SHEPTON MALLET (Charlton Road)		
To Bath (Green Park)	5	6
Wincanton	3	6
From WELLOW		
To Bath (Green Park)	2	0
From WINCANTON		
To Bath (Green Park)	8	6
Salisbury	8	0
Shepton Mallet (C. Rd.) ...	3	6
Sherborne	3	0
Sturminster Newton ...	3	3
Yeovil	3	6

NOTE — The above fares are liable to alteration.

Children under Three years of age, Free, Three and under Fourteen years of age, Half-fare. (Fractions of a penny reckoned as one penny)

Tickets can be obtained in advance at Booking Stations and Agencies.

drive. As Bob was then a registered but not a passed fireman, he could not have driven the pilot engine. Fortunately, the driver became sober in time, but it spoilt the afternoon for the other three because they did not know what to do — whether to see someone at Branksome, or phone Bath — but they were reluctant to get him into trouble.

Driver Bill Gray was very proud of his brown boots which he kept clean and sparkling. One Sunday he worked a 'Sunshine' and he, his fireman and Guard Jack Hopkins went to the beach and fell asleep in deck chairs.

Jack woke with cold feet — the tide had come in. He woke Bill who sadly remarked: 'Look at my poor boots — they're as white as a lily!' Onlookers who had gathered round to see when they would wake up, thought it a great joke.

The return 'Sunshine' left Bournemouth at 7.45pm and although scheduled arrival at Bath was 10.5pm, crews aimed to arrive at Bath before the pubs closed at 10pm. Another engine took the train to Bristol where it arrived at 10.53.

Above: Instructions regarding the diversion of through trains to alternative routes in cases of emergency, June 1940.

Left: A handbill for the period 10 September 1962 to 16 June 1963.

Class 3F 0-6-0T No 7619 (22C, Bath) shunting at Bath *c*1935. The six-wheeled S&D mail brake van is behind the bunker. *S. Miles Davey*

Freight and mineral services

The S&D carried a significant quantity of freight traffic. Apart from that generated by industries adjacent to the line such as brick-making, agricultural engineering, brewing and the dairy industry, there were goods consigned to the area to be sold in shops, or used in workshops and on farms. Additionally there was a very significant coal traffic emanating from 14 pits, stone from five quarries and a fuller's earth mine. There was also the highly important through heavy traffic from the Midlands and Avonmouth to the LSWR. In the first 11 months following the opening of the Bath Extension in 1874, no fewer than 107,529 tons of traffic were exchanged with the MR at Bath, and 89,431 tons with the LSWR at Templecombe, thus proving that the step to create a north to south through route had been a correct decision, because hitherto S&D traffic had been principally of a local nature. Under Joint ownership, between 1876 and 1899, traffic almost doubled regarding train mileage, tonnage and the number of passengers carried. In 1899, Dykes said that some days up to 1,000 wagons were exchanged with other companies.

In 1875, the year following the opening of the Bath Extension, timetables showed six goods trains daily, plus a coal train from Radstock. Two years later, a stone train was added from Binegar or Winsor Hill. By 1894, 17 goods trains ran each way over the northern part of the line, while by 1904, 21 down goods trains left Bath daily and five coal and mineral trains from Radstock, Binegar or Winsor Hill. South of Templecombe, goods traffic on the S&D was lighter and signalboxes were closed at night.

In the early 1900s, the MR and LSWR decided to route as much traffic as possible over the S&D, the MR directing some traffic hitherto travelling via London, while the LSWR diverted traffic previously offered to the GWR at Basingstoke, Salisbury and Exeter. Up to ten up S&D goods trains left Templecombe between 10pm and 5am, while 21 down goods trains ran from Bath plus five coal and stone trains from Radstock, Binegar or Winsor Hill. Sixteen cattle specials ran in October 1906.

In 1910, 203,571 wagons (a daily average of about 650) were transferred between the LSWR and the S&D at Templecombe and sometimes four or five specials a day were required to clear traffic. Much of this freight travelled at night, and between 8pm and 2am it was not unknown for trains to be blocked back for several sections awaiting a path into Templecombe Upper Yard. Several milk trains, occasionally consisting of 25 to 30 vans, from the S&D left Templecombe daily.

The same year saw approximately 900 wagons at Evercreech Junction attached or detached each day.

J. Thornton Burge, son of the stationmaster at Templecombe, in 1911 wrote that 'through vehicles of various kinds are exchanged by almost every passenger train'. The number of fitted vehicles exchanged in 1910 was 22,805. During the winter, rabbit traffic was heavy, while in the early summer months special fruit trains ran from Plymouth with French and Tamar fruit, transferring to the S&D for transit to Edinburgh, Glasgow, Manchester, Derby and other stations. Often there were from 12 to 20 vehicles and sometimes two trains were run to Bath, an MR guard taking charge from Templecombe.

Although goods traffic ostensibly brought in large receipts – £149,303 in 1913 compared with £105,998 from passenger traffic — the end result was not so favourable owing to the fearsome gradients causing heavy working expenses for freight trains. That year, the small goods engines were incapable of handling the heavy traffic adequately and so were replaced by Fowler Class 7F 2-8-0s.

In February 1913, Eyre stated that coal traffic from Radstock was expanding and mining there, unlike in the North, was continuous without winter/summer fluctuations. Radstock provided good house and gas coal and reasonable steam coal which was burned by most S&D locomotives. Mendip stone had been found very satisfactory for road-making and with the developing use of motor vehicles was increasingly in demand. In 1913 J. Thornton Burge wrote: 'At night, very often goods trains are standing one behind the other at block sections for a distance of 20 miles, waiting until they can be dispensed with in the marshalling sidings at Templecombe.'

In both world wars the line proved a vital link between the North, Midlands and South Coast (see Chapter 1).

In 1920 the noon goods Templecombe to Bournemouth (West or Central as required) was

Class 4F 0-6-0 No 44559 (71G, Bath) (ex-S&D No 59) arriving at Templecombe with a down freight on 12 May 1955. The main line to Bournemouth is on the right. *Rev Alan Newman*

Class 3F 0-6-0T No 47465 is ready to bank a freight from Radstock to Masbury, 9 November 1954. *Rev Alan Newman*

Leaning to the curve, Class 7F 2-8-0 No 53807 with a down freight approaches Radstock on 9 November 1954. Empty coal wagons stand on the siding, right. *Rev Alan Newman*

worked by an LSWR engine, as was the 8.20am goods Poole to Templecombe. The 5.50am goods and mineral train Templecombe to Bournemouth Central was required to leave Templecombe with a heavy LSWR goods brake van next to the engine and an ordinary S&D brake at the rear. At Wimborne Junction, the engine was turned and ran to the other end of the train.

With the formation of BR, the S&D was commercially supervised by the Southern Region district superintendent at Southampton, but on 1 February 1958 the Western Region was given control of the line from Bath to Henstridge and this marked the beginning of the end of the S&D. Almost immediately, the WR diverted the Burton beer traffic to the West of England via Taunton, instead of via Templecombe. This traffic had been using the S&D since the opening of the Bath Extension, and in fact the 11am down freight from Bath was called 'The Burton'.

A vacuum-fitted train of 40 or so wagons of Burton beer arrived at Westerleigh Yard north of Bristol, and a Bath engine was coupled on as soon as the other engine came off and ran to Barrow Road shed. The train was taken to Bath where it was re-engined and drawn to Templecombe before proceeding to Exeter behind an SR locomotive. This route was quicker than the more direct route via Bristol where delays were likely. Latterly, staff at Westerleigh Sidings altered labels so that any traffic consigned via Bath actually travelled via Bristol, but because transit by this new route took double the time, traffic was diverted to road and was completely lost to rail.

Perhaps the most surprising economic 'improvement' was the fact that fertilisers consigned from Avonmouth to Blandford

The 11.5am Bath to Evercreech Junction train climbing through Oldfield Park on 12 February 1955. Class 4F 0-6-0 No 43995 is the train engine, while sister No 44096 assists at the rear. The site of the brickworks in the left background is being used by the local council as a controlled tip. *R. E. Toop*

were routed to travel via Bath, Southampton and Bournemouth, a distance of 135 miles compared with 65 miles using the S&D. Such tactics 'proved' that the S&D was uneconomic and should be closed. On 7 September 1964, the night goods trains and the 2.40am 'Mail' from Bath to Bournemouth were withdrawn, thus enabling the line to be shut at night for the first time since 1878. Freight facilities were withdrawn from most S&D stations between 1963 and 1965. When Emborough quarries closed on 21 June 1965, only one daily freight train ran in addition to mineral trains from Writhlington and Norton Hill collieries.

Clark's shoe manufacturers of Glastonbury used to dispatch its traffic by rail, but as BR was only about 50 per cent reliable on delivery by a certain day, the firm changed to road transport.

Norton Hill Colliery closed on 12 February 1966 and following withdrawal of most services over the S&D on 7 March 1966, the only remaining lines were from Bath Junction to the Co-operative siding in Oldfield Park, coal from Writhlington Colliery over a new spur at Radstock linking the S&D with the former BNSR to give an outlet to Bristol, while at the southern end of the S&D, Blandford Forum to Poole remained open to cope with milk from Bailey Gate, army traffic and general goods. All these lines were short-lived: Bath Junction to the Co-operative siding closed on 30 November 1967; the last train from Writhlington ran on 16 November 1973 and Blandford Forum to Broadstone Junction closed on 6 January 1969.

ALTERATIONS IN HOURS OF CLOSING SIGNAL BOXES.

NAME OF SIGNAL BOX.	WEEK-DAYS.		WEEK-ENDS.	
	FROM	TO	FROM	TO
MIDFORD	—	Open	continually	—
WELLOW	—	Open	continually	—
WRITHLINGTON & B'DOWN	4. 0 p.m.	8. 0 a.m.	4. 0 p.m. Sat.	8. 0 a.m. Mon.
RADSTOCK EAST	10. 0 p.m.	6. 0 a.m.	10. 0 p.m. Sat.	6. 0 a.m. Mon.
RADSTOCK WEST	—	Open	continually	—
MIDSOMER NORTON ..	10.30 p.m.	6.30 a.m.	10.30 p.m. Sat.	6.30 a.m. Mon.
CHILCOMPTON	—	Open	continually	—
MOOREWOOD	4.20 p.m.	8.20 a.m.	4.20 p.m. Sat.	8.20 a.m. Mon.
BINEGAR	—	Open	continually	—
MASBURY HALT	5.30 p.m.	9.30 a.m.	5.30 p.m. Sat.	9.30 a.m. Mon.
WINSOR HILL	—	Open	as required	—
SHEPTON MALLET ..	—	Open	continually	—
EVERCREECH NEW ..	10.30 p.m.	6.30 a.m.	10.30 p.m. Sat.	6.30 a.m. Mon.
EVERCREECH JCT. NORTH	—	Open	continually	—
EVERCREECH JCT. SOUTH	—	Open	continually	—
COLE	10.30 p.m.	6.30 a.m.	10.30 p.m. Sat.	6.30 a.m. Mon.
WINCANTON	—	Open	continually	—
TEMPLECOMBE No. 2 JUNC.	—	Open	continually	—
STALBRIDGE	—	Open	continually	—
STURMINSTER NEWTON ..	—	Open	continually	—
SHILLINGSTONE	—	Open	continually	—
STOURPAINE	—	Open	as required	—
BLANDFORD	—	Open	continually	—
SPETISBURY HALT ..	—	Open	as required	—
BAILEY GATE	7.30 p.m.	8. 0 a.m.	Open as	required
CORFE MULLEN	—	Open	continually	—
WEST PENNARD	Last Train 2. 0 p.m.	6.10 a.m. 3.40 p.m.	Last Train Sat. 10.0 p.m. Sun.	6. 0 a.m. Sun. 6.10 a.m. Mon.
GLASTONBURY	Last Train	6.20 a.m.	Last Train Sat. 10.0 p.m. Sun.	6. 0 a.m. Sun. 6.20 a.m. Mon.
WELLS	Last Train	7.50 a.m.	Last Train Sat.	7.50 a.m. Mon.
SHAPWICK	do.	7. 0 a.m.	Last Train Sat. 10. 0 p.m. Sun.	6. 0 a.m. Sun. 7. 0 a.m. Mon.
EDINGTON JUNCTION ..	do.	6.45 a.m.	Last Train Sat. 10. 0 p.m. Sun.	6. 0 a.m. Sun. 6.45 a.m. Mon.
BRIDGWATER	do.	7. 0 a.m.	Last Train Sat.	7. 0 a.m. Mon.
HIGHBRIDGE LOCO. ..	do.	6. 0 a.m.	Last Train Sat. 10. 0 p.m. Sun.	6. 0 a.m. Sun. 6. 0 a.m. Mon.
HIGHBRIDGE "B" ..	do.	6. 0 a.m.	Open as	required
HIGHBRIDGE "C" ..	do.	6.15 a.m.	Open as	required

The hours of opening and closing of Signal Boxes, may, without further notice, be altered to meet traffic requirements. Drivers and Guards must be prepared accordingly.

Opening hours of signalboxes, 6 January 1941.

At one period, the 2.40am 'Mail Goods' from Bath was a particularly heavy train and had three engines from Bath to Combe Down Tunnel: the train engine plus a Stanier Class 3 2-6-2T on the front and a banker at the rear. Passing through Devonshire Tunnel the crew of the banker had to tolerate fumes from three engines, so they often crouched to the floor in order to gasp better quality air. In actual fact they did not get quite three times the fumes produced by one engine, because usually three engines got the train through quicker.

The 2-6-2T came off at Radstock and banked at the rear, thus guarding against runaways, and stayed on the back to Shepton Mallet where it came off and ran light to Templecombe before returning on the 7.5am passenger train.

In later years, one to three BG (guard's brake) vans were loaded in the dock at Bath Green Park station, with mail for Shepton Mallet, Evercreech Junction, Blandford etc, to Bournemouth. The guard booked on at Victoria Bridge Road and walked to his goods brake at the station which was coupled behind the BG.

Instructions dated 16 September 1926 to freight enginemen and guards.

A Class 5 4-6-0 came off shed about 2.20am and stood at Bath Junction. The shunting engine, which doubled as a banker, drew the formed train to the road immediately north of the down main, was cut off and ran out of the way to the turntable road. A Class 2P 4-4-0, which had collected the BG and brake van, placed these two vans on top of the banker on the turntable road. The 4-4-0 then proceeded to Bath Junction while the banker pushed the vans to the rear of the otherwise prepared train into the siding. The banker was then uncoupled.

The BG was placed next to the guard's brake van so that the guard could keep an eye on it and prevent a possible robbery. Meanwhile the 4-4-0 reversed on to the 4-6-0 and was tight-coupled. The guard informed the footplate crew of the train's weight.

SOMERSET AND DORSET JOINT LINE.

Circular O.W. 78.
O.G. 9312.

Operating Section,
Bath,
September 16th, 1926.

FREIGHT TRAINS WORKED BY No. 4 AND 5 CLASS ENGINES.
INSTRUCTIONS TO ENGINEMEN AND GUARDS.

DOWN TRAINS.

ENGINEMEN.

Bath and Midford.

On the Train emerging from Combe Down Tunnel the Driver should apply sufficient steam to keep the couplings well strained. On passing Midford Signal Box the regulator should be opened as necessary and not eased until the Train has reached the level at the top of Midford bank.

Wellow.

When passing the Down Home Signal the regulator should be eased but steam should not be shut off entirely, and when passing the Station platform the regulator should be opened as required.

Writhlington.

After passing the Down Advanced Starting Signal the regulator should be closed and brake applied as required.

Shepton Mallet.

On approaching Shepton Mallet the Train should be allowed to run until the Engine is passing the Down Home Signal, when the hand brake should be applied; this should be released again when passing the Goods Shed.

Wincanton.

When passing over Bridge No. 137 the regulator should be shut and the Train allowed to drift.

Henstridge and Stalbridge.

When running between Henstridge and County Bridge, the regulator should be slightly open, and when passing under the Bridge it should be opened wider, and kept open until the Engine is close to the Down Distant Signal when it should be closed and the tender hand brake applied and steam brake, if necessary, until the Train has passed the Distant Signal when the brakes should be released with discretion.

Shillingstone.

Drivers of Down Trains stopping at the Home Signal must not release the brake after passing over Bridge No. 180.

GUARDS.

DOWN TRAINS.

Bath and Midford.

Gradually apply brake after whole of Train has entered Combe Down Tunnel, increasing, as necessary, to take strain of couplings. On emerging from Tunnel, continue to hold same until Van is passing Midford Signal Box, when brake must be eased, and finally released as Van passes Up Inner Home Signal.

Wellow.

Apply brake at Distant Signal and release immediately after passing over Viaduct.

Braysdown.

Apply brake slightly at Bridge No. 32 and work same, as necessary, to Radstock.

Shepton Mallet.

Release brake near Down Home Signal.

Henstridge and Stalbridge.

Guards should well apply brake shortly after passing Henstridge Station to take strain of couplings until passing under the County Bridge, when brake should be released.

The first engine was called the 'Mail Coupled' and although usually a Class 2P (in the late 1930s, generally Nos 696/7/8/9/700), was sometimes a Class 4F 0-6-0. The 'Mail Coupled' ran as far as Evercreech Junction where some mail was unloaded and the Class 5 topped up with water. Although scheduled to take water at Evercreech Junction, this was sometimes taken at Shepton Mallet. The mail train stopped at Templecombe No 2 Junction to be checked by a carriage and wagon examiner. One minute was allowed at Templecombe Lower for mail exchange. On summer Saturdays, in order not to delay the stream of holiday passenger trains, the 'Mail' carried no freight and was merely just one or two postal vans running on passenger timing and carrying the headcode of lamps top and left, rather than top and right which it did on other days.

After the 'Mail Coupled' came off at Evercreech Junction, it worked a short freight train — no more than a dozen wagons in length due to its poor brake power — to Templecombe before returning to Bath with the 7am — the first up passenger of the day.

Meanwhile the 'Mail Goods' worked to Bournemouth and at about 8.15am the driver ran the engine to shed after turning on the Branksome triangle and the fireman had made a hole in the fire to keep it cool. The 'Mail Goods' crew than went to lodgings either in the permanent way shed, or paid a shilling a day to Mrs Fred Alford, the steam raiser's wife, who provided a single room with clean sheets.

The crew was called about 5pm and arrived at Branksome shed at about 7pm, leaving with the 8pm goods to Bath.

Class 4F 0-6-0 No 44560 (ex-S&D No 60) at Evercreech Junction on 28 June 1963.
The yard is full despite the WR's efforts to get traffic diverted from the 'Dorset'.
Rev Alan Newman

They often returned with the engine they had worked down on, but in the interim it had gone to Bath and back on the 'Pines'. Returning with the goods they had four or five wagons from Branksome and then a full load from Poole, often consisting of wagons of china clay for Stoke-on-Trent and other places in the Potteries. There was a tendency for some of the contents to be dropped, making the rails slippery for subsequent trains. They left the train at Evercreech Junction and backed on to 40 or 50 empties. If the load was over 40, they were banked by a Class 3F to Masbury with a Templecombe engine which shunted at Evercreech Junction. The banker to Masbury was coupled and at Cannard's Grave Summit, the train engine driver shut off steam and the fireman applied the tender brakes for descent. At Charlton Viaduct the fireman wound off the handbrake and the train driver gradually took over the first 20 or 30 wagons. It stopped at Binegar for the banker to be uncoupled.

The 3.30am from Bath to Evercreech Junction was a train loaded with heavy traffic from Avonmouth — grain, cattle feed etc. At Evercreech Junction the wagons were shunted into the down yard and the train crew had breakfast, after which they crossed to the up yard, collected empty wagons and proceeded to Moorewood Sidings tender-first. The 5.50am goods off Bath was timed to reach Moorewood concurrently. The 3.30 engine went into the sidings and drew the stone wagons out. The 5.50 engine then went across, picked them up and placed them on its train. The 3.30 engine then shunted the empty wagons from Evercreech Junction into the siding to replace the loaded ones withdrawn. The 3.30 engine proceeded to Midsomer Norton where its crew were relieved, but the engine itself returned with coal from Norton Hill Colliery to Evercreech Junction, which was why it was worked tender-first to Midsomer Norton, because to haul the heavy load from Norton Hill, it needed to work chimney-first so that the maximum number of sanders were available. Towards Masbury, some 811ft above sea level, the wind seemed to get between the wagons and increase the running resistance.

Although rear banking assistance was usually a help, on one occasion it compounded a problem. It was 1944 and one Saturday evening Driver Charlie Knight and Fireman Fred Epps booked on at 10pm, their engine, Class 7F 2-8-0 No 13808, having been prepared by others. Large lumps of North coal were in the tender. No 13808 backed on to its train which consisted of a full load, and the banker was placed at the rear near Bath Station signalbox.

Fred pushed the tablet catcher out ready to collect the single-line tablet at Bath Junction and was busily engaged in breaking up the large lumps as the engine started. He noticed a violent rock and roll motion, looked around to determine the cause and was amazed to see he was the sole occupant of the footplate! Charlie had gone.

The '7F' turned over and Charlie, luckily unhurt, was hanging on out of the side. Fortunately, two wheel flanges caught in a check rail and prevented the engine from turning over completely on its right side, but went far enough to thrust a buffer into the ground.

The derailment occurred by the Midland Road overbridge near the Belvoir Castle Inn. The steam crane from Gloucester was summoned, No 13808 was cut from its tender and it took eight hours to get the engine righted.

The gas lamp on the bridge, normally always lit following the lifting of the Second World War restrictions, happened to be extinguished that evening, but had it been alight, would probably have disclosed a steel plate approximately 3ft by 2ft across the surface of a rail. It was this which had caused the pony truck to derail. Had the train not been banked, the mishap would not have been so severe, but the banker, not knowing of the derailment, kept on propelling and pushed No 13808 over.

At Midford, the 5.50am local pick-up goods collected wagons of fuller's earth and agricultural machinery, farm implements at Wellow and also wheelbarrows made by a local firm, and dropped off cattle food. This train had six road boxes — for Bournemouth, Exeter, Salisbury, Templecombe, Wincanton and 'Various' (i.e. Shepton Mallet etc).

Work at Radstock took approximately an hour, and nine times out of ten the train picked up coal wagons. At Midsomer Norton gunpowder was put off and paper bags loaded. At Chilcompton wagons of coal from Moorewood Colliery were added as were sundries for the road boxes.

At Binegar, the pick-up goods was usually shunted into a siding as the 9am Bath to Bournemouth would be drawing near. Stone traffic both for road-making and railway ballast was collected. This train rarely called at Masbury, but occasionally collected stone traffic from Winsor Hill if the engine, which came specially to collect the wagons, had been unable to clear all the traffic.

At Shepton Mallet, the guard changed with a Templecombe man on an up pick-up which had left Templecombe about 5.30am. It had been loaded with milk powder and other dairy products at Wincanton and at Cole it had shunted out coal empties and picked up wagons at Evercreech Junction and Evercreech New, with cheese and bags of lime.

Beyond Shepton, its first call was at Binegar and there bulk whisky was unloaded for Oakhill Brewery, presumably travelling from Scotland via London and Templecombe. Also from Templecombe it carried boxes of cartons of cigarettes destined for Bath.

At Midsomer Norton one day Guard Frank Staddon discovered a split box of cigarettes in the Bath road van. He immediately locked the van and phoned to ask the railway police to meet his train at Bath. In fact, no packets were missing, but if he had failed to carry out this procedure and something was missing, he would have been held responsible.

S&D guards were tested on the rules every six months by Harry Helps, deputy chief clerk and controller of the operating section. If they failed to pass the test, they were sent back to the yard as shunters. A goods guard's uniform consisted of serge trousers, waistcoat, jacket, overcoat, cap, leggings, tie, oilskin mac and sou'wester.

One duty was being a porter-guard at Bath — four hours on duty as a guard and four as a porter. While doing this turn, on his sleeve Frank Staddon wore a large metal ambulance badge about the size of the base of a cocoa tin. One day a lady asked him to carry her bag to a taxi. When he got there she said: 'Oh, I shouldn't have asked you to carry my bag, I can see you're not a porter, but a bus driver.'

Guard Elkins uncoupling banking engine Class 3F 0-6-0T No 47496 at Binegar, 5 September 1960. *Author*

At one time Frank lived at 12 Edward Street, Lower Weston, Bath, and when he arrived at work one morning, was told that Control had prevented him from signing on because it claimed that the call boy had called three times and that he had failed to answer. Eventually, Frank persuaded Control to let him sign on, but it insisted that this negligence must not happen again.

As Frank was returning home from duty that day, Mr Smith at 2 Edward Street, told him that during the night vandals had kicked his door and it had been damaged by a hobnailed boot. Frank got Mr Smith to write a letter to the LMS saying that he had been roused and his door damaged. He believed that the mistake probably occurred and the call boy visited the wrong house because the '1' on his sheet was indistinct.

Although a direct junction between the S&D and BNSR at Radstock was not made until 1966, wagons could be exchanged through colliery sidings, though this was a rare event. In June 1962 a wagon of coal was taken from Writhlington Colliery to Radstock West (the ex-BNSR station) via Bath, Bristol, Wells and Frome — so the crow-fly distance of one mile became 82 miles by rail. To offer traffic to its southern partner the S&D sent Radstock coal to Swindon via the LSWR to Andover and then by the Midland & South Western Junction Railway.

Working heavy freight trains over the long 1 in 50 gradients of the S&D required great skill from the footplate crew and the guard. S&D men considered that stopping to pin down wagon brakes at the head of a gradient was an effeminate GWR practice and resorted to it only very rarely. In the early days, two 10 ton brake vans were required to be coupled to the rear of all goods, cattle and mineral trains on the Bath Extension. A brakesman manned the inmost van and the guard the rear.

It was not unknown for an unbraked goods train to run away down the gradient from Masbury, but whistle-blowing and alert signalmen resulted in level crossing gates being closed across roads at Evercreech Junction or Radstock and no serious harm ever befell a train.

Guards had to know the road intimately because if they released their brake too soon, wagons would buffer up and then cause a snatch, with the ever-present probability of breaking a coupling when the engine took the weight again. The dip at Midford caused quite a few breakaways and if there were many wagons, the brake van could not hold them and they would seesaw backwards and forwards up and down the incline at either end until they came under control. Working a goods train over the Dorset, a guard could not sit for long unless there was a banker on the back, for he was almost continuously applying or releasing his handbrake. Between Bath and Evercreech Junction there were 89 changes of gradient, 137 between Evercreech Junction and Broadstone Junction, and 20 from Broadstone Junction to Bournemouth West, making a total of 246, an average of 3.44 changes for every mile of track.

Coal, coke etc	6,930
Other minerals	2,683
Goods and livestock	9,766
Empty wagons	10,665
Engine and van	14
Total wagon miles	30,058

Only 81 miles of the 10,665 empty wagon miles were run in the down direction.

Wagon miles over the S&D on a typical day in 1949

Driver George Prentice was described as a beefy man with thick wrists and broad shoulders. Early in the Second World War he took a train of rolls of barbed wire on the 7.50pm off Bath. Before leaving, the guard came up to him and reported a full load, but in the event it proved well in excess of this. By the time George and his fireman Fred Epps reached Binegar they knew they had a substantial load behind them. They turned over the summit at Masbury and carefully descended to Shepton Mallet.

The '7F' crept very slowly over the top at Cannard's Grave because they had already experienced great difficulty in controlling the descent to Shepton. When they went through the first arch beyond Cannard's Grave, George called to Fred: 'That's it, she's gone. Sit down, there's nothing you can do.' This was pre-Ferodo brake block days and flames poured out from the cast-iron brake blocks, giving sufficient light to see cows grazing in lineside fields.

With the whistle wide open they passed through Evercreech New at an estimated 50 to 60mph. The signalman rang Evercreech Junction and the branch train shunting there was moved out of the way to give them a through road. Eventually George stopped a mile or so beyond Evercreech Junction. The brake blocks were completely worn away. The train was shunted back to the junction and the '7F' taken on to Templecombe to get new brake blocks fitted. Fred was young at the time, and thought it thrilling and was not really afraid.

When a driver required a guard to apply his brakes he sounded the whistle three times. The line was particularly undulating between Midford and Radstock; a 60-wagon train could be on three different gradients at once and a guard had to restrain the wagons from bumping heavily into the engine. His job was particularly difficult during World War 2 when a Red Warning was on and speed restricted to 15mph because when a train was travelling slowly, it was more difficult to keep the wagons off the engine. The guard's job was also made harder by more modern wagons with oil instead of grease axleboxes, oil allowing wagons to run more freely. Some goods guards were not too intelligent and failed to allow for the varying weights of trains. One such guard on a lightly loaded goods applied his brake near Wellow when it was quite unnecessary to do so. The driver purposely took no action and the train ground to a halt. The driver sent his fireman back to ask why the guard had stopped the train.

It was common practice for a guard to take an oily rag, wipe his stove shovel with it and cook bacon and eggs on his brake van heating stove. Another culinary delicacy was onions cooked to eat with his bread and cheese.

On the S&D it was the practice for passenger shunters to become passenger guards and goods shunters, goods guards. Being a passenger shunter was a dirty job — you became filthy coupling and uncoupling corridor connections — in fact your clothes became so greasy that they repelled rain, so you did not need a waterproof in wet weather. On the other hand, being a passenger guard was a clean job. With goods it was the reverse: goods shunting was clean, but a goods guard had a dirty job. Goods guards could operate passenger trains — in fact they were called upon to do so in summer when many extra passenger trains were run — but a passenger guard could not work a goods train. Goods guards were their own masters all the time, but passenger guards came under the superintendence of a stationmaster when within station limits.

One shunter would never shunt a train until he had checked that the stop blocks were intact, because on one occasion he was rebuked as the blocks had been previously demolished, he had shunted without checking, and wagons rolled out into the yard.

In the event of a train getting away down a bank, the temptation was to apply the brakes too fiercely causing the wheels to lock. In the event of this happening, to achieve maximum braking power a driver had to release his brakes to allow the wheels to turn and then re-apply the brake. Some drivers misused the brakes on gradients and enjoyed seeing fire come from them when applied fiercely at speed.

An S&D Class 7F 2-8-0 often wore out its brake blocks making just one or two trips over the Mendips from Bath to Evercreech Junction and back, whereas, say, an engine from Saltley shed might use the same blocks for six months. In order to reduce labour costs of replacing the Class 7Fs' brakes so frequently and also to obviate the rapid wear of slide bars due to dust from the cast-iron brake shoes, in 1943 No 13801 was fitted with Ferodo brake blocks. This trial proved successful and the type was used on all the other members of the class. In addition to offering better breaking power, there was less wear on the slide bars and maintenance was easier as the blocks weighed only 8lb compared with 51lb of a cast-iron block. Care was required with their use because it was all too easy to skid and make a flat, while wagons could be derailed as stopping could be like hitting a brick wall. Because of this feature, some drivers preferred the gentler cast-iron brake blocks. Latterly, if a train was above a certain load, a specific number of fitted vehicles had to be at the front to assist braking. This greatly reduced wear of locomotive brake shoes, but was disliked by shunters as it gave them more work.

LMS Class 8F 2-8-0s continued to use cast-iron blocks. Their braking ability was inferior to that of the Dorset 7s, as a Class 8F had only one steam brake cylinder on the engine and one on the tender, whereas a Class 7F had a brake cylinder for the leading pair of driving wheels (which additionally worked brakes on the pony truck in earlier years) and brake cylinders under both the fireman's and driver's side for braking the intermediate, driving and trailing wheels. Class 7F tyres were riveted on, whereas those of an '8F' were shrunk on and the heat generated by braking could, and did, cause tyres to expand and become loose.

A sharp-eyed shunter at Bath spotted an '8F' arriving off the Dorset with a loose wheel tyre. When taken over to the locomotive depot, it crossed the main lines at half walking pace, with men each side watching for derailment. It was driven at a maximum of 10mph to Bristol where keys were knocked into the flanges and welded on.

Various classes of engine had different braking characteristics. The SR 'S11' class 4-4-0s were loaned to the S&D during World War 2 and sometimes used on freight duties, but their brake power was insufficient. A. H. Whitaker, shedmaster at Bath said, to Fred Holmes, 'You can take 20 minerals over.' Fred replied: 'Yes, if I have the brakes down on 19 of them.'

On another occasion, Fred used an 'S11' to move two ash wagons from Shepton Mallet to the viaduct and it successfully coped with this light duty.

Fred Epps drove what was believed to have been the longest ever fitted train from Poole to Templecombe — 26 bogie vans loaded with pigeons. Although screw-coupled, there was still a certain amount of play and he had to drive carefully to avoid snatches. He said that with a train of that length, he felt a tug when the train was on differing gradients.

An '8F' 2-8-0 had travelled to Bournemouth and Fred had driven it back light engine to Poole Yard. He was going to take twenty bogie vans, but then the guard reported: 'The foreman wants to know if you'll take the rest.' 'Oh, I'll do it to help out, but tell him he must get the signalman at Broadstone to let me have the Broadstone distant off, because I don't want to have to stop on that 1 in 75 bank.' The agreement worked and the distant was indeed off when Fred reached it.

Driver Reg Beasley was on a coal train descending the bank through Midsomer Norton. The Radstock distant signal was clear. Fortunately, Guard Frank Staddon was keeping a good lookout and observed a man on Radstock platform waving and shouting 'Stop the train!' Frank picked up the brake stick and screwed the wheel on hard. At the far end of the platform was a man holding a red flag. When the engine came to a halt, about 20yd in front of it a rail had been taken out — the permanent way men had failed to inform the signalman. Frank said it was fortunate that no buffers became locked as this tended to happen when braking hard.

Frank and the footplate crew did not make an official complaint as this would have cost the permanent way men their jobs. The S&D was certainly a friendly line, like a big, happy family. If a passenger missed the last train, he was usually offered a ride in the brake van of the next goods train.

The S&D had its own method of determining the weight of a goods train. On the MR a 10 ton wagon was a 10 ton wagon with a tare weight and a gross weight, but the S&D used the quarter system. Wagons were equated as follows:

One empty	=	2 quarters
One goods	=	3 quarters
One 8 ton mineral	=	4 quarters
One 10 ton mineral	=	5 quarters
One 12 ton mineral	=	6 quarters

Before departure, a guard would walk along his train looking at each wagon and the label, noting it and the wagon's contents. For instance, if a 12 ton wagon was loaded with grain, coal or stone, he would assess the maximum for that wagon which was 6 quarters. The next wagon might have two girders in it, a relatively light load and would be judged 4 quarters.

A Class 7F was allowed a load of 40 empty wagons, or 17 mineral wagons, from Bath to Midford, Radstock to Moorewood, or Evercreech Junction to Binegar, but when a load was not in excess of five wagons of minerals, the train could be made equal to eighty quarters. If a train exceeded this load, the guard would tell a shunter: 'This one will have to come off'. The guard would then go forward to the driver and advise him of the number of quarters, and as long as it was not an overload, a driver had to accept it.

Guards varied in their skill of making estimates. One very nice fellow with the surname Senior, was very much a 'I'm the guard and I'm in charge of the train' type. One particular Monday, No 13804 seemed not to be steaming freely and the following day the driver took over from his fireman to prove to himself that it was indeed the engine at fault and not his mate. To his chagrin, he found that he produced even less steam than his fireman.

On the third morning the guard came up and said: '79 quarters', and was told by the fireman, 'You can knock that down to 65, because that's as many as we're taking'. The guard looked at the fireman who continued: 'We've had trouble with this engine during the last two days over lack of steaming — the driver knows it and he's reported it. 65 quarters is the maximum we're taking because she's not doing her work. She's only giving the effort of a Class 4 or 5.' Had an engine been in good fettle, a driver would not object to an occasional overload.

Vans of sugar and cattle feed from Avonmouth were heavy and over the LMS between Avonmouth and Bath were classified as 'mineral'. The S&D had only two classes of train:

'passenger' and 'goods' with respective headcode: two white lights, chimney and left-hand (from cab) for passenger and chimney and right-hand for freight, so what had been 'mineral' from Avonmouth became 'goods' which could include relatively light loads.

A banking engine was required to be coupled to a brake van from Radstock to Binegar, and just before Masbury Summit the guard, if in the type of van which had a veranda right at the end, leaned over and unhooked the banker while on the move and placed the uncoupling hook on the smokebox door of the banker.

One driver of a Class 7F hauling a pigeon special, who was very concerned about the effect that the speed might have on its bearings and motion, covered the big ends and motion with a very thick layer of grease, and whenever the train halted, if there was a suitable wagon nearby, would dash across and purloin some of its grease which he then applied to his engine.

If a train in excess of 50 wagons arrived at Bath off the Dorset, its engine could not be released from the arrival road, so if a Bath Junction signalman knew a train exceeded this length, he informed Bath Station signalbox which set the road across to the turntable, where the engine was going anyway. After the train engine was uncoupled, the shunting engine drew the train back up the Dorset for a short distance so that it was clear of the main line to Bath station. It then shunted.

One night when going down through Winsor Hill Tunnel, a driver applied his brake sharply to make sure he could check the train. When he released the brake it caused a coupling to snatch and break, but the driver was unaware of this. As there were only about four wagons in front of the brake van, it was able to draw them to a halt. Guard Dennis Macarthy realising what had happened, ran them by gravity to Shepton Mallet where he almost reached the rest of the train where its engine had stopped for water. When the guard related to the footplate crew what had happened, the fireman remarked that he thought the van's side lights looked rather a long way off.

On another occasion, an up train had shunted at Midsomer Norton and the shunter had failed to couple up the wagons properly, so when the train left, Guard Macarthy's van remained at the station. Macarthy released the brake and followed his train down the 1 in 50 to Radstock where the signalman, just closing the gates, had to swing them open again quickly.

An interesting little-known fact is that after the Second World War for about six weeks, a stone train ran over the S&D *en route* from Broadstone to Liverpool where the stone was shipped to New York for the United Nations building. The blocks were so large that one filled a wagon. The stone was believed to have originated from Portland.

Signalling

At the opening of the Bath Extension, absolute block working without staff or tablet was under the responsibility of the signalman. Additionally, as it was all single line with passing loops, a crossing orders system was organised from Glastonbury which regulated train movements. Due to human failure, this proved unsafe and in due course single-line tablets were introduced. The broad gauge SCR used GWR-type disc and crossbar signals, whereas the DCR used a different type of disc signal. A red half disc indicated 'danger' and when the disc was turned edge-on to a driver, this indicated 'clear'.

When the S&D became a joint line, the LSWR took over signalling responsibility and standard LSWR signals were used, often on lattice posts. In SR days replacement posts were two old rails braced together. The SR rail-built posts had the rails 6 to 9in apart, but the S&D type had them closely bolted together. The SR replaced some lower quadrant with upper quadrant arms and when the WR took responsibility for the northern part of the line, some ex-GWR type signals were used. A rarer type of signal which appeared at Midford and Evercreech Junction, was an X-shaped backing signal. At Midford it allowed a stalled train to reverse to the down line of double track. A calling-on board was found at Midford's up home and at Radstock; the latter indicated to a driver that he could draw up at the platform, but that the level crossing gates were closed.

A particularly interesting self-acting signal was in use at Wellow. Little documentary evidence is available, but one was certainly in use in 1905 and had been replaced by about 1932. A treadle was placed a train length ahead of the advanced starting signal. When an engine passed over this treadle, current from a battery released an electrical catch allowing the signal to fly to danger by its own weight. This allowed the signalman to replace the lever fully in the frame and he was

A train from Blandford hauled by an 0-4-4T approaches Spetisbury *c*1900. The disc and crossbar signal survived until 16 April 1901 and was worked only for trains requiring to call at the station. *Dr T. F. Budden*

The backing signal at Midford, 19 August 1959. Flat-bottomed rail is in position between the running lines ready for re-laying. *Author*

unable to withdraw it again until the train reached the next home signal. Latterly the system required considerable maintenance. When Wellow box was switched out, a signalman had to place a pin in the 'banjo' containing the catch in order to maintain the signal arm's position.

In 1910, an S&D signal notice was issued concerning Coligny-Welch distant signal lamps which were to be used over the LSWR between Wimborne and Bournemouth and said that all distant signals would be distinguished by a chevron to the rear of the spectacle and at night

The lineman sign at Henstridge, 4 May 1963. *Author*

this would be illuminated. This continued in use until replaced by the general use of amber, instead of red.

The S&D signal engineer's headquarters were at Shepton Mallet where old signalboxes were used as huts for such things as paint stores. It was situated east of the station between the down platform and the stationmaster's house.

The telegraph was maintained by linemen of which there were two: one at Bath covering as far south as Evercreech Junction, while his partner at Blandford covered Evercreech Junction (exclusive) to Broadstone Junction and Wimborne. They travelled the line daily. Signalboxes were issued with an oval disc. The white side displayed horizontally indicated that the apparatus was functioning perfectly; white in a vertical position intimated that the lineman should call to correct a minor fault; while reversed horizontally, showing a completely black face, meant that the electrical signalling apparatus was out of order and the signal lineman was required; while black, hung vertically meant that the telegraph lineman and the signal lineman were both needed.

South of Evercreech Junction, signalboxes were generally similar to the LSWR type '2' or type '4'. Wimborne signalbox dated from 1860 and was unusually tall to enable the signalman to have

In pre-Whitaker tablet exchange apparatus days, an 0-4-4T approaches Midford with an up train, leaving the double track. The signalman holds the single-line tablet for collection by the fireman. The engine carries three headlamps, but no definite reason for this has come to light, although one suggestion is that it is a mixed train. *Author's collection*

good sighting on the curve. It was unique for an LSWR box in that the windows of the locking room were identical with those of the operating floor. Also it was all-brick, whereas the LSWR preferred timber for the upper floor. With the opening of the DCR, Wimborne became the busiest junction in Dorset.

Midford was in a dip and it was not unknown for a snatch to cause a coupling to break. Thus a down train might pass Midford, the section behind it cleared and another accepted, only for the signalman to see runaway wagons entering the cleared section. To avoid a potential accident, the track was electrically circuited as far as the descent to Wellow and the next train could not be accepted until the previous one had cleared the track circuit.

Eleven signalboxes controlled single-line sections, and tablet exchange between firemen and signalmen could cause problems:

- Speed had to be reduced;
- Injury could be caused, despite newspaper padding on arms and backs, and firemen sustained bruising;
- The tablet could be dropped and thus time lost when the train had to stop while the fireman went back for it, and perhaps have to search for a considerable time in long grass.

Although exchange apparatus had been designed and was in use on other railways, it was not ideal: speed was restricted and the arms of the apparatus fouled the gauge and could strike passengers or loose tarpaulins.

To obviate these problems, Alfred Whitaker developed a patent design whereby the exchanger arm returned to a position parallel to the track immediately after use, or in places where space was very limited, such as between tracks, the 'falling man' type was used, the impact of collection swinging the apparatus into a sump. At Bath Junction, as passenger and goods trains generally used two different roads, two loop-shaped handles were provided in the floor of the signalbox to enable one of the two 'falling man' collectors to be raised. Initially only one of this type was provided at the junction, goods firemen throwing the tablet into a net, but when Carter's Siding to Wimborne Junction closed in 1933, this made another 'falling man' available, so it was re-sited at Bath.

Another excellent feature of Whitaker's apparatus was that it could be used for exchanges at speeds up to 60mph. In 1903, pre-apparatus times, the 2.22pm ex-Bath reached Poole in 103 minutes, whereas in 1906, following the installation of the automatic exchangers on 1 January 1904, the 2.10pm arrived in 96 minutes — the apparatus had saved seven minutes.

Midford up outer home and 'calling-on' arm, 15 August 1959. *Author*

Whitaker thought of everything: an adjusting screw allowed the height of the locomotive-mounted apparatus to be altered in order to compensate for tyre wear, and an apparatus at locomotive depots was used to check the height.

Firemen were instructed not to place the tablet pouch in the holder until the distant signal had been passed. They were required to watch the exchange being made, using a hand lamp during darkness to illuminate the engine's apparatus.

The signalman at Bath Junction receives the tablet from the driver of BR Standard Class 4 2-6-4T No 80041 working the 16.05 from Wincanton to Bath on 1 July 1965. *Author*

This watching was essential as a miscaught tablet could fly anywhere — on the ground, or on a carriage running board, and much time could be saved if a fireman knew where to look. The collected pouch had to be examined by the driver and placed in a safe position. Some drivers with a warped sense of humour placed the tablet on the shelf above the fire door to get it hot before handling it over. 'The pouch must not be inserted in, or removed from the apparatus while the engine is passing over a bridge' — one can imagine the story behind this instruction. All instances of failure to deliver or pickup had to be reported by the driver in order that the depot staff could gauge the locomotive's apparatus.

The Whitaker tablet catching apparatus at Corfe Mullen, 1965. *Christopher Steane*

In the event of an engine not being fitted with the apparatus, or it being faulty, signalboxes *en route* were advised by the code word 'Pouch' and the tablet was placed in a pouch with a larger handle than was used for auto collection.

Although use of the apparatus could result in dangerous situations — a fireman falling overboard when setting or retrieving a tablet, or someone on a platform being struck by a pouch flying along following a faulty collection or delivery — the only serious accident was to Fireman Christopher Amesbury on 19 July 1923. On approaching Blandford he placed the pouch in the apparatus and then noticed it was the wrong way round. He leaned out and reversed it but before he could get back into the cab, the receiving apparatus badly gashed his right arm. Ironically, it was unnecessary for him to have reversed the pouch.

The Whitaker apparatus was used on other lines including the Midland & Great Northern Railway and perhaps, very surprisingly, the GWR's Norton Fitzwarren to Minehead and the Barnstaple branches, so not quite everything S&D was an anathema to the GWR.

A special Bath banking engine staff was issued for a banker to give protection additional to the tablet carried by the train engine. Returnable to Bath Junction signalbox, it unlocked ground frames at the brick and Co-op sidings. Locking ensured that Bath Junction or Midford boxes could not withdraw another tablet until both the tablet and staff had been replaced.

The Binegar banking key was similar. Although the line was double track, the staff was necessary to return 'wrong line' from Masbury Summit to Binegar where it regained the up road. In the early days of the Bath Extension before the key came into use, the working timetable stated that a

The fireman leans from Class 4F 0-6-0 No 44135 at Bath Junction to catch the tablet from the apparatus in the foreground, the engine not being fitted with a catcher. The train is the 3.20pm from Bath to Templecombe on 28 March 1959. *Author*

Class 7F 2-8-0 No 53807 with the Ian Allan 'Severn & Wessex Express' at Bath Junction, attacks the 1 in 50 gradient on 14 May 1960. The fireman retrieves the tablet from the catcher. *Author*

Lower Bristol Road, Bath: the Red Bridge, Twerton Viaduct, the Bath Electric Tramway, the S&D Single Line Junction signalbox, which closed on 13 April 1924, as did the ex-MR Bath Junction signalbox, both replaced by a new Bath Junction signalbox situated midway between the two. MR, LSWR, GER and GWR wagons can be seen in the background. *H. J. Patterson Rutherford*

Radstock banker must proceed to Masbury and work back as an ordinary train.

For a box to release a single-line tablet, the co-operation of the adjoining box was required and the whole operation was designed to be foolproof. Imagine then the consternation at Midford when the signalman was dusting round the tablet apparatus and the single-line tablet suddenly dropped out of his machine.

He immediately contacted Bath Junction and the duty lineman to notify them of this surprising, and supposedly impossible, occurrence. The equipment in both boxes was duly inspected and no fault could be found. Its makers were called in and when they stripped down the machines, all was in order.

One day a signalman at Bath Junction was looking towards the Lower Bristol Road and watching a tram on the route to Twerton. As it approached the railway bridge, the tram's trolley arm dipped as the overhead wire lowered to pass below the railway bridge. He realised that the arm was pressing the tramway overhead against the underside of the bridge. Could the electric tramway wire interfere with the railway's communication system when the live overhead touched the bridge structure?

When the next tram passed under the Red Bridge, the alert signalman turned the commutator on his single-line apparatus and sure enough, a single-line tablet dropped from the machine. The mystery was solved and the necessary remedial action taken.

Some signalboxes had particularly interesting features. The two boxes at Radstock and the one at Writhlington were worked by seven signalmen working alternate turns day and night, that is, 12 hours on and 12 off. The seventh signalman covered rest days.

At Templecombe the LSWR 'A' box was at the west end and the S&D 'B' at the east end. Most signals worked from 'B' were slotted from 'A' box so that a train could not be admitted to or leave the station without the permission of both signalmen. To avoid trains being kept overlong outside the station and passengers missing a connection, special permission was given for a second train to occupy the platform road. The first train pulled towards 'A' box; the second stopped at the home signals and was then admitted to the station by a 'calling-on' arm.

A particularly vivid flash of lightning struck Blandford signalbox on 23 June 1906. Wires fused and windows were blown out by the force of the explosion and the signalman had barely time to escape before the box started to burn furiously. All the telephone, telegraph and train tablet apparatus was destroyed and the cost of the damage was about £500.

Winsor Hill signalbox and down tunnel, 31 July 1959. *Author*

– 5 –

Locomotives

IN the early days, small engines crawled up banks and went all out down the other side, while the 1874 Fowler 0-6-0s slipped in Midford Tunnel, a heavy train could pull them backwards. For the opening of the Bath Extension the locomotive stock was boosted by nine 0-6-0STs built by Fox, Walker of Bristol. The boiler was large for a tank engine, the diameter being 4ft 3in and the length of the barrel 10ft 6in. Ostensibly intended for banking, in practice they were used on goods and express passenger trains. No 1 was converted to a tender engine in 1888 and in 1890, No 8 converted to a side tank and had its 4ft diameter wheels replaced with those of 4ft 6in. No 1 was reconverted to a saddle tank in 1908, the same year that No 8 became an 0-6-0 tender engine.

In 1900, the S&D locomotive stock comprised:

Passenger engines

Type	*Number in class*
2-4-0T	2
2-4-0	2
0-4-4T	13
4-4-0	8
	25

Goods engines

Type	Number in class
0-6-0ST	7
0-6-0T	1
0-6-0	39
0-4-2T	1
0-4-0	2
	50

S&DJR 0-6-0T No 8, formerly a saddle tank. *Author's collection*

Change in the next 17 years was dramatic, for in 1917 the stock consisted of:

Passenger engines

Type	Number
2-4-0T	2
0-4-4T	13
4-4-0	13
	28

Goods engines

Type	Number
2-8-0	6
0-6-0ST	8
0-6-0	41
0-4-2T	1
0-4-0T	2
	58

S&DJR 0-6-0ST No 9, as rebuilt 1899. *Author's collection*

S&DJR 0-6-0 No 1 at Bath locomotive depot *c*1895 having been converted in January 1888 from an 0-6-0ST. It was eventually reconverted to a saddle tank in December 1908. *Author's collection*

A summer 1930 view of LMS No 1500 (formerly S&D No 1), recently re-numbered and re-lettered. To its right is 4-wheel Sentinel No 7190 (ex-S&D No 101) at Radstock. No 1500 was withdrawn in November 1930, while No 7190 was new in February 1929. *Author's collection*

Two Radstock 0-4-0ST shunters, Nos 26A and 45A, on 16 March 1929 in their twilight years. No 26A was withdrawn in December 1930 and No 45A in August 1929. Coal was kept in the bunker beside the firebox. *Colin Roberts collection*

Only two ex-SCR engines remained: 1861 2-4-0s rebuilt as 2-4-0Ts No 27A and 28A. Fifteen of the locomotives on this list were built when the S&D was an independent company. The remaining engines were built in Joint times, of MR design adapted to S&D conditions, such as being given smaller driving wheels to cope better with the severe gradients. 0-6-0s were often used on passenger trains.

0-4-4T

When the MR and LSWR took over the S&D in 1875, a locomotive shortage was temporarily eased by the loan of MR 0-4-4Ts Nos 6, 1262/3. The LSWR's engineer's department complained that the front-coupled engines damaged the track, so their speed was limited to 50mph. When they were inspected, No 6 was found to be in good condition, No 1262 had broken bogie springs, while No 1263 had weak springs and was considered dangerous above 35mph.

The type proved successful, so in 1877, nine were ordered from Avonside, Bristol. It was very odd that the S&D version was cabless despite the fact that the MR version of 1875 had cabs. Not surprisingly, the S&D roofed the weatherboards at an early date, which must have made working over Masbury on a winter's night that much more delightful. Nos 52-55 built by the Vulcan Foundry in 1884/5 were supplied with cabs and were slightly different from those constructed by Avonside in having marginally higher side tanks which were extended slightly forwards. This batch of 0-4-4Ts was the first Johnson engine to have an entrance door, MR engines not receiving them until 1889. The Avonside engines had brakes on the bogie wheels, but these were removed

S&DJR 0-4-4T No 12 with its well-ventilated cab on the up road at Evercreech Junction soon after it arrived new on the line in November 1877. *Author's collection*

S&DJR 0-4-4T No 55 near Broadstone in 1914. *Author's collection*

later. During 1891-9 the S&D rebuilt the Avonside engines with new Deeley boilers pressed to 160lb (Johnson boilers were 140lb), and MR-type cabs. The cylinders were bored to 18in from the original 17in x 24in. These 0-4-4Ts worked all main line passenger trains, including expresses, until 1891 when 4-4-0 tender engines appeared. The tank engines gave a good account of themselves and two trains averaged 31¼mph between Bath and Wimborne with three stops, all on a single line and with steep gradients. An 1891 booking from Shepton Mallet to Bath was 35 minutes, which required an average speed of 37.3mph.

Harry (Stumpy) Groves was driver of 0-4-4T No 11. Stumpy could neither read nor write and was press-ganged into working on the footplate, this being the only alternative to the sack, for his employment as builder's labourer on such tasks as building Highbridge locomotive water tank ended. Born 13 May 1839, he was first employed by the SCR from 1 December 1861. As a driver he received 7s 6d a day, or £2 5s a week from 12 October 1878 until he retired, aged 71, on 13 May 1910.

Driver Isaac Hardacre on engine No 13 was rather temperamental and if kept a minute late at

Class 1P 0-4-4T No 58072 (71J, Highbridge) at Midsomer Norton with the 6.5pm Bath to Binegar train on 25 March 1955. *Rev Alan Newman*

Highbridge, would be a minute late arriving at every stopping place to Templecombe.

One Saturday afternoon in 1926 Bath received a phone call. A 200 ton passenger train was arriving from the Midlands destined for Bournemouth. Bath was desperately short of engines, in fact the only one it had was No 8 in use as a wash-out boiler and minus its tender. As an 0-4-4T had just set out light engine for Templecombe, this was the nearest available. (It was normally restricted to a load of 130 tons between Bath and Evercreech.) It was returned from Radstock, bankers fixed up and water assured at Chilcompton, Shepton Mallet and Evercreech Junction. The 0-4-4T was so short of water when it reached Shepton that the fusible plug was almost at melting point. The average number of gallons used per mile for this class was normally 33, giving a distance of about 30 miles. It reached Templecombe No 3 Junction where another engine was available to work the train forward.

Once Ron Gray was on an 0-4-4T working the 5.5pm from Bath to Templecombe. The engine had originally worked from Highbridge and when topped up there, the water must have had a salt content because although the tanks had been filled at Bath, the engine primed badly when working hard. When it stopped at Shepton Mallet both injectors went off because the tanks were empty. He filled the tanks with fresh water and experienced no more trouble. Incidentally, the 0-4-4Ts had no slacking pipe to keep the dust down.

In 1930, only 12 0-4-4Ts remained to be transferred to LMS stock. The last S&D 0-4-4T to be withdrawn was No 32, as LMS No 1230, which was scrapped in June 1946, aged 69, with a mileage of 1,643,238.

Bath was short of locomotives in April 1955 and 0-4-4T No 58072 was used for trains in the area, the first time for several years. The class had been generally displaced by the arrival of Class 2P Stanier 0-4-4Ts in 1947. These were unpopular and on one occasion a member of the class took the 6.5 pm Bath to Binegar, but was seriously short of steam and so never appeared on the S&D again and was confined to Bath to Bristol trips.

Ex-S&DJR Sentinel No 102 as LMS No 7191 (22E, Highbridge) shunting at Radstock on 5 September 1949. The panel on which '7191' is painted pulls out and forms a hopper to load coal into the cab bunker. The short wheelbase enabled it to traverse a sharp curve. The wagon to the left of the Sentinel is branded 'Patent Shaft & Axletree Company, Wednesbury'. *S. W. Baker*

Sentinel 4-wheel shunter

Because of the low 'Marble Arch' at Radstock carrying the branch from Tyning Colliery to the GWR, which was impossible to raise, engines working this part of the yard of necessity had to be of low height. Until 1929, when they proved life-expired, 0-4-2ST No 25A and 0-4-0STs Nos 26A and 45A were operated. They were replaced by vertical boiler, 4-wheeled Sentinels Nos 101 and 102 which could pass under the arch when propelling wagons to Ludlow's Colliery.

Of unusual design, a pair of 100hp high-speed vertical two-cylinder engines drove a reduction gear from which power was taken by chains to both axles. Steam was produced in a water tube boiler with side firing. The exhaust was discharged through the chimney in the roof making the cab very hot in summer, but delightful in winter. The 600gal water tank was between the engines and the boiler. Running costs averaged only about £650 pa so they were economic. The original intention was to work with only one engineman, but the unions opposed this. A bunker in the cab held 10 cwt of coal, a side flap forming a coal chute.

After examination at Highbridge Works on arrival, they spent practically all their working lives at Radstock, having repairs and examinations carried out there. Occasional visits were

made to Bath for repairs or the boiler removed by Barrow Road's sheer legs. They also visited Derby Works for general repairs. When both Sentinels were temporarily out of use in 1931, ex-Lancashire & Yorkshire 0-4-0ST No 11202 was used and re-appeared in subsequent years; similarly, No 11212 in July 1946. No 7191 spent over three years at Kettering, returning to Bath on 28 November 1936. The arch was demolished in 1960 and as there was no further need for them, No 102 as BR No 47191 was withdrawn in August 1959 and No 47190 (ex-No 101) in March 1961.

Above: 'Large' 4-4-0 No 71 at Bath *c*1910. The coaches have side chains in addition to screw couplings. *Author's collection*

Right: Ex-'Large' 4-4-0 No 78 as LMS Class 2P No 321, on the turntable at Bath, 9 July 1932. *Colin Roberts collection*

Right: 'Small' 4-4-0 No 18 built at Derby in May 1891 and withdrawn September 1931, at Branksome *c*1928. Notice the good headroom in the cab, also the coniferous trees, left. *Author's collection*

4-4-0

In 1891, the 0-4-4Ts were largely replaced on faster services by 'Small' 4-4-0s, a 5ft 9in wheeled version of Johnson's MR 4-4-0s. In due course heavier trains required a stronger engine and 'Large' 4-4-0s appeared in 1903, with superior steaming capacity and a higher working pressure. In the spring of 1913 MR '483' class (perpetuated by the LMS as a Standard Class 2P) No 499 with superheated boiler was tried over the S&D. It was successful and showed improved performance at pulling away from stations, so was joined by No 519. No 499 was returned to the MR in autumn 1913 and two superheated 4-4-0s, S&D Nos 70 and 71, ordered. In due course, some of the older S&D 4-4-0s were rebuilt to this design.

Having 7ft 0½in diameter wheels proved no disadvantage and they were eminently suitable for S&D gradients, the short valve travel enabling them to be driven on relatively long cut-offs under conditions of both light and heavy steaming. Had examples of the class been modified for S&D work by being given smaller wheels, although having a higher tractive effort, the boiler would not have produced sufficient steam when working hard over a distance.

Their LMS derivatives with 6ft 9in wheels were rostered to take 200 tons, i.e. about six coaches, without assistance between Bath and Evercreech Junction. Before the Second World War the down 'Pines Express' was booked to pass Masbury, 18.7 miles from Bath, in 39 minutes, involving a speed of 18mph on the 1 in 50 bank up from Radstock. This involved a power output equal to no less than 82 per cent of their nominal tractive effort. A maximum speed of about 60mph was reached on favourable gradients.

An LMS Standard '2P' with a load of seven coaches in fog and on slimy, greasy rails, slipped to a standstill by Oldfield Park brickyard. Fireman Bob Ford climbed down, took sand from the boxes, sanded the rail for 30ft and added fine chippings from the ballast. They managed to start and continued up the incline.

One day, Fireman Ted Smith paired with Driver Bill Brooks was on 'Large' 4-4-0 No 67 working the 3.45am down and 10.10am return passenger. For this type of engine a haycock fire was best, with the firebars showing at the sides. A locomotive inspector boarded the footplate and insisted it be fired with coal in the firebox corners. Objecting to this treatment, the engine was shy for steam and lost nine or ten minutes by the time it arrived at Bath. When the guard appeared with a Lost Time ticket, Driver Brooks tried to make the inspector accept the ticket, but he refused. Bill wrote in his report that the lost time was due to carrying out the inspector's instructions.

In the coal crisis of 1921, 4-4-0 Nos 67 and 68 were converted to oil burning and were used on expresses. Chopped sleepers had to be carried in the tender in case it was necessary to rekindle the fire by placing oily cotton waste on the end of a stick and igniting it from the oil lamp carried in the cab.

Deeley Class 4P 4-4-0 No 995 was tried over the S&D in August and September 1925 as the type had proved well suited to the gradients of

Top: Women cleaners at Bath during the First World War. 'Large' 4-4-0 No 70 was built in May 1914 and withdrawn as No 40322 in March 1953. *Gordon Dando collection*

Above: 'Large' 4-4-0 No 68, later LMS No 325, in the 1920s. Notice the brake cylinder between the bogie wheels. *Gordon Dando collection*

Class 2P 4-4-0 No 40509 (71H, Templecombe) leaving Midsomer Norton on 11 May 1954 with the 4.35pm Bath to Templecombe.
Rev Alan Newman

the Leeds–Carlisle line, but as new Compounds were taking over, a new use was being sought for the class. Although No 995 was liked by S&D crews, it used considerably more coal than a 'Large' 4-4-0 and so was not considered worth the extra expense.

Despite a successful trial of a 'Crab' 2-6-0 in 1927, slightly modified Fowler LMS 4-4-0s were supplied to the S&D in 1928 as Nos 44–46. These were to have been LMS Nos 575/6 and 580, their numbers actually stamped on the motion.

In November 1933, ex-S&D No 44, as LMS No 633, was fitted with a Dabeg feed water heater at a cost of £425, but savings proved insufficient to cover its cost, although the engine retained the apparatus until November 1959, when withdrawn from service. The water was preheated prior to being pumped into the boiler, the pump being worked off the return crank on the link motion. No 633 was fitted with an injector in case the pump failed and it also had patent firebars as did No 634. The firebars were designed in one piece and could be removed only when the boiler was washed out. The plan of dropping fire through lifting the bars started in the Second World War to avoid throwing out a fire which could be seen by hostile aircraft. Other depots in postwar years reverted to throwing the fire out, but Bath continued the practice of dropping the fire. The blacksmith at Bath made a special hook to lift bars of Bulleid Pacifics.

In pre-war years heavy S&D expresses required a 4-4-0 and Class 4F 0-6-0 which provided power at the expense of four sets of wages and a coal consumption of about 90lb per mile. In 1936, Nos 630–632 almost monopolised the working of the 'Pines Express'. Nos 696–698 were frequent visitors and together with Nos 633–635 (ex-S&D Nos 44–46) were the most popular with drivers working passenger services over the route. 4-4-0s left the S&D in 1962 when Nos 40696/7 and 40700 were withdrawn, among the last of this wheel arrangement to work on BR. This class of engine, together with BR Standard Class 9F 2-10-0, was arguably the best passenger engine to operate over the S&D. Apart from problems of firing, the hilly nature of the S&D could catch out a fireman of any class of engine. He had to ensure that water was sufficiently high above the firebox crown when passing over a summit so that it was not dry when water ran towards the front of the boiler.

Class 3F 0-6-0 'Bulldogs'

In 1894-5 piloting of heavier loaded goods trains over the main line became too common, so five Johnson 5ft 3in 0-6-0s were ordered. Derby could build them for £1,960 each and the LSWR for £1,980, so as Derby was cheaper and could also deliver earlier, this price was accepted. Apart from the S&D vacuum ejector layout, they were identical with MR engines. The ejectors followed S&D practice by being in the cab and using the right-side hand rail as a brake pipe.

Numbered 62–66, the class proved superior to the 'Scotties', an earlier 0-6-0, and earned the name 'Bulldogs'. They steamed well, were economical on coal and quite speedy on a passenger train. Five more were ordered in 1902 from Neilson, Reid & Co at £3,185 each (Nos 72–76). As they were a diverted MR order, they were delivered painted Midland red. They differed from the earlier series in having deeper frames, being pressed to 160lb instead of 150lb and having larger tenders. The ejector was similar to Midland practice.

In the early 1920s they were given 'G7' boilers. All ten remained on the S&D until the Second World War when some were transferred. During 1933-5 their average annual mileage was 25,396 — the highest for an LMS 0-6-0, and they ran 96,763 miles between general repairs; they consumed an average of 45.3lb of coal per mile, the lowest of all LMS Class 3F 0-6-0s and lower then their MR sisters, and also had the lowest repair

'Scottie' 0-6-0 No 43 at Bath depot; it was withdrawn in October 1914. *Author's collection*

cost at 9.09d per mile. They were in service for an average 238 days a year. The last of the class (BR No 43216, ex-No 72) was withdrawn in 1962.

Stanier Class 3P 2-6-2T

In the spring of 1938, Class 3P 2-6-2Ts Nos 179, 180 and 181 were shedded at Bath and Templecombe intended for use on local passenger workings. These engines proved poor steamers and rather than replacing the Class 1P 0-4-4Ts, the 2-6-2Ts tended to be given shunting and banking duties. Even so, by the time a '3P' reached Claude Avenue Bridge about ½ mile from Bath Junction, boiler pressure had dropped from 200lb to 180lb and with little chance of pressure being regained. Stanier '3Ps' liked a low and bright fire with coal placed on little and often; S&D men were used to heavy fires, and did not take to them.

Class 3F 0-6-0 No 43216 (71H, Templecombe) (ex-'Bulldog' No 72) at Templecombe on 12 May 1955. *Rev Alan Newman*

Class 3P 2-6-2T No 181 by the water softener, Bath, *c*1940. *Author's collection*

Class 3F 0-6-0T

The Fox Walker saddle tanks' duties were taken over in 1929 by seven LMS Standard Class 3F 0-6-0Ts (Nos 19–25) purchased at £3,500 each and allocated to Bath, Radstock and Templecombe. Unlike the 2-8-0s which were painted black, these Bagnall tank engines were given the S&D unlined blue livery as they were expected to work local passengers services, although in the event this was rare. Unlike LMS locomotives of the same type, they were equipped with screw, not lever-operated, reversing gear.

Some time after they started working, they were fitted with a slot bolted to the cab side to enable a tablet catcher to be inserted to collect the banking tablet at Binegar. Each winter one member of the class at Bath was fitted with a snow plough, No 47496 (an ex-LMS locomotive of the same type) being chosen in 1960. It was a day's work for four men to take the buffers off and fit the plough weighing 3½–4 tons using an overhead gantry. A fire was lit when the first cold snap was expected — usually about the beginning of December — and the engine kept in low steam continuously through the winter, the fire being made up

Above: S&DJR 0-6-0T No 22 in unlined blue livery. It was the longest lasting engine of S&D origin in BR ownership, not being withdrawn until 10 June 1967 as No 47313. *Author's collection*

Right: LMS Nos 7153 (right) and 7152 (left) at Templecombe in blue livery on 7 June 1930. 'SDJR' has been painted out and 'LMS' applied and '7153' is painted on the smokebox door, leaving the S&D numberplate in position with the number 22 blacked over. *H. C. Casserley*

Left: Driver Newman, right, and Class 3F 0-6-0T No 47557 at Norton Hill Colliery, 14 August 1959. The pet pipe for damping coal and washing the cab floor and the socket for the tablet catcher are to his left. *Author*

only three times daily. The weather, or weather forecast, was watched carefully so that the boiler was not being washed out when the locomotive was needed for ploughing duty. One year, a plough was fitted to each end. This caused a problem when it became trapped in a drift, because as the coupling hooks had been removed when the ploughs were fitted, there was nothing on which the rescuing engines could hook a chain.

Top: S&DJR 0-6-0 No 57 by Highbridge weighbridge. The original classification of '5P4G' is on the cab side. *Author's collection*

Above: Class 4F 0-6-0 No 44560 (ex-S&D No 60) just ex-works. In the foreground are the remains of the oil storage tanks and in the background is a Stothert & Pitt crane. *Basil Robbins*

Class 4P Compound

In December 1924 LMS Compound No 1065 was compared with S&D 'Small' 4-4-0 No 67, the conclusion at that time being that the Compound was unsuitable for the line. The next compound to work the line was No 1050 on 5 August 1939. No 1046 was sent to the S&D in September 1940 to replace a 'Black Five' 4-6-0 required for other wartime duties. The Compound was used only on semi-fasts and locals and was returned to Bristol by Christmas. Going from Evercreech New to Shepton Mallet it could not gain sufficient speed to start compounding, but leaving Shepton, it would compound up to Masbury and usually reach there in under time. Firemen enjoyed working on her as less coal was burnt. No 1046 was allocated to pull about the same sort of tonnage as a Class 4F 0-6-0: seven coaches, 225 tons.

Class 4F 0-6-0 'Armstrong'

Five Standard MR Class 4 0-6-0s were ordered from Sir W. G. Armstrong, Whitworth & Co Ltd, their builder's name giving rise to the sobriquet 'Armstrong'. Numbered 57-61, they proved a very useful addition to the S&D stud. Being more powerful than the older 0-6-0s, their arrival allowed a reduction in the number of engines required and caused at least one fireman to have to return to cleaning. Although really freight engines, they proved suitable for mixed traffic, being as much at ease on an express passenger as heading a ballast train. They rode quite well at speed; in fact the heaviest expresses, including the 'Pines' in the 1930s, were unusually headed

Class 5 4-6-0 No 5042 at Bath, July 1938. The class was originally known as 'Six foots', later as 'Mixed Traffics' and finally, 'Black Fives'. *Rev Alan Newman*

by a Class 2P 4-4-0 piloted by a Class 4F. Although the '4F' had a higher tractive effort than a '2P', the boiler capacity was the same and so a '4F' was limited to 230 tons over the Mendips. Their haulage capacity was exceeded only by Class 5 4-6-0s, and '7Fs', 265 and 315 tons respectively.

Fireman Bob Ford found the 'Armstrongs' were not free-steaming and if an inch of water was lost on a run with eight coaches, the level could not be regained unless you could get both injectors on as it ran into a station. He considered No 4559 the best S&D '4F'.

The 'Armstrongs' were well-maintained. Although banking and shunting duty was good for running an engine in after shopping, a good engine was spoilt if it made only short runs. Unlike some of the ex-S&D 4-4-0s, Nos 57-61 (as Nos 4557–4561 and as BR Nos 44557–44561) remained on the S&D until withdrawn in the 1960s with the exception of No 44560 which spent its final month at the ex-GWR shed at Gloucester.

Class 4 Ivatt 2-6-0

The end of July and early August 1948 saw Bristol's Nos 43012 and 43013 working the 'Pines Express'. In the summer of 1948 No 43036 worked S&D services. No 43017 was tried on a Bournemouth to Bath passenger train, but steaming was erratic and the injector could only be on for a short time without lowering the pressure. Poor steaming required an engine of this type to be assisted by a '2P' 4-4-0.

'Black Five' 4-6-0

Stanier Class 5 4-6-0 No 5288 was tried over the S&D on 11 March 1938. The load of the test train was varied *en route*, being observed at Broadstone with 13 bogie coaches (four SR and nine LMS) in both directions. The engine was turned on Branksome triangle. On the return journey the train was stopped at the Broadstone home signal on a rising gradient of 1 in 75. When the signal cleared the engine restarted the train with ease, getting away smartly and accelerating rapidly through the station. The trial was a success, so six of the class were allocated to Bath. Regular workings were introduced over the S&D as from 2 May 1938, No 5432 working the 10.20am Bath to Bournemouth semi-fast and No 5440 the 'Pines Express'. The 10.20am from Bath was worked alternate days by Bath and Saltley engines, starting on Mondays with Bath, Tuesdays with Saltley and so on. Up to 20 May 1938 Nos 5239, 5249, 5270, 5271 from Saltley had visited Bournemouth.

A Class 5 could take 265 tons unaided over the Mendips compared with 190 tons for a '2P' 4-4-0 which meant that '2Ps' took up to six coaches, '4Fs' eight coaches, Class 5s eight coaches, (unless one was a 12-wheeler), and Class 7F ten coaches.

One day, Driver Bob Ford had No 5440 on the down 'Pines' with a load of ten coaches. When going slowly he found that acceleration was impossible. At Chilcompton his speed was about 5mph and he was in full forward gear and full

Class 7F 2-8-0 No 53804 passes Bath MPD with a Nottingham to Bournemouth West train, the 11.55am ex-Bath on 19 July 1953.
Rev Alan Newman

regulator. He wisely sanded the rails as a slip at that power would have caused serious damage.

He said that engines of the same class had different characteristics. Of the Class 5s at Bath '5440 was the queen'. No 5194 was different from the others inasmuch that it burnt more coal at the front of the box than it did in the back corners.

During the Second World War most of the Class 5s were removed from the S&D for other duties. Bath was intended to be a depot where 22 engines for S&D working would be oil-fired. On 15 February 1947 installation work on an oil fuel plant commenced and on 23-26 September 1947 the three storage tanks were tested by being filled with water. The Class 5 oil burners, Nos 4826/30, were confined to the S&D. They used about 250 gallons of oil for the 71½ miles from Bath to Bournemouth. Oil-fired locomotives needed their firebricks replaced frequently. One S&D fireman who had worked on oil-fired engines in the Middle East when on wartime service, asked why bottles were not thrown in to glaze the bricks and prolong their life, and this suggestion was adopted.

From the fireman's point of view, oil-firing was a success: it provided all the steam required and no time was booked against such an engine. Fumes in Devonshire and Combe Down tunnels were no better, or worse, than with coal-firing. With an oil-fired locomotive there was a temptation for the initial steam raising from cold to be done too quickly which would lead to tube problems due to rapid and unequal expansion. The undulating character of the line with its wide fluctuations in steam demand caused variations in firebox temperatures which could also lead to tube leakage problems.

At Bath oil was pumped direct from tank wagons, filled at Avonmouth and stored at the rear of the coal road, to the tender of an engine standing on the shed's No 2 road, so the special tanks at Bath were never filled with oil. After all the expense of installing plant and converting engines, it was discovered that due to a postwar shortage of foreign currency, no money was available to purchase foreign oil. The storage tanks were cut up and removed, while the engines were reconverted to coal-firing.

Class 7F 2-8-0

By the mid-1900s, freight traffic on the S&D required more powerful engines than those available. In January 1907, Derby proposed two 0-8-0 designs, but the LSWR's civil engineer rejected them unless almost £35,000 was spent on strengthening bridges, relaying track and lengthening sidings. It was eventually decided to leave things in abeyance, but ensure that any future track renewal and bridge strengthening would be capable of accommodating heavier locomotives.

When M. F. Ryan succeeded A. W. Whitaker as locomotive superintendent in 1911, he discovered that a reduction of 6 tons in weight carried by coupled wheels would necessitate the civil engineer having to spend only £2,050 to allow the line to carry an eight-coupled

S&DJR 2-8-0 No 80 new at Derby in 1914 in photographic grey, showing the tender cab. *Author's collection*

Two ex-S&D engines at Bath on 28 May 1936: 'Bulldog' No 64 as LMS No 3201 (22D, Templecombe), and No 87 as LMS No 13807 (22C, Bath). This was the Stephenson-built, larger boiler version of the '7F'. *Rev Alan Newman*

locomotive and if fitted with a tender cab, the need for longer turntables would be avoided. The weight reduction was to be achieved by adding a pony truck.

Six engines were ordered from Derby, the first, No 80, arriving at Bath on 1 March 1914. The boiler, a 'G9AS' type, was the same as that fitted to LMS Compounds and MR rebuilds. The outside cylinders were inclined at 1 in 12 to clear platform faces. The short-travel valves were ideal for slogging up over the Mendips. Too heavy for a bridge near Bath locomotive depot until it was rebuilt in November 1914, they were initially shedded at Radstock, men from Bath travelling to Radstock to man and clean them.

Vacuum equipment was fitted for use when hauling coaching stock and steam-operated sanders worked for forward and reverse running. On 25 March 1919 No 82 was fitted with dry sanding gear as an experiment and drivers were requested to report whether it was better than the original steam sanding. Results suggested that dry sanding was better.

The engines ran chimney-first in the down direction and as they could not be turned, token apparatus was fitted on both sides. In due course, the brakes were removed from the Bissell truck. Due to a small bearing area, axleboxes were deficient, so in September 1919 No 85 was modified by adding a mechanical lubricator to the axleboxes of the coupled wheels. The scheme proved a success, so the rest of the class was modified in 1921.

Tender cabs proved draughty in the open and liable to fill with fumes in tunnels and an obstruction when handling fire irons. No 82 had its tender cab removed in 1918 and footplate crews deeming this a success, the rest of the class was so modified by December 1920. For several months in 1918, the MR tried No 85 on heavy freight working between Toton and Cricklewood. In August 1921 No 84 was converted for oil-firing, but reconverted after a few weeks.

In 1924, five more 2-8-0s were ordered from Robert Stephenson & Co Ltd, at a cost of £6,666 each. The first, No 86, was given a fine finish and exhibited at the centenary celebrations of another S&D — the Stockton & Darlington Railway. The Stephenson-built engines had a larger boiler,

Class 7F No 53807 (82F, Bath) at its home depot on 21 August 1964. It was given this smaller boiler in June 1954 and in October 1964 became the last S&D '7F' to be withdrawn.
Rev Alan Newman

5ft 3in diameter compared with 4ft 7⅞in of the 'G9AS' type fitted to the first series. This non-standard 'G9BS' boiler used the same flanged plates as the boiler fitted to 'Big Bertha', the Lickey banker 0-10-0. Other changes included left-hand drive, hand-operated screw reversing gear and Lambert sanding apparatus which supplied a mixture of sand and water to the rail. This had the advantage that there was no need for sand to be dried, and crosswinds at Masbury or wherever, did not blow the sand off the rails. Some crews used the same principle on other sanding gear: if they found sand failed to drop they placed the slacking pipe into the sand box. By washing it down the sand quickly ran out, but sometimes it was the only way to get adhesion.

The modifications made in the second series of 2-8-0s proved successful so the first series was altered, although retained its right-hand drive. Lack of spare boilers for the 1925 2-8-0s caused a problem, so when a boiler change was necessary a 'G9AS' pattern was used as fitted to Compounds. No 53806 was the last with a large boiler, retaining it until 1955.

On 9 June 1931, E. S. Cox of the Chief Mechanical Engineer's Department wrote a report to S. J. Symes, locomotive assistant, that mechanical failures with the '7Fs' were low but steaming was indifferent with both large and small boilers. The 11 engines suffered six hot boxes in the previous eight months owing to severe hammering on the steep gradients. He commented that the bearing surface was rather small. Frame fractures were almost unknown. Steam sanding on the original engines had been found unsatisfactory and hand sanding substituted, but a small amount of moisture around the valve caused sand to cake and create a blockage. Lambert's wet sand on the Stephenson-built engines was satisfactory as regards slipping, but the mechanism was delicate and needed considerable maintenance. Grit from the brake blocks caused the white metal in the slide bars to wear and the average life of a standard brake block was just ten days. The tyres loosened due to the heat from the brake blocks on down gradients, but he said rivet fastening would cure this.

On the S&D's absorption into the LMS in 1930, Nos 80-90 became LMS Nos 9670-80 only to be renumbered 13800–10 on 27 February 1932, to make way for new construction. In July 1930, Nos 9671/6 were drafted to Toton for working heavy mineral and freight to London, followed by

No 9675 a month later, the latter engine on her second secondment to these duties. The three locomotives had returned to their own territory by the end of October 1930.

When built, a '7F' was one of the most powerful 2-8-0s in the country. In LMS times, the wheels were re-tyred to 4ft 8½in instead of 4ft 7½in, reducing the tractive effort from 35,932lb to 35,296lb. In 1933-5 the average annual mileage of the class was 23,573; 88,734 miles were run between general repairs, 65.91lb of coal consumed per engine mile, and a locomotive was in service for an average of 243 days a year. The cost of repair was 15.51d per engine mile. In the 1946-7 oil conversion programme, had it not been aborted, all 11 engines in the class would have been converted.

In 1959, No 53800 was the first of the class to be scrapped and all six engines of the Derby series attained over a million miles, No 53804 achieving 1,091,772. The Stephenson series averaged 930,000 miles. In November 1963, No 53810 was the first of the second series to be withdrawn, while No 53808 was the last to undergo a general repair. This was done in April 1962, and although really a non-standard engine, it speaks highly of the design that four were not withdrawn until 1964, No 53807 lasting until October. Two survive in active preservation, Nos 88 and 89.

The first recorded passenger train to be worked by a '7F' was *c*1924 during a locomotive shortage. Manned by Driver H. Jennings (killed on No 89 in 1929) and Fireman F. Hancock, it ran from Bath to Bournemouth in express time, but shot a lot of coal through the chimney in the process. It ran up to 50mph, although not necessarily offering crew comfort at this speed. The *Bath Weekly Chronicle* of 6 November 1937 said that in August 1937 a '7F' was used once or twice on slow passenger trains to Bournemouth. The first post-Second World War use of a '7F' on a passenger train was on 5 August 1950. It had the great advantage that it could haul ten coaches, whereas Bulleid Pacifics and 'Black Fives' were restricted to eight. As well as saving the use of a pilot engine, it also saved a crew, a very important factor. In the summer of 1952, use of '7Fs' for passenger working passed from emergency to regular procedure. The scheduled running time for a '7F' between Bath and Bournemouth was 144 minutes and 142 for Bournemouth to Bath compared with 133 and 130 minutes respectively for a '4F' 0-6-0. As many as five '7Fs' in one day have been noted on summer Saturday expresses and on more than one occasion one made two double trips from Bath to Bournemouth in a day — 286 miles, no mean achievement for a heavy freight locomotive on express work, some approaching 40 years of age.

Class 7F 2-8-0 No 53803 climbs the 1 in 50 by Claude Avenue Bridge, Oldfield Park, Bath, in September 1952.
Rev. Alan Newman

S&D 2-8-0 No 80 on 6 March 1914 and not a week old, attacks the 1 in 50 at Bath Junction. The MR Bath Junction signalbox which closed on 13 April 1924 may be seen towards the rear of the train. The locomotive is on test and has an indicator shelter on the front. *Author's collection*

On one of the first visits of an S&D 2-8-0 to Bournemouth with a heavy pigeon special, on reaching Broadstone, an LSWR pilot joined the crew. Beyond Poole he glanced back and saw the length of the train and ordered the driver to stop, believing he could not breast Parkstone Bank with that load. The S&D driver was unfazed and said: 'I'm in charge of the train and we don't require assistance, thank you.' He was right, and she climbed it in fine style. On reaching the summit the pilotman acknowledged: 'Driver, you've a wonderful engine here. We haven't a single engine on the South Western which, on her own, could have climbed that bank with this lot.'

The first six '7Fs' were right-hand drive and the last five left-hand. As drivers preferred a fireman to fire from his side of the cab, a fireman needed to be ambidextrous. Some drivers actually drew a line down the centre of the footplate and warned firemen not to cross it.

When Nos 86-90 arrived in 1925 an inspector travelled on the footplate to investigate their capabilities. They steamed well, but instead of leaving them alone, he had them taken to Highbridge Works and a larger diameter blastpipe fitted — with the result that they were not so free-steaming. The man from Robert Stephenson & Co was so disgusted that he went home early. Crews had to rectify the situation by using a jimmy. As the '7Fs' had a tool box in their tenders containing two breakdown hooks, it was found that these could be placed in the blastpipe to sharpen the exhaust. The incompetent inspector was eventually sacked.

Class 8F 2-8-0

In 1941, three LMS '8Fs', Nos 8028/67/95, were briefly allocated to Bath and although to a certain extent they were successful for S&D work, the '7Fs' undoubtedly had better brakes and tractive effort; therefore the S&D was in no hurry to part with its 2-8-0s. With the withdrawal of the '7Fs' in the early 1960s, the '8Fs' became the principal freight engines on the line.

Footplateman Bob Ford said that the '8Fs' had no problem pulling weight, as they were powerful, free-steaming and had a reserve of power which the '7Fs' lacked. He considered the '7Fs' were just good enough to do the job when everything went absolutely perfectly. The '8F' cabs were more comfortable and their tenders offered better access to the coal, and the injectors were able to replenish water rapidly if the boiler was used as a reservoir on a steep bank, but braking was a different matter. Braking down the eight miles from Masbury Summit to Radstock, or the eight miles from Masbury to Evercreech Junction, the '8F' brake blocks grew very hot and one locomotive shed a tyre. For some time it turned

GWR-built Class 8F 2-8-0 No 48444 leaves Norton Hill Colliery sidings on 27 October 1965. The falling gradient of 1 in 50 to Radstock is perceptible. *Rev Alan Newman*

round the wheel and was not noticed by the driver and fireman because the tender handbrake was screwed on hard, no wheels were skidding and there was no reason for them to suspect that the brake on one wheel was ineffective. It was not until the tyre moved out and was visible to the driver that he became aware of it.

MR and LMS engines on loan

In 1877, when tank engines were banned from running south of Evercreech Junction until track improvements had been carried out, the MR loaned 2-4-0s Nos 51A, 53A, 58A and 59A.

The *Bath Chronicle* of 21 September 1911 reported that 'some years previously a Midland Railway bogie passenger engine fitted with exchange apparatus was tried over the Somerset and Dorset, and in the 1890s a heavy Midland Railway goods engine made experimental trips over the Somerset and Dorset'. On 18 September 1911, MR 0-6-4T No 2023 arrived at Bath, was equipped with the Whitaker exchange apparatus and tried the following day on a Bath to Bournemouth passenger train. The conclusion of the test was that although a powerful engine, it was unsteady at speed, while its restricted water capacity caused problems. The same locomotive was derailed at 50-55mph at Ashton-under-Hill on 25 February 1935 killing its driver.

Horwich 2-6-0 No 13064 in red livery was tried over the S&D in November 1927 and the conclusion reached 'That the engine was not capable of keeping time on the banks' and the outcome was that the S&D received three more 'Large' 4-4-0s, Nos 44–46.

No more 'Crabs' appeared until 1942 when some replaced Class 5 4-6-0s removed for other duties. Apparently, they had a good turn of speed, for D. S. M. Barrie recorded No 2766 reaching a maximum of 74mph at Sturminster Newton. The line's maximum speed limit was 70mph. The Stanier version of the 2-6-0 was too heavy for the S&D.

Circa 1942, Driver Ralph Holden, 6ft 3in in height and an ex-Coldstream Guardsman, travelled on the cushions from Bath to Wincanton, there to relieve Templecombe men on the wartime equivalent of the up 'Pines'. 'Crab' No 2766 arrived about 17 minutes late, but he gained three minutes to Evercreech Junction, 'almost flew' over the Mendips and arrived at Bath on time. Hauling a load of 250-270 tons it was never above the fourth notch on the bank. Bob Ford considered that a 'Crab' was the best engine for climbing that he had ever had as a fireman and believed it superior to a 'Black Five'.

Ron Hacker remembers seeing a red LMS 4-2-2 at Bournemouth West *c*1928 which had hauled an inspection saloon from Bath. This was perhaps the only time that a single-wheeler had traversed the line. For some months in 1932 ex-MR 2-4-0 No 155 worked services from Templecombe.

Former London, Tilbury & Southend Railway 4-4-2T No 62 *Camden Road* as LMS No 2103, at Bath on 16 July 1936. A former MR Pullman car is grounded beyond the platform. *Rev Alan Newman*

Between 1 October 1935 and 22 August 1936 ex-London, Tilbury & Southend Railway 4-4-2T No 2103 was shedded at Templecombe and Bath. It worked a return trip from Templecombe to Bath, but proved very heavy on coal, primed badly and its water capacity proved insufficient for running from Templecombe to Bath without being replenished. It was soon retired from this service, Class 1P 0-4-4T No 1387 returning to this duty after a month's absence and No 2103 used on Bath to Bristol trains.

A 'Jubilee' class 4-6-0 arrived at Bath on a train from the North about 1946. The train was too heavy for the allotted engine to take it southwards alone and as no other assistant engine was available, the '5XP' banked it to Combe Down Tunnel. Much to the relief of the locomotive control office, because the class was banned from the Dorset, it proved to have just sufficient clearance of Devonshire Tunnel.

At the end of April 1950 ex-MR Class 3P 4-4-0 No 40741 was used over the Mendips, when shedded at Templecombe for six months.

LSWR and SR locomotives on loan

Even before the start of the Joint era the LSWR was ready to provide power at times of locomotive shortage. When the DCR opened between Wimborne and Blandford on 1 November 1860 it supplied 2-2-2WT No 15 *Mars*, 2-4-0 No 41 *Ajax*, and on the opening of Templecombe to Cole, 2-4-0 *Hood*, and 2-2-2s Nos 53 *Mazeppa*, 58 *Sultan* and 61 *Snake*, and 0-6-0 No 49 *Bison*. When the Fox Walker 0-6-0STs were banned in 1877 from working south of Evercreech Junction until the track had been improved, the LSWR loaned 'Gem' class 2-4-0s Nos 56 *Meteor*, 57 *Mentor* and 67 *Aeolus*, 'Volcano' class 2-4-0 No 231, and 'Lion' class 0-6-0s *Aurora* and *Mazeppa*. (The original *Mazeppa* had been scrapped and its name given to a new engine.)

On 24 April 1916 an ambulance train was hauled to Bath by LSWR 'C8' class 4-4-0 No 299, this probably being the first appearance of an LSWR locomotive north of Templecombe since the loans of 1877.

In 1928, the Rev Alan Newman saw 'H16' class 4-6-2T No 518 at Bath having arrived on a freight from the south, running light to turn on the Mangotsfield triangle. Presumably its weight precluded it from passing over two weak bridges to gain access to the Bath turntable.

The Second World War saw quite a lot of SR locomotives working over the S&D including 'S11' 4-4-0s Nos 395–404. S&D crews discovered that Nos 399, 400/1 needed careful adjustment of the water level in the boiler because they primed easily. They found the steam reverser a bugbear on this type because when pulled back it sometimes went into reverse gear.

One day Arthur Elliott, running shed foreman at Bath, told Fireman Bob Ford: 'You've got a Southern today. This brass wheel works the

SR 'S11' class 4-4-0 No 400. Driver Bill Jones of Bristol Barrow Road shed complimented the class by saying his experience was that 'it ran like a well-oiled sewing machine'. As BR No 30400 she was the very last of the class and was not withdrawn until October 1954, outlasting her sisters by three years. *Rev Alan Newman collection*

blower,' but as he turned it, Bob corrected: 'It's the large injector,' so Elliott replied: 'I'll let you get on with it as you know more about it than I do.'

Bob wondered about the use of a brass pointer on the gauge glass, but by trial and error found it indicated the recommended water level, and if the water was above the mark, the engine would prime. The engine had a flat firebox similar to the LNWR pattern Bob had met with when at Ryecroft shed.

'U1' class 2-6-0 No 31906, on trial over the S&D, is seen here at Radstock working the 4.25pm Bath to Bournemouth West train on 8 March 1954. *Rev Alan Newman*

No 404 was painted black and had a steam reverser but no steam brakes, only vacuum. She took a full load of 210 tons out of Bath, was smooth running and sat down on the rails. Bob took the tablet at Bath Junction and 'it walked up the 1 in 50 bank as if there was nothing behind her'. She emerged from Combe Down Tunnel with a full pressure of 175lb. At Midford only one safety valve was blowing off. Boiler pressure continued to rise and Bob was most relieved when they received the 'Right away' and steam could be used. The engine ran freely and Bob was impressed.

Next day he had No 403 painted green. The SR engines were used for a fortnight and he told Arthur Elliott that they were much better than the LMS Standard '2P'.

For a week a locomotive inspector travelled with them on the 8.30am from Bath to Templecombe. The load was six coaches, parcel van and two milk tanks for Wincanton, making 236 to 240 tons, so it was over the limit and normally would have been worked by a Class 4F 0-6-0 which would not have found it an easy task.

Chief Inspector Foulkes from Derby announced that he would come to experience the 'S11s' and see if they were acceptable. On arrival he said:

'Don't take any notice of me, I'll make my own mind up.' The first day went well. At Radstock on the third day Bob's driver whispered: 'Doing too well' and deliberately left her halfway up the reversing rack to stall her and so had to reverse before she would go forward, but they made up lost time.

On the return trip to Bath, the engine blew off at Shepton Mallet. Bob did not turn on the injector as the water level was up to the brass pointer. Foulkes ordered: 'Put the injector on.' Bob said: 'No.' Foulkes insisted, so Bob turned it on.

They left Shepton on the down gradient but when she began to climb over Charlton Viaduct, water came out of the chimney. Foulkes remarked: 'Now I know your reason for not turning it on.' Foulkes also congratulated Bob for knowing how to fire a flat box.

When SR 4-4-0 No 401 was transferred to Bath in the week ending 27 September 1941 it missed meeting LMS 4-4-0 No 401 by just a few days.

'K10' class 4-4-0s Nos 135/7/8 and 388/9 also worked over the Dorset during the war, while 'T1' class 0-4-4Ts Nos 3 to 6 were allocated to Templecombe. 'T9' class 4-4-0s Nos 303/4/7/12 arrived in October 1941 and were returned over the years, the last being No 304 in May 1945. It was usually shedded at Templecombe and used either piloting 4-6-0s or working a stopping train to Bournemouth. Subsequently 'T9s' were very occasionally substituted for failed engines on Bournemouth to Bath services, No 30728 working up on 10 November 1955. No 30706 worked to Bath several times in 1956 and No 30120 was loaned to Templecombe from 21 to 27 July 1957 and on 26 July piloted the 7.35am from Nottingham to Bournemouth. No 30310 was a last-minute substitution to work the 1.10pm from Bournemouth West to Bristol as far as Bath on 17 April 1958 owing to the brick arches on BR Standard Class 4 2-6-0 No 76014 collapsing. No 30310 returned on the 7.5pm to Bournemouth. No 30706 appeared on 26 April.

In 1941, four ex-South Eastern & Chatham Railway 'F1' class 4-4-0s were in the course of transfer from the SR to the LMS at Gloucester. They travelled via Templecombe and while in transit, one was commandeered to work a passenger train from Templecombe to Bournemouth and back.

'U' class 2-6-0 No 31621 on 1 March 1954, the first day of its trials over the S&D, heads the 11.40am Bournemouth West to Bath through Radstock. *Rev. Alan Newman*

Contrasting locomotive power: Class 3F 0-6-0 No 43436 and 'West Country' Pacific No 34044 *Woolacombe* climb through Lyncombe Vale with a down express on 11 July 1953. The '3F' had recently emerged from Derby following a general repair and would be the equal of a run-down '4F'. *W. J. Jerome*

'West Country' Pacific No 34040 *Crewkerne* climbs to Midsomer Norton with the 10.17am Bath to Bournemouth West on 14 July 1953. The ex-GWR Bristol to Frome line is at the foot of the S&D embankment. *Rev Alan Newman*

On 8 October 1948, 'U' class 2-6-0 No 31624 worked a football special to Ashton Gate on the Bournemouth to Bath leg of its journey. On 1 May 1950, the same Mogul piloted Class 5 No 44839 on the 'Pines Express' in both directions, but it was not a success as the WR restricted its speed to 45mph. Class U No 31621 and 'U1' class 2-6-0 No 31906 were tried in March 1954, but were not generally adopted, although members of the class appeared periodically. Between 1950 and 1958 Templecombe had a 'G6' class 0-6-0T as shunter, followed by a 'Z' class 0-8-0T. About the same period, during an engine shortage, a '700' class 0-6-0 worked station pilot duties and services from Templecombe including the Bason Bridge milk train. 'Q' class 0-6-0 No 30548 worked Poole to Bath on 9 October 1953 and No 30541 Bournemouth West to Bath on 27 December 1962.

The first Pacific to travel over the S&D was Bulleid 'Battle of Britain' class No 21C149 *Anti-aircraft Command* with a 12-coach Christchurch to Bath excursion for Bournemouth & Boscombe Football Club to Ashton Gate, Bristol, on 6 November 1948. Driver Ron Gray acted as pilot from Broadstone to Bath. He suggested to the driver that it might be an idea to take on water at Evercreech Junction. Here there was not a lot of coal in the tender, but the fireman said: 'It's alright, there's not much further to go,' blissfully ignorant of the amount of steam required. Up the 1 in 50 between Evercreech Junction and Shepton Mallet the engine slipped and half an hour was lost! The driver of 4-4-0 No 505 in front had to have the reverser 'right down the rack'. They had to stop to raise steam at Shepton and arrived at Bath 45 minutes late.

The Bulleid Pacifics did not slip if handled correctly. If a driver had his eye on the steam chest pressure gauge and kept it below 90lb, an engine would rarely slip, but if over the mark, it would. The reason one driver liked the Pacifics

Class 2P 4-4-0 No 40527 (71H, Templecombe) and 'West Country' Pacific No 34093 *Saunton* head a Sheffield to Bournemouth West train out of Bath on 31 July 1954. The first brake third is an ex-GWR vehicle. Class 4F 0-6-0 No 44150 stands beyond the grounded coach. *Rev. Alan Newman*

Ian Allan 'Trains Illustrated' excursion Waterloo to Bath via Templecombe passes Radstock on 25 April 1954 headed by spotlessly clean 'Schools' class 4-4-0 No 30932 *Blundells* and a filthy Class 2P 4-4-0, No 40601.
Rev Alan Newman

was because of the electric light. Over the Mendips the wind was prone to blow out the gauge and headlamps. This would cause a signalman to stop the train and if it was very windy, the lamps could not be lit in situ, but had to be carried into the cab.

On 25 November 1949, No 34092 *Wells* travelled light engine from Templecombe to Wells for its naming ceremony. It was later renamed *City of Wells*.

From 13 to 25 March 1951, No 34109 *Sir Trafford Leigh-Mallory* worked over the S&D, initially with the 11.40am Bournemouth to Bath and the 4.25pm to Bournemouth. It was anticipated that the class would replace the Class 5s on the S&D. The trial proved fairly successful and Pacifics were used that summer. At first, loads were determined at ten coaches, but then it was found that they tended to slip on gradients so the maximum load was reduced to 270 tons (eight coaches), the same as for a Class 5. Crews found them rather unsuitable for hard slogging up the banks. With a wheelbase of 57ft 6in there was little room to spare when using the 60ft turntable at Bath. One fireman was reputed to have filled the firebox of a 'West Country' Pacific at Poole and allowed it to travel all the way to Bath without any more firing.

Initially, Bath fitters did not understand that the steam reverser on a Pacific needed lubricating, but when they were educated, the reversers were all right from then on. One 'West Country' was not steaming well so the driver told the fireman to place a shovel of sand on the brick arch. He did so, the driver opened the regulator, the sand cleaned the tubes and from then on 'she worked like a good 'un'. A 'West Country', probably No 34037 *Clovelly*, on an up train encountered problems at Binegar. The heat from the brake blocks ignited the oil bath of the chain driven valve gear and flames surrounded the engine. It stopped on the Bath side of Radstock.

No 34042 *Dorchester* had a reputation for being a very bad steamer. Early one summer Saturday morning, Driver Fred Epps booked on with Fireman Sam Stainer. At 2.30am they went to the engine board and discovered that they were to have *Dorchester.*

They set off from Bath with a full head of steam, 250lb. This had fallen to 180lb by Claude Avenue bridge, 1¼ miles from Green Park station, but they managed to reach Combe Down Tunnel with the water winking at the bottom of the gauge glass.

On the return journey, when they reached Radstock the coal supply was so low that Sam had to sweep it forward from the back of the tender. Fred conceded that the class was marvellous at running — he could close the regulator and it ran smoothly for miles, but said that when he notched up, the steam reverser sometimes went back.

The first modified 'West Country' to work over the S&D was No 34039 *Boscastle*, in 1959.

LNER 'B12' class 4-6-0 No 8569, with No 8523 right. *Rev Alan Newman collection*

LNER engines working over the S&D

In the Second World War LNER 'B12' class 4-6-0 No 8549 with its crew was stabled at Templecombe under the S&D foreman and was attached to an ambulance train ready to move at a moment's notice. The crew — drivers, firemen and guards — lived with their train and worked in rotation. Ambulance trains over the S&D were restricted to 45mph. The 'B12' class was used on this duty because their short wheelbase and low axle loading gave them very high route availability. The class was unusual in that inside cylinder 4-6-0s were rare. Although fitted with Westinghouse brakes, a vacuum-air proportional valve allowed the driver of a pilot engine — most likely vacuum fitted — to work in the normal manner and apply the air brakes on the train engine and coaches to an appropriate degree. On D-Day, 6 June 1944, No 8549 arrived at Bath with an ambulance train off the S&D, as did No 8525 on 13 June and No 8549 again on 5 July.

Running times for ambulance trains, 18 August 1940.

Running Times for Ambulance Trains.

	minutes
Templecombe (Upper)	0
Evercreech Junction	20
Binegar	45
Radstock	55
Midford	65
Bath Junction	73
Bath Station	75

	minutes
Bath Station	0
Bath Junction	2
Midford	10
Radstock	20
Masbury	40
Shepton Mallet	45
Evercreech Junction	55
Templecombe (Upper)	75

A maximum speed of **45 miles per hour must not be exceeded** at any point during the journey and all restrictions which impose a slower speed than this must continue to be observed.

Special care must be exercised by Drivers of the loaded trains.

BR Standard Class 5 4-6-0 No 73047 with a Bath to Bournemouth train, climbing the 1 in 50 out of Bath on 13 October 1961. The trees on the right are in Twerton cemetery, the resting place of many ex-S&D employees. *R. E. Toop*

BR Standard engines

New Class 4 2-6-0 No 76018, on her way to Eastleigh from Horwich Works, Lancashire, via Willesden, was appropriated by Willesden shed to work a train to Birmingham. On its arrival the LMR at Birmingham was well aware that the only proper route to the SR was via Bath and the S&D. Bath was desperately short of good engines in the summer months so on 5 July 1953 No 76018 was observed there being fitted with a tablet catcher. It did eventually arrive at Eastleigh.

As a result of altered engine workings introduced on 7 March 1955, Class 4 2-6-0 No 76012 from Eastleigh worked the last up passenger train of the day to Bath and the first down the following morning. In 1956, Class 4 4-6-0s took over some of the passenger duties of '2P' 4-4-0s and 4F 0-6-0s, especially the 4.25pm from Bath to Bournemouth. S&D crews liked their free steaming, their comfortable cabs and easy riding. Their only problem was that between 60 and 70mph a fore and aft movement developed between engine and tender, and if allowed to continue led to all the fire being at the front of the box and the crew ankle deep in coal shaken from the tender.

Although not generally rostered to work the 'Pines', which was usually headed by a Class 5 or Bulleid Pacific, on one occasion Class 4 4-6-0 No 75073 with double blastpipe and chimney kept to time between Bournemouth and Bath despite a load of 450 tons — well over the maximum of 365 tons, although it was piloted by a '2P' 4-4-0 over the Mendips. Peter Smith in 'Impressions of the BR Standard Class 4 4-6-0' in *Model Railways*, October 1975, wrote that when Branksome crews ran an unofficial competition to climb the 1¼ mile-long 1 in 60 Parkstone Bank the fastest, the four-coach 4.25pm from Bath to Bournemouth behind Nos 75071/2/3, sped up it at about 60mph.

On 4 November 1963, a Class 4 2-6-4T was tried from Bournemouth to Bath. A full circle had been turned and it was back to tank engine working again. The Class 4s were successful as long as the bunker was completely filled with coal, as little of the 3½ tons was left after a single trip, while the 2,000gal side tanks needed frequent topping up at water columns.

One of the very few good things that the WR did for the S&D was to introduce Class 9F 2-10-0s. On 29 March 1960, No 92204 with Driver Bill Rawles made successful trial runs, so for the summer service Nos 92203–92206 were allocated to Bath. Their initial limit of 390 tons was later raised to 410 tons (12 coaches). Due to a lack of steam heating they were transferred

BR Standard Class 4 4-6-0 No 75009 (82G, Templecombe) and Standard Class 5 4-6-0 No 73049 leaving Bath on 6 July 1962, with an express to Bournemouth. *Rev Alan Newman*

Standard Class 4 2-6-4T No 80067 (83D, Templecombe) preparing the 4.35pm Bath to Templecombe on 4 May 1964. *Rev Alan Newman*

Class 9F 2-10-0 No 92220 *Evening Star* at Bournemouth West heading a stopping train to Bath on 30 September 1963. Its shed plate has been removed. *Rev Alan Newman*

elsewhere for the winter and replaced by Class 5 4-6-0s. At long last, the '9F' gave the S&D a locomotive which did not need a pilot engine. For 1961, Nos 92000/1/6/12 were at Bath from June until September and the class re-appeared in 1962, with the last of the line, No 92220 *Evening Star*, hauling the final 'Pines Express' over the route. The '9Fs' could not be used on freight as the Evercreech Junction turntable was insufficiently long to turn them.

Two four-car DMU sets pass Bath Junction signalbox with a Birmingham to Bournemouth excursion c1960. The blind reads simply 'Excursion'. *Author's collection*

Ex-War Department locomotives

Ex-WD class 2-8-0 No 90125 was tried over the S&D in January 1959, but its braking was found inadequate and then on 9 December 1959 the WR conducted clearance tests over the S&D with No 90693. Clearance was satisfactory, but again braking capability was not.

GWR and WR locomotives

In 1932, the half-day excursion from Avonmouth and the Bristol district stations to Bournemouth West was routed via the S&D from Highbridge, a GWR engine working throughout, the S&D supplying a pilotman. On 11 August 1932, the train was hauled by 4-4-0 No 3367 *Evan Llewellyn*. (Evan Llewellyn was a GWR director from 1898 to 1914; was the GWR trying to tell the S&D something?)

The WR conducted clearance tests with ex-GWR types, 0-6-0PT No 3604 and 0-6-0 No 2251 appearing on 23 December 1959. Results were satisfactory and in March 1960 No 3218 was transferred to Templecombe to work passenger and freight trains between Templecombe and Highbridge, with Nos 2219, 3210, 3215/6 following later that year.

Ex-GWR 0-6-2T No 6641 was also tested in December 1959, but proved useless. It drew loaded coal wagons from Midsomer Norton to Radstock where the signalman wisely made sure the level crossing gates were open in case the engine failed to control its train. The driver commented that if the signalman had not opened the gates, he would have done it for him.

Diesels

DMUs never ran regularly over the S&D, an appearance being a very rare event. A WR cross-country unit worked an excursion sponsored by the Gloucestershire Railway Society on 10 May 1958, while the same year, a Whit Sunday excursion from Birmingham to Bournemouth comprised four two-car Derby units and reported

A Swindon three-car cross-country unit at Bath Green Park on 10 May 1958, working a Gloucestershire Railway Society special from Cheltenham St James to Templecombe, Lyme Regis, Yeovil, Frome, Radstock, Stapleton Road and Cheltenham St James. Notice the newly-installed loudspeaker in the top right-hand corner of the picture. The 'cat's whiskers' depicted here were later replaced by a yellow panel to assist permanent way men to judge the speed of the train's approach. *Author's collection*

TABLE 'E' continued—MAXIMUM LOADS FOR DIESEL LOCOMOTIVE HAULED PASSENGER, PARCELS, MILK AND FISH TRAINS ON BRANCH LINES

The loads quoted are the absolute maximum authorised for the various types of locomotive and are not in any way related to any timing schedules. Reference to the Regional and Divisional Locomotive Route Availability Notices and relative publications will give other appropriate restrictions, which must at all times be observed.

SECTION		CLASS OF LOCOMOTIVE										
		D11–D147	D6XX	D8XX	D1XXX	D15XX D16XX	D6300 –D6305	D6036 –D6357	D67XX D68XX D69XX	D7XXX	D95XX	
From	To	Tons	Tons	Tons	Tons	Tons	Tons	Tons	Tons	Tons	Tons	Tons
Bath Green Park	Masbury	—	—	—	—	—	270	305	425	495	130	—
Masbury	Corfe Mullen	—	—	—	—	—	450	500	550 †	550 †	215	—
Corfe Mullen	Bournemouth West	—	—	—	—	—	330	370	525	550 †	160	—
Bournemouth West	Corfe Mullen	—	—	—	—	—	415	460	550 †	550 †	200	—
Corfe Mullen	Evercreech Junction	—	—	—	—	—	415	460	550 †	550 †	200	—
Evercreech Junction	Binegar	—	—	—	—	—	270	305	425	495	130	—
Binegar	Bath Green Park	—	—	—	—	—	550 †	550 †	550 †	550 †	270	—
Templecombe Upper	Templecombe Junction	—	—	—	—	—	—	—	—	—	—	—
Masbury	Templecombe Upper	—	—	—	—	—	—	—	—	—	—	—
Templecombe Upper	Evercreech Junction	—	—	—	—	—	—	—	—	—	—	—

†—525 tons for Passenger Trains.

Maximum loads for diesel hauled trains if ever authorised to work over the S&D.

23 minutes early at Templecombe No 2 Junction. Had DMUs been used regularly, what a view could have been experienced from a front seat!

Circa 1961 a Class 08 shunter was used when track was being relaid in Combe Down Tunnel as it obviated fume problems. It had a Bristol Bath Road driver, with a Green Park pilotman. It failed and an '8F' 2-8-0 had to tow it back to Bristol. The Bath driver travelling on the dead '08' as a rider grew very cold and was glad to step on to the '8F' to get warm on the return journey to Bath.

On at least one occasion *c*1964, a 'Peak' class 1Co-Co1 diesel-electric was used for banking a train to Combe Down Tunnel.

Following closure of most of the S&D, the Radstock West to Midsomer Norton & Welton trip, Mondays to Fridays, was made with a 'D95xx' 0-6-0 diesel-hydraulic.

Locomotive allocations

Bath (including Radstock and Branksome)

10 November 1945

Sentinel	0-4-0T	7191
0F	0-4-0ST	11202
1P	0-4-4T	1324/34/48
2P	4-4-0	497, 518, 696/7, 700
3F	0-6-0T	7275, 7316, 7465, 7496, 7542, 7557
3F	0-6-0	3734
3P	2-6-2T	115, 181
4F	0-6-0	3875, 4096, 4102, 4402, 4523, 4557–61
5P5F	4-6-0	4844, 5056, 5440
7F	2-8-0	13800–10
		Total 43

12 May 1951

Sentinel	0-4-0T	47191
0F	0-4-0ST	51202
2P	4-4-0	40568/9, 40601/96/7/8, 40700
2	2-6-2T	41240/1/2/3
3F	0-6-0T	47275, 47316, 47465/96, 47542/57
4F	0-6-0	43875, 44096, 44235, 44422, 44523/33/57/8/9/60/1
4	2-6-0	43013/7/36
5	4-6-0	44826/30/9, 5440
7	2-8-0	53800–10
WC	4-6-2	34040–44
		Total 53

May 1959

Sentinel	0-4-0T	47190/1
2P	4-4-0	40601, 40696/7/8, 40700
2	2-6-2T	41241/2/3, 41296, 41304
3	2-6-2T	82041
3F	0-6-0	43682
57xx	0-6-0PT	3742
3F	0-6-0T	47275, 47316, 47465, 47496, 47557
4F	0-6-0	44096, 44146, 44422, 44523, 44558–61
4	4-6-0	75071–73
5	4-6-0	73019/28/47/49/50–52
7F	2-8-0	53800–10
		Total 49

Templecombe

10 November 1945

1P	0-4-4T	1251, 1406
2P	4-4-0	634, 698
3F	0-6-0	3198, 3248, 3260, 3356, 3792
4F	0-6-0	4146, 4417
		Total 11

12 May 1951

2P	4-4-0	40505/9/63/4, 40634
2F	0-6-0T	30274
3F	0-6-0	43194, 43216/8/28/48, 43356
4F	0-6-0	44102/46, 44417
		Total 15

May 1959

2P	4-4-0	40563/4/9, 40634
2	2-6-2T	41248
57xx	0-6-0PT	9651
3F	0-6-0T	47542
3F	0-6-0	43194, 43216/8/48, 43427/36
3	2-6-2T	82039
4F	0-6-0	44102/35, 44417/57
		Total 18

General S&D shed notes

In 1930, when S&D locomotives were absorbed into LMS stock, Bath, Radstock and Branksome came under shed code 8, while Bristol Barrow Road and Templecombe were coded 5.

In the 1935 'garage' scheme, the sheds came under the Bristol district and were coded: Bath, Radstock and Branksome 22C and Templecombe 22D. Under SR Eastleigh auspices, Bath and Radstock became 71G, Templecombe 71H, and when under the WR from 1958: Bath and Radstock 82F and Templecombe 83G.

Coaling was generally by uncovered cranes hoisting wheeled tubs directly from wagon to locomotive. Often two jibs were used and as a loaded tub was lifted, the empty was lowered. Bath used a stage with 10cwt tubs. As Bath used soft Welsh coal which had less sulphur content, it was safer for use in the single-bore Devonshire and Combe Down tunnels. As they were single-line bores with very limited clearance above the chimney, any smoke which the engine was issuing would be forced up to the roof and then come down to the footplate. It was not uncommon on a summer's day, or a humid day when the air was still, for a footplate crew to dip their clean wipers in a bucket of cold water and place it over their faces. You could enter Devonshire Tunnel at 8 to 10mph with a heavy load behind and in the 447yd tunnel the fumes were very dense, particularly if you were on a second engine, or a banker. It was quite common for an engine to emerge saturated with water and drying out with yellow sulphurous fumes. Drivers and firemen have been down on their knees with their faces padded, seeking the freshest air — and this was even with Welsh coal.

Welsh coal could not be tipped mechanically like the harder North (Derby) coal. Welsh coal was very dusty and so required a greater supply of primary air through the ash pan. When using Welsh coal, dust had never to be shovelled on a fire unless the engine was moving and the fire burning well. When an engine was stationary Welsh coal had to be put on by hand.

Radstock coal was heartily disliked by Bath men. John Stamp once used some on the 5.15pm Bath to Poole goods, a heavy train. The coal 'melted' and sealed the firebars so that little air could pass. By the time Binegar was reached, pressure on the '7F' had fallen from 190lb to 120lb and the water was out of sight in the glass. They stopped at Binegar for 20 minutes to raise sufficient steam to reach Masbury. Another stop was made at Evercreech Junction to raise steam to attain Templecombe as they faced a rising gradient from just before Cole to approaching Wincanton. It struggled up this gradient and with a steam pressure of 100lb, they took it into Templecombe shed and another engine came out to take it onwards. The firebars were fused and long, black 'icicles' hung down. Some clinker was kept for A. H. Whitaker to inspect. He ordered that no more Radstock coal was to be used at Bath.

An S&DJR warning notice. *Rev Alan Newman*

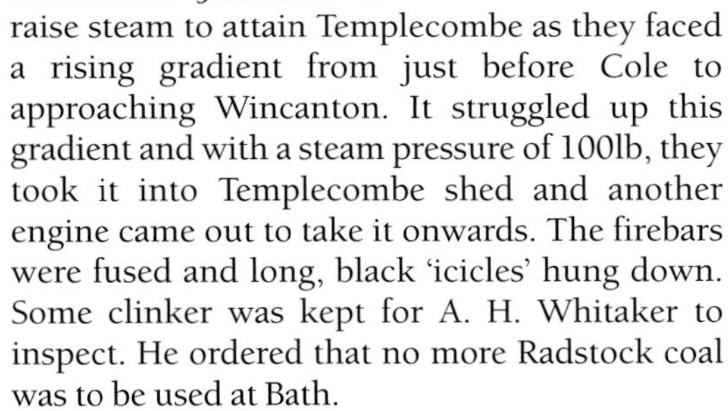

Before a driver signed off duty he filled out a 'Repair' card or a 'No Repair' card. In his early days of driving, Bob Ford omitted to place such a card in the box and he had been home for half an hour and was enjoying a meal when a call boy arrived with a 'Repair' and a 'No Repair' card stating: 'The foreman says we can't use this engine until you've put your report in regarding her.' Until he was authorised by Bob, that foreman was unable to send her out into traffic. It was no use getting a fitter to examine an engine because some faults were only revealed when an engine was driven. A driver was always glad to fill in a repair card because if an engine was a duffer and not corrected, he might be given it for the next shift.

The interior of the S&D shed at Bath, 5 June 1965: Class 8F 2-8-0 No 48760 built by the LNER at Doncaster and No 48732 built by the LNER at Darlington are seen here shortly after allocation to the depot. No 48760 has not yet acquired a shed plate. *Rev Alan Newman*

Bath shed

As the existing Midland Railway shed was too small to be used additionally by the S&D, on 5 May 1874 the MR accepted the tender of Samuel Robertson, of Bristol, for building a two-road shed of timber, measuring 160ft x 30ft. Traffic developed to such an extent that this shed was quite inadequate for the increased number of S&D locomotives, so Robertson added an almost identical shed immediately to the south of the original S&D shed. In 1883–4 the shed frontage was equalised by the first shed being lengthened by approximately 100ft and the second by 65ft. The shed then consisted of four roads plus the workshop road.

The fitting shop was electrified in 1909 and a dc motor drove three lathes, two drillers, a shaper and a grindstone. In January 1934 a balancing table for weighing locomotives was installed. As the shed was below the main line and fairly near the river level, it was occasionally flooded.

The original 42ft diameter turntable was replaced in 1878 by a 46ft table and a 60ft table in February 1935, at an approximate cost of £3,375. The table's centre pillar protruded and fouled an engine fitted with a snow plough. When the turntable was under repair, locomotives were sent to turn on the triangle at Mangotsfield, it being quite common to see four coupled together.

Class 4F 0-6-0 No 44558 (ex-S&D No 58) on the turntable at Bath MPD, and Class 9F 2-10-0 No 92214, 7 June 1964. *Author*

'Scottie' 0-6-0 No 41 by the timber-built coal stage, Bath, *c*1923. *Rev Alan Newman collection*

Bath S&D locomotive depot viewed from the top of the water softener *c*1935. A Bath to Bournemouth express leaves behind two Class 2P 4-4-0s. Notice the neatly trimmed coal stack. *Author's collection*

Right: Class 7F 2-8-0 No 53810 (82F, Bath) at its home shed on 31 July 1961 showing the new brick-built coal stage. An ash wagon stands beyond the loco's front buffer beam. *John Cornelius*

Below: Coal wagons converted for coke-carrying by the addition of three planks, seen on the flooded 'Boat Road' at Bath MPD, 5 December 1960. Part of the two-span bridge leading to Green Park station is in the background. When the River Avon subsides the wagons' oil axle boxes will require attention from the carriage & wagon department due to the contamination of the oil with water. *John Stamp*

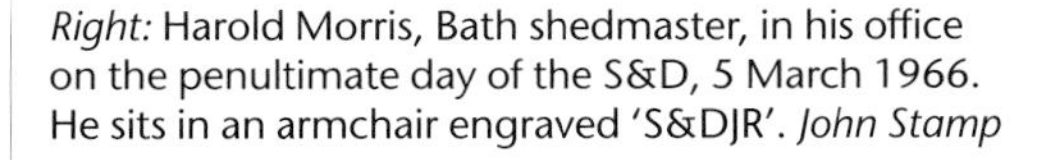

Right: Harold Morris, Bath shedmaster, in his office on the penultimate day of the S&D, 5 March 1966. He sits in an armchair engraved 'S&DJR'. *John Stamp*

Bath shed details 1927

In 1927, the S&D shed at Bath accommodated 25 engines.

Annual rent payable to the LMS for:

	£	s	d
Engine shed and accommodation	661	9	3
Shear legs	65	15	6
Sand furnace	23	17	6
Water tank and pipes	17	0	10
Pumping plant	20	12	10
Turntable	25	4	0
	£813	19	11

also

	£	s	d
Maintenance	550	0	0
Rates and taxes	175	0	0
Signalling expense	180	0	0
Maintenance of telephone	38	0	0
	£943	0	0

Numbers of running shed staff at Bath 1927

Drivers	37
Firemen	28
Chargeman cleaner	1
Cleaners	15
	81

Shed staff 1927:

	Weekly wage per person	Total wages per annum
2 foremen	5 0 0	520 0 0
3 steam raisers	2 11 0	397 16 0
6 labourers	2 8 0	748 16 0
3 bar boys (passed cleaners)	2 2 0	343 4 0
3 boiler washers	2 11 0	397 16 0
3 tube cleaners	2 9 0	382 4 0
1 stores issuer	2 11 0	132 12 0
1 office cleaner	1 15 0	91 0 0
		£3,013 8 0
4 coalmen	2 11 0	530 8 0
		£3,543 16 0

Artisan shop staff 11 May 1936

Leading boilersmith	1
Leading fitter	1
Grade 1 fitter	6
Grade 3 fitter	1
Assistant fitter	6
Tuber	2
Blacksmith	1
Blacksmith's striker	1
Total	19

Coal at Bath 11 May 1936

Welsh: Tredegar; Waun Llwyd; Wyllie; Bedwas; Windsor
Radstock: Somerset Collieries

Weekly consumption of water, about 800,000 gallons

Sources: from Devonshire Tunnel; pumped from River Avon and Bath City water available on standby.
– ¾ ton of sand dried daily.
– Water softening plant capable of treating 17,000gal per hour.

Time allowances 1930

		Hr	Min
Signing on			10
Preparation	Class 7F	1	0
	Sentinel (driver only)		30
	Other classes		45
Coaling at Bath, any amount			10
Coaling at Stations where coal crane is used up to 60cwt			15
Coaling at Stations where coal crane is used over 60cwt			20
Coaling of Sentinel			10
Disposal	Class 7F	1	0
	Class 2P and Class 3 and 4 tender engines		40
	Sentinel (driver only)		15
	Other engines		30
Signing off			10

S. & D. J. Rly. Loco. Dept.

Time allowed for preparing Engines.

Engines Nos. 80 - 85	60 minutes.
All other classes of engines	45 minutes.
"Sentinel" engines	30 "

Time allowed for disposal of Engines.

Passenger Tank Engines .. .. / Ordinary Goods Tender Engines	30 minutes.
Goods Engines 62 - 66 and 72 - 76	40 ~~35~~ minutes.
Passenger Tender Engines .. .. / Goods Engines 57 - 61	40 minutes.
80 Class Mineral Engines	60 minutes.

Time allowed for engine preparation. This document was duplicated in Bath Locomotive shed office c1925.

Radstock shed

The two-road shed was built of stone, probably in the mid-1880s. It contained two types of tank engine: large six-coupled engines for banking main line trains and small four-coupled engines for shunting colliery sidings. In 1914, the first six 2-8-0s were temporarily shedded at Radstock as they were too heavy to cross certain bridges to reach the S&D shed at Bath.

Circa 1937, Radstock had seven sets of men and five engines, three large and two small. A Sentinel shunter had a two-day washout every 14 days and while it was out of use the other Sentinel would be employed unless it was undergoing repair, in which case an ex-Lancashire & Yorkshire 'Pug' would be used. As there were no goods trains to be banked on summer Saturdays, Radstock men were sent to Bath to assist with the preparation and disposal of the many engines in use.

The coaling crane at Radstock shed, 1966. *Christopher Steane*

Templecombe shed

The first shed was a single-road timber construction opened in 1863. In 1877, it was replaced with a two-road timber shed, 140ft x 32ft, accommodating nine locomotives. It was rebuilt in brick in 1951. The 30ft diameter turntable was replaced by a 50ft table *c*1880.

Water was in short supply and engines were expected to fill at a previous watering point. Old tenders were filled either at Shepton Mallet or Blandford, run over a sump at Templecombe Upper to feed the 25,000gal tank in the locomotive depot below. Later, reliable supplies were piped from Milborne Port. The pressure in the depot's hydrants was now so good that until a booster pump was installed at Bath, the 2-8-0s' roster was arranged to allow them sufficient time at Templecombe for a washout. The gas works also supplied the LSWR at Templecombe.

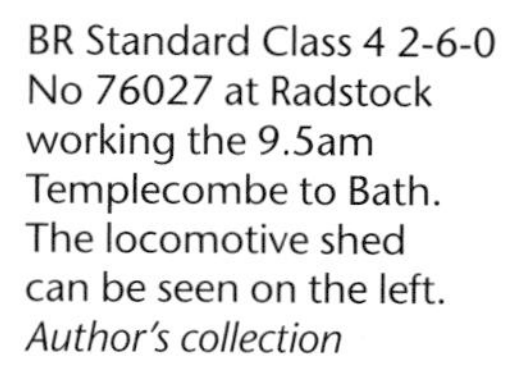

BR Standard Class 4 2-6-0 No 76027 at Radstock working the 9.5am Templecombe to Bath. The locomotive shed can be seen on the left. *Author's collection*

Templecombe shed *c*1960 with Class 3 2-6-2T No 40171, Class 2P 4-4-0 No 40634 and Class 2 2-6-2T No 41248. *Author's collection*

Templecombe locomotive depot on 6 December 1965 with a driver oiling the motion of Class 2 2-6-2T No 41291. Having just released a supply of coal into its bunker, the coal crane attendant is at work. No 41291 has brackets on either side of the smokebox for carrying SR codes. The turntable pit is whitewashed to prevent mishaps to locomotives and men. *Rev Alan Newman*

Templecombe, 12 May 1955: BR Standard Class 4 2-6-0 No 76029 passes the locomotive depot with the 12.55pm from Bournemouth West to Bath. Visible on shed are Class 7F 2-8-0 No 53803 and Class 2P 4-4-0 No 40527. *Rev Alan Newman*

Wimborne shed

The first shed is believed to have been a one-road timber building *c*1863, access being by turntable. A two-road shed, also of timber, was built alongside. They were sited in the fork of Wimborne Junction. A steam pump supplied three water tanks. In 1909, a new shed of timber was constructed using the existing two pits, but was rather larger than the original and measured 130ft x 35ft. It closed on 22 January 1923, but the 44ft diameter turntable continued in use until 6 July 1931. When the shed closed, its driver and fireman were transferred to Templecombe, the passed cleaner to Bath, the pumper to Blandford, and the district foreman to Templecombe which was already in his care plus Branksome.

Just before closure the shed had just one engine, a 'Scottie' 0-6-0. It left at 6.15am and ran light to Bailey Gate to collect wagons put off overnight. The engine then went to Blandford and worked the military camp branch before returning.

Branksome shed

The S&D shed was built on land leased from the LSWR. The original single-road shed was of brick. In 1895, a new shed, 120ft x 30ft was built by the S&D to an LSWR design. It had a deal frame clad in corrugated iron. The two roads held a total of four locomotives. The 12,000gal water tank was fed from the LSWR mains.

Branksome never had its own locomotive allocation and, at least latterly, was not used for coaling. It closed as a Second World War economy measure, but reopened afterwards. Five sets of men booked on there in BR days, including the set for the up and down 'Pines Express'. There were three steam raisers and four cleaners, the latter also used for general shed duties such as shovelling coal forward in preparation for a locomotive's return trip. SR locomotives and men also used the shed. Someone who lived near the shed complained of smoke nuisance from fire-raising, so to obviate this, fires were built up with coke. The turntable was removed *circa* spring 1955. The shed closed officially in January 1963, but continued to be used until 2 August 1965.

General information on locomotive working on the S&D

If Radstock coal was put in a bunker or tender at Bath, the fireman went to a pit by the water softener, collected three or four buckets of limestone and placed it on the bars to prevent clinker sticking to them like toffee. The Radstock bankers used only local coal so they required limestone and their fires had to be cleaned after every trip.

The curvature of the S&D twisted engines and made them rough. If Derby sent a good engine to Bath they advised 'Don't use it over the Dorset'. If Bath did and it made a couple of trips, Derby could tell because it was rougher.

Most S&D drivers used a jimmy — a ring with a wing nut bolt which would just fit round the top of a blastpipe collar and a bar on a hinge which could be lifted over and allowed to lie and split the blast, thus giving the fire a more powerful pull. When used it created a whistling sound. If an engine was a poor steamer, the use of a jimmy increased its steaming ability. Fitters made the jimmies unofficially and a blind eye was turned. One driver placed a jimmy on his blast-pipe at Queen Square, but it was insufficiently tight so when he opened the regulator, the jimmy was blasted through the glass roof.

All S&D drivers had a brass hook which fitted on the brake quadrant to keep the steam brake in the off position on goods trains and thus save a small volume of valuable steam.

Although a notice fitted in a glass-fronted frame in the cab gave written instructions that

The railwaymen's hostel at Wimborne on completion, 1902.
R. Atthill collection

SR 'N15' class 4-6-0 No 748 *Vivien* and S&D 'Large' 4-4-0 No 71 at Branksome shed on 28 April 1928. *H. C. Casserley*

whenever an engine was working, the small ejector must be constantly on, in reality it was not. As soon as a '7F' started to move its train up a bank the small ejector was turned off, but as soon as a summit was reached it would be turned on, as then the demand on the boiler had temporarily receded.

Another steam-saving dodge was to insert a farthing into a blowdown valve. When water softening plants were installed by the LMS in the 1930s, its locomotives were fitted with continuous blowdown valves to reduce the surface scum formed by the chemical action of the softened water, and therefore help prevent priming. Every minute 1 to 1½ gallons of water were lost through this valve and this could be an important factor on an engine shy for steam.

In the 1930s, most of the older S&D men were reluctant to learn the Midland roads and they tended to pass this attitude on to the young firemen and passed firemen. They signed for road knowledge Bath to Bournemouth, and if pushed might sign for Westerleigh or Avonmouth, but would not sign for Gloucester or Birmingham saying that signal lamps were 'like stars in the sky'.

If a good 'foreign' engine arrived at Bath, especially in the summer when demand for locomotives was high, the shed foreman did his best to keep it for a week or two, but if it was a duffer, it was quickly returned to Birmingham. Temporary tablet catchers were fitted to tenders of visiting engines and did not require holes. A Bulleid Pacific or a BR Standard engine required a bracket welded on the tender, so this was only done for locomotives regularly working over the S&D.

One night Bob Ford was returning on a 'Sunshine' with Driver Wally Lake. The tablet was taken at about 30mph passing Midford and by the time Bob crossed the cab to reach in the arm they had almost reached Combe Down Tunnel. Wally warned: 'Less than 50 yards to go Bob. Leave it.' Bob was unsure if the catcher jaw would foul the tunnel side, but it was certainly not safe for him to lean out. In the event, the catcher was unharmed.

S&D crews believed steam sanders more economical with sand than gravity ones as sand was blown under the wheels by a pipe angled to the rails, whereas a gravity pipe just dropped it, but the steam sander placed it where it was needed.

As engines of up S&D trains were usually disposed of on arrival at Bath, to ease his work, as a fireman approached Radstock coming down from the Mendips, he usually took his irons down, and levelled the fire. Unless there was an unforeseen occurrence he would not need to fire her again. If he felt that there could be an insufficiency of steam for the 1 in 100 climb from Midford to the far end of Combe Down Tunnel, he would place a round in the box as quickly as possible after passing Midford, so that no smoke was made in the tunnel.

At least one S&D driver never wore a watch believing that if the company wished him to have one, it would have supplied it. He was given one only when he retired. He did all his timing by estimation and looking at station and church clocks. He claimed that when driving, if he could count the sleeper ends going by, he was going too slowly and losing time.

SOMERSET AND DORSET JOINT LINE.
Locomotive Department,
HIGHBRIDGE.

No. 307. December 3rd, 1928.

NOTICE TO DRIVERS.

The following speed limits must be strictly adhered to, even though expresses are delayed by so doing, viz :-

Place.	Reason for Restriction.	Speed per hour.
DOWN JOURNEY.		
Bath Junction	Junction Facing Points	20
Midford	Facing Points	None
Radstock	Curve on Level Crossing	20
Winsor Hill	Crossings & Curve	25
Wyke	"S" Curve	25
Templecombe No. 3	Junction Facing Points	20
" No. 2	" " "	20
Stalbridge	Loop " "	20
Sturminster	" " "	20
Shillingstone	" " "	20
Stourpaine	" " "	20
Blandford	" " "	20
Corfe Mullen	Junction Facing Points	25
Broadstone	Junction & Curve	20
Branksome	Junction Facing Points	25
UP JOURNEY.		
Broadstone	Junction & Curve	20
Blandford	Loop Training Points	20
Templecombe No. 2	Junction	20
Wyke	"S" Curve	25
Evercreech Jct	Junction Facing Points	25
Midsomer Norton	Slip	20
Radstock	Curve on Level Crossing	20
Midford	Loop Trailing Points	20
Bath Junction	Junction Trailing Points	20

a fresh timing is being issued.

R C Archbutt
Res. Loco. Sup't.

Speed limits 3 December 1928.

Locomotive Superintendent's notices

7.6.18 [During water shortage] Drivers are taking on too much water at Templecombe — only just sufficient must be taken to get to the next water column at which they are booked to stop.

11.10.19 Water in tank of saddle tank engines must not be changed unless it is too hot to bear on the hands. Much water is being wasted through drivers emptying and refilling their tanks every hour or so. (They would have done this because an injector will not work with warm water and saddle tanks were particularly prone to warming the water within.)

9.9.19 In future the following clothing will be supplied to enginemen — Annually: two suits of jean overalls, one serge jacket, one cap. Every two years: one reefer jacket or one overcoat.

27.7.20 Cleaners are entitled to two suits of overalls annually; one overcoat after performing 25 turns or shifts of firing duty.

13.9.20 Men can keep old uniform unless they leave the service, but inscribed buttons and badges to be returned.

28.4.20 Not enough notice taken of speed restriction through tablet changing. 10mph in daylight and 4mph at dusk.

16.7.20 Houses are being built at Evercreech New, Ditcheat and Lamyat and will be completed for tenants by the spring. Rents anticipated to be 7s–8s week + rates.

21.10.20 Houses for railwaymen being built at Templecombe.

25.11.20 Screw jacks which have been carried on engines for many years have now been removed.

20.10.21 Drivers and firemen are to try to prevent blowing off as the railway is at present working at a loss.

10.8.22 There is a large increase in the amount of water taken at Branksome. Water is expensive there and drivers must please take as little as possible at that point.

23.2.23 Water may be taken from the LSWR [sic — amalgamation has occurred!] but water must not be taken unless specially required. A water ticket must be obtained.

14.4.23 Agreed that water may be taken at Wimborne without charge.

20.8.23 Increased coal consumption January–July of 2.13lb per engine mile is equal to 1,056 extra tons of coal burnt this year, representing £1,527.

11.9.23 Consumption of water at Branksome is too heavy. Only sufficient water must be taken at Branksome to enable a locomotive to run to Blandford.

Average mileage of various locomotive classes

Type		Miles per calendar month	No of months to run 20,000 miles
4-4-0	'Large'	3,385	5.9
4-4-0	'Small'	2,546	7.9
0-6-0	'Armstrong'	2,541	7.9
0-6-0	'Bulldog'	2,390	8.4
0-4-4T	Nos 10–55	2,093	9.6
2-8-0	Nos 80–90	2,021	9.9
0-6-0	'Scottie'	1,671	12.0
0-6-0T	Nos 19–25	1,569	12.8
0-6-0ST	Fox, Walker	1,323	15.1
0-4-0T	Sentinel	678	29.6

— 6 —

Accidents

ACCIDENTS, including minor ones, reveal details of S&D workings and something of the historical period. There is an interesting contrast between today's sanitised accounts in newspapers of accidents, omitting details some may consider gruesome, and the issues from the Victorian era which reveal the much harsher sociological climate where death and hurt entered people's lives more frequently.

On 30 September 1872 an accident occurred between two passenger trains at Stalbridge causing minor injury to two occupants. In the Board of Trade report, Col W. Yolland remarked that the S&D 'does not appear to be provided with all the appliances for working traffic safely'. Stalbridge was not constructed as a passing place 'and with a proper amount of supervision the fact that the up distant signal not being lighted at night for years could not have escaped being noticed'. He said that the collision would not have happened had the driver and fireman of the 7.55pm up train kept a proper lookout as they approached the station.

On 5 October 1874, as the 6.20am from Templecombe to Bath reached the high embankment close to Pecking Mill Viaduct crossing a stream and the Castle Cary road between Evercreech Junction and Shepton Mallet at about 30-35mph, the engine gave a lurch and Driver George Carter exclaimed: 'Mate, we're off the road.' Fireman Philip Thorne rushed to apply the handbrake, but had hardly reached it when the engine, a 2-4-0, came to the viaduct. No 18 fell into the stream where she lay on her side. The brake van derailed, but the coupling between the van and the three coaches snapped and the coaches were not derailed. Driver Carter of Bath was killed and Fireman Thorne of Highbridge injured. Traffic was obstructed for the rest of the day, but trains were worked up to each side so that passengers could walk by the scene of the accident.

It happened through subsidence of the embankment causing the left-hand rails to be 8–10 inches lower than those on the right. The *Bath Chronicle* commented: 'The line, since its opening, has not been considered too safe by more than one competent judge, and signs have not been wanting of the line not having properly set'.

At the inquest, Permanent Way Inspector Hooper said that he had examined this length of line daily and saw it last on Saturday, 3 October and ordered the ganger of each length to check the line before the first passenger train of the day ran.

Colonel Yolland wrote in his report that Colonel Rich, when making a report three months earlier, had criticised the poor workmanship of the contractor and only agreed to the line being opened to the public on the understanding that bridges, viaducts, cuttings, embankments and tunnels were carefully watched for some years. On 4 January 1875 the early morning goods ran into a landslip near Midford, considerably damaging the locomotive's firebox. Consequently the first passenger train from Bath ran for about two miles and returned to Bath Ticket Platform where fares were refunded. Traffic resumed at 1pm.

On 7 October 1875, 2-4-0 No 6 running tender-first heading the 3pm from Templecombe to Glastonbury, comprising three four-wheeled coaches and a six-wheeled brake van, left Cole 18 minutes late and at 30mph the tender derailed on newly laid track improperly canted. No one was injured largely because an alert guard noted dust rising from the ballast and immediately applied the brake.

Above: The aftermath of the Foxcote accident, 7 August 1876. *Author's collection*

Right: Elizabeth Edgell's tombstone in Clandown churchyard. She was killed in the Foxcote accident, but her daughter, buried with her, died naturally. *Rev Alan Newman*

As the S&D was a single line, in addition to the Absolute Block system, trains had booked crossing points in order to pass trains running in the opposite direction. If a train was running late, a decision had to be taken as to how long a train could be held at an appointed crossing place waiting for its belated opposite number. Caleb Edwin Percy in his office at Glastonbury was responsible for crossing trains running out of course and was in contact with stations by means of the single-needle telegraph.

Bank Holiday Monday, 7 August 1876 had been very busy with 17 extra trains run. The 7.10pm from Wimborne to Bath was an up relief consisting of 13 coaches plus two vans hauled by 0-6-0ST No 5 driven by John Bishop. The guard was in the front van, a brakesman in the rear van and a porter, acting as brakesman, in a carriage in the centre of the train. Because it was hauled by a powerful engine only a couple of months old and good at climbing the banks, it reached Radstock 15 minutes before Percy's calculations. Stationmaster John Jarrett at Radstock tried to contact Percy for instructions, but was unable to get through. Instead of holding it until an answer was received, he foolishly sent it on at 11.2pm.

Now between Radstock and Wellow stations, Foxcote signalbox (renamed 'Braysdown Colliery Sidings' and later still 'Writhlington') had been opened the previous year when a colliery siding was put in. There was no crossing loop, the box merely working the siding and passing on trains. It had no communication with Glastonbury.

Right: Writhlington Colliery and signalbox opened on 1 July 1894, opposite the site of the former Foxcote signalbox. The locomotive, with a train of loaded Braysdown Colliery wagons, is 0-4-2ST No 25A. All the wagons are dumb-buffered. *M. J. Tozer collection*

Things were slack at Foxcote. Regulations required the train books to be examined by John Jarrett but he had omitted to do so; only the home signals were lit; both distant signals were unlit because they had run out of oil and it was the frugal practice of the S&D not to light them on moonlit nights.

In charge that evening was Alfred Dando, a young fellow of 20. Formerly a miner, he was appointed porter at Radstock on 22 May and as he showed promise, was appointed to Foxcote box and after a week's training there, took charge. When the 7.10pm up arrived, as the block was still occupied by the previous up train, Alfred held his signals at danger. The driver saw him using the block telegraph. In due course the block was clear and the train sent forward.

Unfortunately things were every bit as slack at Wellow as they were at Foxcote and Radstock. Stationmaster James Sleep had been on duty from 5am until 6.30pm for £1 3s 0d a week, but on such a busy day he should have remained at his post and not gone off to quench his thirst at the Hope & Anchor, Midford. Sleep had been stationmaster for nine months, previously being a signalman at Evercreech Junction.

Assisting him, and in charge during his absence, was 15-year-old Arthur Hillard, also in charge of the telegraph, but a rule stipulated that the telegraph clerk was not allowed to signal 'Line clear' unless authorised by the stationmaster.

A special carrying spectators from the Bath Regatta at Kelston should have left Bath at 9.15pm, arrived Radstock at 9.45 and returned, picking up at Midford about 500 members of the Young Men's Liberal Association from Bath who had been on a picnic. (The small platform there must have been very crowded.) Its departure was held up due to a coach shortage and for an up train to clear the signal line. At 10.23pm Bath telegraphed Percy to inform him that it had left, although in reality it did not leave until 10.43. Percy verified that it passed the ticket platform at 10.48. (If these times are accurate, this gives an average speed of 16½mph.)

In due course the 12 coaches plus two brake vans arrived at Wellow, with Sleep travelling on it from Midford. At 11.3pm it was sent on by Hillard who claimed that he had received 'Line clear' from Foxcote.

Now two trains were approaching each other head-on between Wellow and Foxcote.

Driver John Hamlin on 0-6-0ST No 7 heading the down special found Foxcote distant 'nearly down to Caution' and shut off steam to ease oscillation round the 30 chain curve. He saw the red signal, applied the brake, blew his whistle and saw the up train approaching him about 25yd away, but was able to place his engine into backward gear before the crash 247yd east of Foxcote box. Henry Pullin, assistant guard of the down train and in the rear van, when he heard the whistle acted and had his brake fully applied when the collision occurred.

Only the down engine was derailed, but the first three coaches of its train were smashed — guard's van, third class and first and second class composite coaches, killing ten adults and two children, plus the guard.

In all, 28 passengers and six railway employees were injured. Elizabeth Treehorn, wife of the Wellow baker and standing on Wellow platform 2¾ miles away, heard the crash.

Driver Bishop on the up train had only just started, saw the down excursion approaching at about 12mph and had only time to close the regulator. None of the passengers on the up train were killed and its coaches were only slightly damaged.

One man was pinned for three to four hours between the buffers of the locomotive and the guard's van. Although stimulated with brandy, he died within minutes of release. The wounded were taken to neighbouring houses and then five to the Royal United Hospital (RUH), Bath, in a trap from the George Inn, Wellow. Mr Coombs of the Bell Hotel, Radstock, 'supplied a liberal quantity of spirits' to the wounded and his hotel, the Waldegrave Arms, Radstock, accommodated passengers unable to complete their journey.

The corpses were taken to the barn of the adjacent Paglinch Farm belonging to Mr Oxenham, and laid out to be identified. Unfortunately, they proved a magnet for the ghoulish and both the coroner and the local vicar addressed the crowd, saying that they hoped only immediate relatives would view the bodies. 'Notwithstanding the distance from Bath [about seven miles] hundreds of the inhabitants of the city visited the spot during the day.' By noon Tuesday the line had been cleared for traffic. Numerous articles belonging to the killed and injured were stolen from the wreckage including a bag belonging to Miss Noke which contained her ticket confirming that she was insured with the Railway Passengers Association Co, entitling her to £1 10s 0d per week in

VERSES WRITTEN UPON THE LATE

Dreadful Railway Accident

NEAR RADSTOCK,

On the Night of the 7th of August, 1876, when a Train from Bath came into Collision with a Train from Bournemouth, by which Calamity 13 Persons Lost their Lives.

Tune—" DRIVEN FROM HOME."

How often we see as we pass thro' the world,
Our poor fellow creatures to eternity hurl'd;
By the cold hand of death so quick snatch'd away—
Neglect is the cause very often we say.
In the best of good health you depart from your friends,
No thought of the danger your journey attends;
These poor Radstock people, alas! did not know
They were travelling to death every mile they did go

CHORUS.

They were travelling that night from pleasure to death.
On the railway near Radstock they drew their last breath,
Disfigured and mangled till almost unknown,
Thirteen poor creatures are driven from home.

The seventh of August was boat-racing day—
From Radstock to Saltford many had took their way
Free and light hearted no care to annoy,
With their friends and their neighbours the day to enjoy.
They spent the time happy till the Bath Train did start,
And then for their homes once more did depart;
It was their last journey upon the railway—
Thirteen were doom'd not to see the next day.

They had nearly reach'd Wellow, when without any sign
A train which came from Bournemouth was on the same line!
They ran into each other in one moment's breath,
And soon spread around them destruction and death.

Bruised, maim'd, and mangled on the railway they lie;
Limbs torn and shattered in agony to die;
In many a home in Radstock to day
They're mourning for those kill'd upon the railway.

Poor Thomas Wills, the guard of the train,
A part of the carriage had crush'd thro' his brain;
A wife and six children are now left alone—
The stay of the family is snatch'd from his home
Limbs were torn off, and were seen on the ground,
And one headless body cut off there was found;
The scene on that night made the stoutest heart quail,
And to hear the poor wounded their suffering bewail.

Think of the fate of that poor Radstock man,
Jammed with the buffers against the guard's van;
In most fearful pain for three hours he lie,
And when he was rescued it was only to die.
Children and mothers, men and their wives,
Even dear little infants, alas! lost their lives;
Altho' without warning in a moment they fell—
They're gone with the angels in heaven to dwell.

They are laid in their graves, they'll never return;
From their sad fate we can all of us learn;
In full health and strength we are travelling to death—
The very next moment may be our last breath.
I'm sure we all hope upon the last day,
Surrounded with friends we may all pass away;
In this sudden manner it is dreadful to die,
But God's will be done on earth as on high.

A contemporary poem inspired by the Foxcote disaster of 8 August 1876.

case of accident. The police eventually recovered this ticket.

Messrs Powell & Powell, upholsterers and auctioneers of 8 Union Street, Bath, provided coffins for the 11 adults and two children for £46. They were conveyed to Oxenham's farm on 8 August by special train.

Following the crash, Henry Pullin, assistant guard of the down train, proceeded back towards Wellow and laid detonators. Charles White, who shared duties at Foxcote with Alfred Dando, was in the second coach of the down train, his vehicle being smashed when the coach behind mounted it. Knocked unconscious, after 15 minutes he recovered and went to the signalbox. The down home signal, although alight at the time of the accident, went out soon after through lack of oil. The lamp from the up home was taken to help illuminate the accident scene. Rescue work was also helped by the light of bonfires made from the wreckage.

George Alfred Quick, later chief clerk at Bath S&D locomotive depot, was unofficially taking a ride to Radstock on the footplate of the down special. He jumped off before the collision, so injuring an already defective leg that it had to be amputated. Known as 'Crutchy Quick' he certainly lived up to his surname. One driver arrived at Bath, went to him and said that he had been given green signals all the way to Bath — although in truth he had run through many reds. He also mentioned that he had a revolver. Quick said: 'Let's see.' The driver took it out of his pocket to show him. Quick, quick as a flash, whipped it into an open drawer, locked it and threw the key to someone on the other side of the office. The driver was mad and had to be removed to Wells Asylum. Quick retired from Bath depot in May 1922.

Early on Sunday, 13 August 1876 two engines drew wagons to the accident scene at Foxcote to remove the wreckage. It was not all cleared away until late that afternoon.

The inquest revealed that the single-needle telegraph was abused by clerks. Percy's clerk at Glastonbury had teased his counterpart Herbert John the previous day and when Locke asked 'Where is down special?' John gave enigmatic replies.

Behind the up relief was the regular train and the accident prevented it from proceeding beyond Radstock. As some of its passengers were anxious to be ready for business the following day, they walked to Bath, while others 'by paying liberal prices' obtained transport. Those who walked from the wrecked train at Foxcote did not arrive at Bath until 6am 'exceedingly tired and footsore, as well as being generally out of sorts.'

Various events were organised to raise money for the widow and children of Guard Wills on the down train, and £600 was collected. In all, the Joint Committee paid about £9,000 in compensation and four children orphaned by the accident were offered employment, three eventually rising to become stationmasters and one a head office inspector. The two 0-6-0STs, Nos 5 and 7, arrived at Derby on 12 August 1876 for repairs which cost £685 and £743 respectively. Patching of their frames necessitated an extension of the front overhang by 8 inches. The damaged coaches were repaired at a cost of £1,416.

At the time of the Foxcote disaster there was an unfortunate spate of accidents in the area: Captain Tyler was in Bristol reporting on the Flax Bourton accident of 27 July 1876; there was a minor accident at Hampton Row just east of Bath on 14 August; and a collision at Temple Meads the same day.

At the inquest on the Foxcote accident the jury considered for three hours and came up with a verdict of the accident being caused by the criminal carelessness of James Sleep. It said that John Vorce Garrett, although not guilty of manslaughter, deserved severe censure for sending on an up train without a crossing order; Caleb Percy deserved severe censure for not providing a crossing order and Abraham Difford, General Superintendent of the line, was open to the severest animadversions for not maintaining discipline. Sleep was allowed bail for £100, two sureties being given of £50 each.

Captain Tyler's report of 28 October 1876 highlighted defects of regulations and workings, his main points being:

1. Foxcote signalbox broke the undertaking that only one engine be in steam between Radstock and Wellow at the same time.
2. The Foxcote signalman was inexperienced, unable to use the telegraph and almost unprovided with oil for signal lamps.
3. Responsibility for safe working should not have been given to a 15-year-old boy on duty for 15¾ hours when the accident occurred.
4. The Crossing Agent's Train Advice Book did not contain a column for entries for Radstock and some other stations.
5. The Superintendent failed to issue a timetable for the up relief.
6. The driver of the up relief had received no crossing orders.
7. The stationmaster and telegraph clerk at Wellow allowed the down train to leave without its being taken on block by Foxcote.
8. They accepted the up relief from Foxcote before the down train had time to reach Foxcote.
9. The Radstock stationmaster allowed the up relief to leave without any crossing instructions.
10. Both drivers failed to ask for crossing orders or telegraph passes.
11. There were too many instruments on the telegraph circuit to allow sufficient telegraphy of trains.

Tyler said that Sleep, who had resumed charge of Wellow station following his evening at Midford, was directly responsible for the accident having allowed a down train to start without having it put on the block and secondly for having permitted the up train to leave Foxcote before the down could have reached Radstock.

Hillard, due to his age and long hours of duty, was considered free of consequences. Abraham Difford contributed by not providing a time for the relief train and allowing lax discipline and long hours of servants.

Tyler added that a combination of block telegraph and train staff working offers the highest degree of safety but 'safety must more or less depend upon strict adherence to simple rules, and on the employment of responsible agents, carefully selected and closely watched. Accidents happen when discipline is lax, supervision careless or insufficient. Accidents are not caused by the system, but living agents by whom the system is worked.' This view was not quite in accord with Difford who believed that arrangements for working the S&D were 'very good and even better than with a staff'. He used the interesting reasoning that if the staff system had been properly working on the night in question no accident would have occurred, and neither would it have happened if the S&D's system had been working properly.

At the Somerset Spring Assizes on 14 March 1877 James Sleep was charged with manslaughter of Elizabeth Edgell. Bailey for the accused, asked why the S&D directors, who in providing 17 special trains that day and having earned 17 special sums of money, failed to provide special watching of this traffic.

The Wincanton accident on 26 February 1877 was caused when MR 0-4-4T No 1262 on loan to the S&D was derailed, killing the driver. The locomotive's wheels can be seen on the right above the inverted coach. *Author's collection*

The jury found Sleep guilty, but recommended him to mercy considering his 'high character'. The judge sentenced him to 12 months' imprisonment without hard labour.

The outcome of the accident was that the block system was improved at a cost of £1,100; Caleb Percy was dismissed with one month's salary in lieu of notice; James Sleep and John Jarrett were dismissed and a 'general revision of staff' carried out. Difford was demoted to goods manager on condition that he performed 'his duties to the satisfaction of the company'.

As rails on the extension were of poor quality, new rails were purchased from the Rhymney Iron Co and the Ebbw Vale steel works. Many sleepers were replaced, as was the fencing while the Bath to Evercreech Junction telegraph wire was tripled. Although the original S&D company was morally responsible for the accident, as the Joint Committee had taken over 25 days before the accident, it was they who were legally responsible. The electric train tablet was installed on the single-line sections in 1886.

On 24 October 1876, an axle broke on the leading van of the 12.30pm down express causing a derailment near Spetisbury, so acting on instructions from the Board of Trade, Captain Tyler, chief inspector of its Railway Department, spent three days carefully examining the S&D. He began at Bath and worked southwards, accompanied by his secretary who took copious notes. He recommended a speed limit of 25mph between Templecombe and Blandford.

The 6.10am on 26 February 1877 left Wimborne, the train consisting of a guard's van, one second class, one first class and two third class coaches laden with about 50 passengers. It departed Templecombe 11 minutes late behind MR 0-4-4T No 1262 built two years previously and on loan to the S&D.

A mile south of Wincanton a 24ft long newly laid rail, made at Ebbw Vale in 1873, broke in the centre causing No 1262 to derail and run along the sleepers for about 200yd before completely turning round and turning over. The van behind the bunker was smashed and the first two coaches greatly damaged. The two third class coaches, although derailed, remained upright. Apart from one passenger who broke a collar bone, the others were only bruised.

Driver Thomas Moorland of Albert Buildings, Bath, was found severely scalded beneath the engine and Fireman Jack Crick from Brougham Hayes Buildings, Bath, was badly cut and bruised. Guard James Ashford, although injured and having his coat tails torn away, returned towards Templecombe to place warning detonators, while one of the passengers proceeded forward to inform Wincanton. Actually, Wincanton was aware that something was amiss because a Bath guard, Coggan, on leave and waiting for his train home, noticed the engine lights disappear. He told Stationmaster Hayman who sent for a doctor and telegraphed Bath and Templecombe for their breakdown gangs. He immediately sent a trolley and men to the scene of the accident. The injured were placed on the trolley and brought back to Wincanton for medical attention, a special train conveying the rest of the passengers to Bath.

The breakdown train from Bath arrived just after midnight. Including men from Templecombe, 70 to 80 men cleared the debris and laid new track. The night was clear, so they were able to work without the light of fires, although some were made with the wreckage. The line was opened at 6am next morning, the only delay being to the night goods trains. Unfortunately, 60-year-old Driver Moorland died two days later. The 0-4-4Ts were then banned from travelling south of Evercreech Junction until the track was renewed. No 1262, renumbered 1236 in 1907, was withdrawn in November 1934.

On 13 December 1878, the 7.15am down passenger train passed safely through Combe Down Tunnel but shortly afterwards masonry was forced in and about 20 tons of sand and stone fell about 100yd in from the north portal, completely blocking the tunnel. Fortunately the authorities, worried about the effect of severe frost on the tunnel, kept two men constantly patrolling and it was one of these who found the fall shortly before the 8.20am goods from Bath was due. Horse brakes were ordered and used to convey passengers and luggage between Bath and Midford for the rest of the day, the road journey delaying passengers by about an hour. The tunnel was lined with four courses of brickwork and one of stone through much of its length. The rest was cut through sandy marl, which was tough and reliable.

The 12.15pm from Wimborne on 20 March 1879 arrived at Bath Junction and was stopped at the home signal. Driver Henry Bullard used the opportunity to get down and examine his engine and discovered a boot and part of a man's foot attached to the sand pipe. When he arrived at Bath station he informed the locomotive foreman and a search party left on an engine taken from the 2.40pm goods. Almost halfway through Combe Down Tunnel, 36-year-old permanent way man Frederick Francis was found with both legs severely damaged and a badly injured hand. Conscious, he held the hand of one of the men who had discovered him and said: 'It's a bad job. I don't know what happened.' He was taken to the RUH, then situated in the Lower Borough Walls, only ¼ mile from the Midland station. He was admitted at 4.40pm and died 25 minutes later, leaving a widow and six children.

A gang of about 20 men employed repairing the tunnel walls only 618yd away from him were quite unaware of the incident. This gang was protected by three watchmen who laid a detonator on the track and drivers also whistled a warning. Francis had a separate duty and was working by himself tightening fishplate bolts.

The cause of the accident was inexplicable. He was sober and not deaf, manholes were available and even if not used, where he was found there was a space of 2ft 9in between the train and the tunnel wall. A manhole was 28yd on one side of him and 32yd on the other. Joseph Lowe, permanent way superintendent from Shepton Mallet, said: 'The pressure of the air and the vibration of a hand lamp would tell anyone that a train was in the tunnel.'

Shortly after 8pm on 14 August 1880, Driver Philip Thorne, who had been fireman when an accident occurred near Evercreech Junction on 5 October 1874, felt his engine, hauling a down goods, strike an obstruction. He reported this fact to the Wellow stationmaster so the driver of a crowded up Mendip excursion was warned. On approaching the spot, he observed a fishplate and hammer on the track, while a short distance beyond, a sleeper, which must have been placed after the goods had passed because it was completely across the line. The culprits were not found.

On 9 March 1881, the midnight goods from Bath passed through Wellow and unfortunately the new signalman forgot to return the signals to danger. When the 1.30am goods from Bath approached at about 2am, although Driver James Dark held an order to cross an up train at Wellow, when he saw the signals clear, assumed that he was to proceed. A quarter of a mile beyond the loop he saw an oncoming train, applied the steam brake and his fireman the handbrake. Driver George Williams and Fireman James Short on the up goods did not jump off, but stayed on the footplate and reversed their engine. The engines struck head-on, one mounting the other. Williams was thrown from his engine and apart from bruising, neither of the crews was hurt. Six wagons were wrecked, but the locomotives were able to reach Bath. A large breakdown gang did well to clear the track by 10am and only one passenger train had to be cancelled. Damage amounted to £700.

On 8 December 1881, 0-4-4T No 14 working the 12.18pm from Bath to Bournemouth was rounding a curve about a mile from Wimborne Junction when the leading brake van fell over on its side and the following four coaches derailed. The only vehicle remaining on the track was the through Birmingham to Bournemouth West coach. No passengers were injured, but the guard was unconscious for six days. The accident was caused through two rails being insecurely fixed.

A banking engine, 0-6-0T No 8, running bunker-first on 2 March 1882 after giving assistance, was returning from Masbury crewed by Driver Edwin Ridout aged 33 and Fireman Robert Baker, aged about 25. They stopped at Chilcompton for water and despite having an order to cross a down passenger train at this station, having filled his tanks, Ridout set off against adverse signals and while the fireman was still on the tank top.

George Powell the stationmaster, ran after the engine on the right-hand side of the line and sent Elijah Oxford, signalman, on the left. Although they waved and shouted, they were unobserved by the engine crew. Powell told Oxford to follow and see the result, while he returned and telegraphed Bath of the occurrence.

Meanwhile, the 1.35pm passenger train from Bath plodded up the gradient from Midsomer Norton. Driver Alfred Dade and Fireman John Rainey, both of Wimborne, on the footplate of 0-4-4T No 32, about midway to Chilcompton saw the approaching light engine. Dade opened his whistle and kept it sounding, applied the steam brake and reversed his engine. Thomas Beakes, passenger guard, saw the banking engine when it was about 12yd in front of his train, pinned his brake and braced himself for the crash. The passenger train was stationary when struck by No 8 at an estimated speed of 20 to 30mph.

The impact threw Dade out of one side of the cab and Rainey the other. Ridout was not so fortunate. The gauge glasses broke and the impact and the force of the steam threw him over, or through, the wire fence for a distance of 30 to 40yd. He was badly scalded, and in fact one large piece of flesh which peeled off his arm was buried on the spot.

Ridout was placed in a third class compartment and taken to Paulton Cottage Hospital where he died soon after arrival, but not before saying: 'Yes, it was all my own fault.'

Fireman Baker, not so seriously injured, was taken to the RUH. The locomotives and five coaches were not derailed and none of the 50 to 60 passengers injured except for one receiving a cut. The line was blocked for only an hour.

At the inquest with a verdict of accidental death, the jurymen gave their fees for the benefit of Ridout's widow and four young children.

The funeral on Sunday afternoon, 5 March, was most impressive. A large number of employees from the S&D, MR and GWR assembled near his home at 40 Dorset Street, Twerton, and marched in procession to St James' Cemetery where the service was taken by the Vicar of Twerton, the Rev Stokes Shaw. A dozen S&D employees acted as bearers and others as pall bearers. Next came J. F. Hewitt, locomotive department foreman; chief inspector G. H. Eyre; H. Martin, MR stationmaster at Bath; George Quick, locomotive time keeper; and Mr Seymour, crossing agent. Then followed S&D firemen in order of seniority; MR drivers and firemen; S&D crossing office staff; S&D guards and brakesmen, and lastly men employed in various capacities on the MR and GWR. Friends and relatives of the deceased brought up the rear.

Ridout had risen quickly through the ranks. He started as an engine cleaner on 16 October 1871, became fireman on 1 May 1874, on 15 April 1878 was passed for driving and on 1 March 1880 became a driver. From 24 February 1882 he was paid 6s 6d a day.

The night before the funeral S&D driver Jesse Board, getting off a goods engine to ask permission to attend Ridout's funeral, severely cut his knee on the bottom step. Due to this injury he was taken to the RUH and detained.

Soon after 4am on 25 October 1883 and shortly after the double-headed goods train from Evercreech Junction to Bath had left Shepton Mallet after taking on water, due to a coupling breaking, seven wagons ran off the line. Five of these plunged 60ft over Charlton Viaduct. Stationmaster Hawkins, woken by the falling trucks which severed the telegraph wires, proceeded to Binegar and telegraphed for a breakdown gang which arrived at about 5am. The permanent way was undamaged, but a considerable length of parapet wall had been demolished. Traffic resumed at 9.20am, and only two trains had been delayed.

In teeming rain on 18 May 1884 0-4-0ST No 45 *Bristol* was pushing 13 empty coal wagons over the Tyning loop at Radstock when the fireman inadvertently directed the train to the wrong line and it smashed into a rake of loaded wagons drawn by horses Jeannie and Sarah. Both were killed and seven wagons damaged. *Bristol* was crewed by a 67-year-old driver and a lad of 14, the latter travelling on the buffers of the leading wagon to attend to points and couplings.

Locomotive superintendent W. H. French was severely censured for permitting such manning and was ordered to draw up rules and put them

Seen here at Midsomer Norton is 0-6-0ST No 2 which narrowly avoided explosion at Chilcompton on 4 August 1884. *Author's collection*

into effect within 48 hours. An amount of £1,830 was authorised to re-lay sharp curves to make colliery lines suitable for steam power so that horses could be dispensed with.

On 14 August 1884, 0-6-0ST No 2, following a banking turn, was returning light to Radstock. It was held at Chilcompton as a goods was occupying the single line. A permanent way man nearby noticed steam escaping from the firebox casing. He told the driver, but as the signals had been pulled off, Driver Reddy made a quick inspection, believed the fault not serious and set off. He had second thoughts and stopped at Midsomer Norton signalbox and was alarmed at the quantity of steam escaping from the firebox. He and his mate both threw out the fire and managed to manipulate the safety valves to reduce the boiler pressure. No explosion took place thanks to their quick thinking, but his fireman was badly scalded when operating the safety valve.

The 11.45am from Bournemouth to Bath was being worked by 0-4-4T No 53 on 31 July 1885, the train consisting of a brake van, five-compartment third class coach, two four-compartment first/second composites, a six-compartment MR bogie third class, an MR four-compartment first/third composite and a brake van. The MR coaches were running through to Birmingham. The Rev Poole King of Clifton, Bristol, recounted: 'The train left Bournemouth and ran very smoothly up to Binegar where it ran into a luggage train. I was lying on the seat of a first-class carriage, of which I was the only occupant, and the shock of the collision threw me on the other side of the apartment (sic). I was in no way injured though my coat was torn, and I got out of the carriage directly. I believe I was the first to get out, and I went in the waiting room of the little roadside station and prepared all the cushions I could get, as well as I could for the injured and also sent for some water. The engines, so far as I could see, were not telescoped, but the trucks were. The first two carriages of the passenger train were smashed up into each other, and half of the next carriage was very much injured. There was wonderfully little noise, so I don't think the train could have been very full. Of course, the women screamed. By the time I had got the cushions ready in the waiting room they brought in a man, who I think was one of the drivers. His head was very much injured. I bathed and washed him clean with water, taking great pieces of stone out of his head, and left him in charge of another. Then I went to assist in getting out the guard, whose name is Beakes. He was on top of the carriage completely jammed in with broken *debris* and luggage, and we were nearly an hour getting him out. Both of his legs were most severely injured, one being nearly cut-off, and his head was severely bruised. He was sensible all the time, and did not appear in much pain — only complained of pain in his legs. When I say not much pain, I mean not in agony. He was quiet and perfectly sensible until he was put in the train to come down here [Bath]. There were others injured; I do not know how many or whom. I gave myself up to attending to the one guard, and bestowing on the poor fellow what care I could.'

Class 4F 0-6-0 No 44422 now happily preserved, approaches Binegar with the 4.35pm from Bath to Templecombe on 31 July 1959. *Author*

The interior of Binegar signalbox, December 1965. *Christopher Steane*

What happened that morning was that Colonel Rich had arrived to inspect the newly-doubled line Binegar to Chilcompton and faulted some of the locking bars in Binegar signalbox. As these locking bars affected only sidings and the down starting signal, Rich was justified in giving permission for opening the double track and he left before noon.

About 1.35pm William Edwards, an LSWR signal fitter set to work to correct the interlocking and removed No 12 locking bar to be drilled and tapped by his assistant Ben Burfield. Signalman William Applebee had come on duty at 9.30am and was one of only four relief signalmen, having been selected because of his experience. Fitter Edwards believed he had informed him of the removal of the locking bar, but was unsure and Applebee could not recall the statement.

The brass plates had been removed from the levers, but their numbers had been chiselled in. In setting the road for the 11.45am, Applebee unfortunately pulled black points lever No 11, instead of blue locking lever No 12 and because the locking had been disconnected, was able to turn the up passenger train to the down road where 'Scottie' 0-6-0 No 48 stood with front and rear brake vans, 25 wagons and 0-6-0ST No 5 banking.

At a speed of 20 to 25mph No 53 collided with No 48 smokebox to smokebox, the leading wheels of the passenger engine leaving the rails. In view of the fact that the leading third class coach No 4 was smashed, except for the first compartment, the injury list of 14 passengers could have been greater.

Some had lucky escapes. Inside the end compartment of the third class coach Miss Edith Woods, Mrs Cecilia Roberts and Mr George Turland were saved through collapsing timber protecting them from serious injury, while in another compartment the force of the collision burst open a door, ejecting a child to the permanent way. The mother, Mrs Elizabeth Newdick, jumped after it. Both were only bruised. Mrs Annie Charles, wife of a County Cork coastguard, was killed, her body when freed from the wreckage initially laid on the grass and then placed in the ladies' waiting room which had been used for treating the injured, in addition to some being cared for in the stationmaster's house. Splints were improvised from broken pieces of wood from the wreckage.

A special train conveyed the injured to Bath where they arrived about 6pm and were taken by cab and stretcher to the RUH. Shortly after 7pm the up line was cleared for traffic, the 2.30pm Bath to Bournemouth express running wrong line. The next train was the 2.10pm Bournemouth to Bath stopping passenger which had been held at Shepton Mallet for about 2½ hours. Light from fires and torches illuminated the scene and by 3am all vehicles had been removed from the track which at the point of collision had been bent 5 inches outwards. The down line opened to traffic at 6am on 1 August.

Thomas Beakes, aged 49, the front guard was fatally injured and died soon after having his legs amputated at the RUH. He was the oldest guard on the line, having joined the B&E at Burnham-on-Sea some 30 years previously and entered S&D service when that company began working its own trains. He later moved to Bath where he lived at 10 Dorset Street. He left a widow and five children, nearly all earning. He was also the guard in the accident on 2 March 1882 when Driver Ridout was killed. His funeral was at St Peter's Church, East Twerton, and the procession was similar to that held for Ridout, except that the S&D band was in attendance. About 2,000 attended the committal in Twerton cemetery. His son John Beakes became chief traffic inspector and later chief clerk and controller of the operating section of the S&D at Bath Queen Square.

Driver Alfred Bruford on the passenger engine, No 53, received a fractured skull, while his fireman Fred Hole received lesser injuries. Both came from Wimborne. Driver James Morley and Charles Rowsell, the leading guard of the goods train, were on the platform talking to Stationmaster Nathaniel Meech when the collision occurred, covering all three with fragments. The fireman, enjoying his midday meal on the footplate was knocked over, but only bruised. The tender of the goods engine was thrown onto one of the trucks, while the first six wagons comprising three 8-tonners containing small coal and three empties, were all smashed. Except for its first two vehicles, the passenger train was hardly damaged. Some of the luggage from the front van was thrown on the station roof. The front passenger brake van and the following three coaches were all fitted with chain brakes and all four could be worked either from the engine or the leading guard's brake. The guard in the tail brake could only work the brake in his van. Driver Bruford applied his steam brake on all eight wheels at the facing points and the rear guard had his brake on.

In his report to the Board of Trade, Colonel Rich said that if the passenger train had had a good automatic continuous brake, the collision would have been less severe as it could have braked in the 160ft between the points and the down goods. He recommended that when alterations were made to the locking gear, the work be carried out when no trains were running, or if this was impossible, all trains to be brought to a halt and pass slowly. Signalman Applebee was tried for manslaughter but acquitted.

To prevent a repetition of this accident, signalboxes were issued with reversible metal badges with 'Disconnected' on one side and 'Workman' on the other. If a lever was disconnected a badge was attached displaying the appropriate side, while if a workman was engaged at points or a signal, the lever operating them would show 'Workman'.

It is understood that the Highbridge breakdown train, returning from Binegar with wagons loaded with material from the scene of the disaster, was misdirected into a siding at Glastonbury and was itself another breakdown when it struck the stop blocks. Products from Oakhill Brewery had so blurred the senses of the gang that some were riding home perched on top of the debris. A portion of the panelling, with the first class coach number '4' in its centre, adorned the wall behind the seat of the carriage and wagon department foreman's office at Highbridge.

Driver Bruford was involved in another accident at Binegar only six months later. On 3 February 1886 a down goods consisting of 22 loaded wagons, headed by 0-6-0 No 36 and banked by 0-6-0ST No 9, approached Binegar along the recently doubled track. Ahead was the single-line section to Shepton Mallet. Driver George Darke on No 9 said that if a train driver wished to stop at Binegar, he would indicate this to the banker by blowing his whistle three times.

The head guard of the down train, William Coggan, said: 'On leaving Chilcompton station I make it a rule to get outside my van to see whether the up train is waiting there or not. If I do not see it, I keep an eye out all the way to Binegar station. At Binegar station, finding my train was running through, and the up train was not there, I got out of my van with the object of getting into my mate's van in order to get to the banking engine at the back of the train to get the driver to whistle to the front driver to stop the train. It was too foggy to show the front man a light. Before I could get to my mate's van the collision occurred.'

Although the 1.20am from Bath was due to cross the 12.15am from Templecombe at Binegar, as Driver John Cadby, who had been a fireman on an engine in the 1876 Foxcote crash, saw green signals, he believed that he must have passed the up train on the new double-track section. This was quite feasible because if his engine was slipping, he needed one hand on the regulator and the other on the sanding lever and to operate the latter, he had to stoop 18 inches. He was thus very occupied. At the inquest William H. French, the locomotive superintendent, said that although Cadby should have stopped, seeing the signals off would delude anyone; 99 out of 100 drivers would have done the same as Cadby and proceeded.

Cadby passed on to the single line and 387yd from the station was struck by 0-4-4T No 53 which had left Shepton 30 minutes late with eight wagons loaded with sacks of barley, 25 empty wagons and two brake vans, and was assisted in the rear by 0-6-0 No 39.

Neither No 53 nor No 36 was derailed by the crash, but the tender of No 36 was pushed into the air. The down train received little injury — just one wagon smashed and one damaged, but 19 wagons out of the 35 of the up train were destroyed.

When news of the accident was telegraphed to Bath, a breakdown gang of a dozen men and Mr H. G. Terry, surgeon of Green Park, were dispatched. As the fireman of the up train could not be found — just before the impact he had jumped from the footplate — as did his driver, torches were used to try to locate him. It was not until 100 navvies who had been engaged on doubling the line's earthworks and who had been borrowed to help clear the wreckage came on the scene, that Charles Wiseman aged about 23 of Wimborne was found after about five hours, beneath a smashed truck with his skull crushed.

The up driver, William Kinnersley of 14 Dorset Street, East Twerton, Bath, Driver John Cadby of 27 Dorset Street and his fireman William Hamblyn of Radstock were placed on an engine and Surgeon Terry recommended that they be taken to the RUH. The men thought otherwise. Hamblyn got off at Radstock and the other two left at Bath goods shed and walked to nearby Dorset Street, though later Kinnersley was admitted to the RUH.

The 7.20am from Bath to Evercreech Junction was cancelled, but subsequent passenger trains ran, with passengers and luggage transferred past the accident site. By 1.40pm the line was clear and normal traffic resumed. Only half a dozen sleepers had been broken or displaced.

George Henry Eyre, assistant superintendent of the S&D, had examined Signalman Cox on 11 January when he started at Binegar and said of him: 'He was a very efficient man and thoroughly understood the working of the signals and telegraph.' He added that a supernumerary worked in the box for 20 days until Cox was given sole charge. Two signalmen worked at Binegar doing alternate weeks of day duty 7am to 6pm, with a week of nights 6pm to 7am. At the time of the collision Cox had been on night duty for three consecutive nights.

The accident was caused through Cox lowering the down signals before the up train had entered the loop, he admitting that he had forgotten about the up train. The coroner recommended the jury to find him culpably negligent, saying, perhaps uncharitably: 'Whether Cox was half asleep, stupid, or half-demented I cannot possibly make out, but the mental confusion contributed materially, if not entirely, to the death of Charles Wiseman.'

After two hours of deliberation the jury brought in a verdict of manslaughter. While the inquiry was being held, Cox's child died and the jury gave its fees, amounting to £2 5s 0d, towards his funeral expenses. It recommended that drivers be better instructed regarding Rule 359 that a driver must in no circumstances start from a station where he was scheduled to cross another train, before that train arrived unless he had received a written order on a green form to proceed to another station. It also recommended that a train staff or tablet be introduced immediately on single-line sections. The jury also considered that the hours of night duty were too great.

Vandalism, which could have resulted in an accident, happened about 3pm on Sunday 24 February 1889. Some lads unlocked a permanent way trolley on an embankment in Lyncombe Vale and sent it off down the line through Devonshire Tunnel. The alert signalman at Bath Junction saw it approaching and directed it into a siding. It had run 1½ miles. Normally no S&D trains ran on Sundays, but had the trolley been released half an hour earlier, it would have collided with a special train chartered to convey Arthur Rousbey's Opera Company from Bath to Greenwich, the S&D being used to Templecombe.

On 3 July 1889 a breakdown train left Bath containing permanent way staff and when travelling at 40mph 300yd north of Cole station, one of the brake van axles broke, derailing the van which turned round and fell on its side across the up line, fatally injuring Walter Ashford of Twerton. He was brought back to the RUH but died the following day without regaining consciousness. Walter, aged 21, was the son of passenger guard James Ashford involved in the Wincanton accident of 26 February 1877. Walter was a member of the United Patriots' Benefit Society and at the time of his accident had in his pocket a current copy of the *Railway Herald* to which was attached an insurance coupon entitling the relatives to £25.

The van and the rest of the breakdown train were normally stabled in a siding at Bath. The train had been examined by the locomotive foreman, whose responsibility it was, on 17 July 1886 and it was found to be in good condition. The van was new in 1862, rebuilt in1880 and its previous trip was to Radstock on 15 June 1889.

At the inquest all parties were exonerated from blame as wheel tapping would alert to a flaw in the wheel, but not the axle. Ashford was buried in Twerton cemetery, a large crowd attending and the S&D band playing the 'Dead March' from 'Saul' headed the procession.

At 5.14pm on 23 December 1890 William Gosney, signalman at Broadstone Junction received a bell signifying that the 2.15pm Bath to Bournemouth express passenger had left Bailey Gate. About the same time he was notified a light engine had left Wimborne Junction. Although he had set the road for the S&D train, correctly he kept all signals at danger until the light engine had stopped. As soon as it halted, Gosney pulled off the S&D signals for the express which was running about 70 minutes late.

Meanwhile, Fireman Albert Stone climbed down from his engine, LSWR double-framed Beyer Goods 0-6-0 No 290, to check that its headlamp was all right. When he returned to the cab Driver William Squires set off believing he had the road, but in fact the signal immediately ahead of him was red, the green signal further on showing for the S&D express.

As Signalman Gosney looked up after making an entry in the train register he saw No 290 moving towards him. He called: 'Where are you coming to?' He ran out of the box towards the oncoming engine, but it failed to stop. He returned to his box and threw all signals to danger. The light engine passed the box and stopped between it and the station platform.

Driver Squires said he heard Gosney call: 'The Somerset train is close on us' [it is interesting that LSWR men should call it the 'Somerset' as Bath men referred to the S&D as the 'Dorset']. Hauling seven coaches and a brake van, 0-4-4T No 54 struck the tender of No 290, kept to the track for 80yd before being derailed by a set of tender wheels and slewing across the track between the platforms, blocking both lines. A buffer from the light engine was found in a garden 40yd distant.

The guard's van next to the engine telescoped into the first class coach behind, killing one of the ladies who had intended spending Christmas with friends. The other three ladies in her compartment escaped with injuries. The assistant guard in the front van had a narrow escape.

The inquest jury's verdict was 'manslaughter' against the driver and fireman of the light engine, and both were arrested. Signalman Gosney was exonerated from blame. Major Marindin at the Board of Trade inquiry found the driver to be the principal cause, the fireman less so. Signalman Gosney was to blame for the action he took when No 290 moved. Instead of running from the box and calling to the driver, he should have thrown all signals to danger, or displayed a red hand lamp. He was to be blamed for an error of judgement, rather than breaking the rules because had he not stopped the light engine, it might have got clear.

At Dorchester Assizes Driver Squires was acquitted of manslaughter and the case against Fireman Stone dismissed. The LSWR gave Squires a severe reprimand.

The real cause of the accident was fatigue — for Squires and Stone had been at work since 6.25am and had only five hours' rest after working 14¾ hours the previous day.

An 18-coach excursion train returning from Bournemouth to Worcester on 10 July 1894 was hit at Templecombe by 0-6-0 No 57 hauling a goods and running through signals. A Pullman car on the excursion was struck and the sides of seven coaches and a brake van scraped, tearing off doors, footboards and panels. The Pullman car was knocked off the road and its vacuum pipe severed. Bath station was notified immediately and the RUH telephoned — technology was up-to-date — and warned to make preparations to receive possible cases. This warning proved needless as no passenger was injured and 0-6-0s Nos 46 and 24 heading the excursion received no damage.

On 5 February 1895, 0-6-0 No 46 was returning light tender-first from Masbury after having banked a goods train. It ran through danger signals at Binegar and collided with the rear of the 12.10am Templecombe to Bath goods headed by 0-6-0s Nos 20 and 23. One goods guard was injured so severely that he never worked again.

The 7am from York to Bath was unlucky on 20 July 1911. At Bath it became two trains: one ran non-stop to Poole and Bournemouth where it arrived at 4.7pm and the other half called at principal intermediate stations and arrived in Bournemouth at 4.54pm. That day the engine of the non-stop portion failed on the gradient through Oldfield Park, Bath, and the train had to return to Bath for a fresh engine thus causing a delay of about ½ hour.

When the semi-fast portion following it approached Midford a cloud of dust and stones was thrown up in front of the engine. The driver stopped to ascertain the problem and found his engine and the first van dragging along a quantity of barbed wire which had been lying on the track. It was removed and the train proceeded. A bundle of wire had rolled down the slope in the grounds of Midford Castle and burst through the iron fence separating the park from the railway. The cost of repairs to sleepers and chairs was borne by the wire's owner.

On 25 September the same year, between Wellow and Radstock, a spark from the engine of the 2am goods from Bath ignited two wagons of waste paper consigned to Glastonbury. Immediately the fire was discovered the wagons behind those aflame were detached and the front portion run to Radstock. The truck bodies and contents were consumed by fire leaving only the frames and wheels. The *Bath Chronicle* reported that a fire on a goods train was not uncommon, but 'usually a few buckets of water frequently nipped trouble in the bud.'

Working on railways can be fraught with danger and accidents occurred to railway staff. One such happened on New Year's Day 1912.

The 3.20pm from Bournemouth to Bath called at Shillingstone and after it left, Richard Spencer, assistant coal yard manager, noticed Samuel Crane standing on the footboard. Crane, a checker aged 41, had been employed at the station for 23 years and was also chairman of the parish council. About five minutes later, Spencer saw him lying face downwards and bleeding copiously. His injuries were fatal.

When tail traffic from an up train needed to be placed in a siding at Shillingstone, in order to save the time and trouble of the engine shunting it, the coupling was unscrewed at the station and then when the train moved off and had cleared the points at the entrance to the sidings or loading dock, the coupling would be lifted off with a pole, sometimes when the train was stationary and sometimes when on the move. After the points had been changed, the uncoupled wagon would gravitate back into a siding.

It transpired that while standing on the running board uncoupling the Blandford to Shillingstone horse box, Samuel Crane fell and the box ran over him.

The coroner's jury brought in a verdict of accidental death 'whilst in the discharge of his duties, and that none of the officials or railway staff were in any way to blame'. The jury expressed its sorrow to the widow and eight children and desired that their fees should be given to them.

On 28 May 1912, the 12.20pm from Bath to Bournemouth comprised three cattle trucks, a luggage van and three passenger coaches. The wagons contained seven bulls and six heifers belonging to Viscount Portman of Blandford and had been exhibited at the Bath & West Show held that year actually at Bath. The three prize-winning beasts travelled in the second van and this had a special compartment for the two herdsmen who travelled with them.

As the train was ascending along the embankment before Devonshire Tunnel, the herdsmen heard the beasts stamping and could smell burning. They slid back the door separating the compartments and were met by a burst of smoke and flame; the straw bedding was alight and being fanned by the draught of the train's movement.

One herdsman pulled the communication cord and before the train stopped, took a flying leap on to the track and sustained a wound over his eye. The other man jumped, but by then speed had been reduced and he was uninjured.

The cattle wagon was a flaming furnace so any attempt to rescue the animals was out of the question; one could not get within half a dozen yards of it. The beasts were silent, probably suffocated. The blazing vehicle was uncoupled and a space of 12yd left at each end. Railwaymen tried to douse the flames with buckets of water from the engine, but all to no avail. The charred remains of the beasts were buried in a nearby field.

This event prompted a letter to the *Bath Chronicle* asking why railway companies were not obliged to carry fire extinguishers on a train as their availability could save lives of people as well as animals.

On 6 March 1929, a coupling failed on a down goods and wagons ran back down the gradient. Some derailed and smashed into Bridge No 200 carrying the Bournemouth Road over the S&D north of Blandford St Mary, blocking both lines and scattering tons of coal and tarmacadam over the permanent way. S. F. Redman, locomotive clerk at Bath, suggested that the 'Pines Express', which was shortly due to depart from Bournemouth West, be diverted through Salisbury and over GWR lines to Bristol. His proposal was adopted and while having lunch, he saw it pass the closed Twerton-on-Avon station at 1.5pm, instead of leaving Bath LMS about 12.30pm.

On 20 November 1929, 2-8-0 No 89, built four years before by Robert Stephenson & Co, was working the 3.25pm from Evercreech Junction, due at Bath at 6.15pm. Its load was 32 private owner wagons each loaded with 8 to 10 tons of coal, one laden goods wagon, three empty wagons, one empty oil tank and a 20 ton brake van. The estimated weight of the train was 493 tons, so the engine was loaded almost to the maximum, 169 quarters, against the 172 quarters permissible. (An 8 ton loaded mineral wagon = 4 quarters.)

As No 89 was steaming poorly and had lost 13 minutes between Evercreech Junction and Masbury, at Radstock, Guard Christopher Wagner, aged 50, suggested that if they stopped at Wellow, Driver Henry Jennings, aged 57, who had become a passed driver in 1915 and a driver in 1919, should ask the signalman to hold them there until they could get a clear run through Midford and so not have to restart near the foot of the bank. Jennings sent this message by the Wellow porter, but left before the signalman received it.

The Blandford derailment, 6 March 1929: S. Sealy, District Controller, Bath is on the right; A. H. Whitaker, District Locomotive Superintendent in charge of the Bath breakdown gang, wearing a bowler hat, is standing in the four foot. The right-hand arch was built when the track was doubled, 29 April 1901. *Author's collection*

They were stopped at Midford outer home to allow the 5pm down passenger and 5.15pm down goods to pass. The 'calling-on' arm was then lowered, and No 89 and its train moved forward through Midford on to the single line and then backed to the down road in order to allow an up passenger train to pass. So that he could get a better start, Jennings reversed about 300yd from the signalbox to place the train on the end of a falling gradient and as the engine was standing on the down line, the tablet catcher was not within reach of the delivery column, so to avoid slowing for collection by hand, Jennings collected the tablet from the signalbox and walked to his engine. Making good use of the time at Midford, Fireman Maurice Pearce cleaned the fire of clinker and believed his good, clear fire would take him to Bath without further firing.

When the signal came off, they accelerated and passed Midford box at about 15mph, but by the time they entered Combe Down Tunnel speed had fallen to 4mph. One thing in Driver Jennings' favour was that he was going tender-first, so the chimney was behind him and fumes less likely to be a problem.

Soon after entering the tunnel, which proved exceptionally hot and smoky, Fireman Pearce, who had transferred from Radstock to Bath only the previous weekend, was forced by the choking fumes to wrap a coat round his head and sit down, after which he remembered nothing — gases had rendered him unconscious. Jennings gallantly stuck to his post at the regulator, but he too was overcome and fell into unconsciousness. At the post-mortem a medical officer found at least 75% saturation of blood with carbon monoxide.

No 89, now with two insensible men on her footplate, plodded up through the tunnel. The other side was a gradient of 1 in 50 down to Bath. Helped through Lyncombe Vale by the weight of the 38 vehicles behind her, No 89 picked up speed, plunged into Devonshire Tunnel and out the other side. Guard Christopher Wagner applied the handbrake in his van, but without the help of the locomotive and tender brakes it was little more than a gesture.

The train sped round the curve by Bath Junction and, at a speed of probably 50 to 60mph, derailed at the second set of points in the goods yard, ran between the tracks for about 50yd before striking the shed and overturning, wagons piling in a great heap, 30 destroyed or beyond repair. The near end of the office cabin used by Railway Clearing House staff was demolished killing Inspector John Norman, aged 58, in charge of the yard. One curiosity was that a pencil on the office table was driven into a sleeper for about half its length. Jack Loader, an Old Sulian like the present author, formerly employed by the S&D but who had been transferred to the LMS at Gloucester and, returning to visit his parents at 4 Canterbury Road, was taking a short cut through the yard. He was killed when struck on the head by part of a gas lamp standard. All three casualties were buried in Twerton cemetery, Bellott's Road, adjacent to the S&D.

Railwaymen quickly arrived at the scene and extricated the footplate crew from the debris, laying them on wooden benches. Both were thickly covered in coal dust. Jennings was just alive, but died on his way to the RUH. Pearce was alive, though badly injured. Guard Wagner was also seriously hurt. Anticipating a derailment on the curve at Bath Junction, he jumped from his van and on landing received a compound fracture to both legs. Ironically had he stayed in his van he would have been unharmed, for after the crash it still stood upright with his oil lamp burning brightly, standing at the base of the handbrake column.

A live coal from No 89 was flung through an open bedroom window in Albert Buildings where it caught the house alight, but was soon put out. A. H. Whitaker said that when he arrived at the scene no pressure was showing on the gauge; the reverser was in almost full gear and locked, while the regulator was a third open. The sand valve was open, but all the sand used.

Newspaper photographers arrived from London by the first train on 21 November, but were denied permits. Determined not to be outwitted, they boarded an outward train from Queen Square station which luckily for them came to a standstill close by the scene of the accident and so were able to obtain their pictures.

Stothert & Pitt's rail-mounted crane was used to assist clearing the debris, although on its way to the disaster it became derailed. No 89 was repaired and returned to service, continuing to work over the S&D until its withdrawal in June 1964, and was eventually saved for preservation.

Drivers gave conflicting evidence regarding conditions in Combe Down Tunnel. Some claimed it difficult to breathe when going slowly, while Driver Hockey, who had driven No 89 on the day prior to the accident, caused laughter when asked if he preferred going tender-first. He replied: 'Yes, if we were not dealing with weather.' He continued, 'I would prefer going through a

Class 7F 2-8-0 No 89 overturned at Bath on 20 November 1929. On the left is the wrecked office cabin, while to the right, a flagman stands in the four foot controlling passing trains. *Author's collection*

tunnel tender-first. Ninety times out of a hundred we would examine the top of the tunnel, the atmosphere was so clear. If we were engine-first, it had only to make a slip or two and it was difficult to see whether the engine was going backwards or forwards. Once I asked my fireman to see which way we were going.'

The general consensus of drivers was that if the tunnel was entered from the Midford end at a fair speed, they were not in the tunnel long enough for conditions to become serious; trouble only came if they had to stop at Midford and then restart with a heavy load.

Guard Christopher Wagner told Colonel Trench that he considered that they passed through Combe Down Tunnel slower than usual and that the atmosphere was thicker than normal. On more than one occasion he looked out and turned his lamp on the wall to check that the train had not stopped. Colonel Trench believed that they had been in the mile-long tunnel for 11 to 13 minutes compared with the normal time of 13 minutes for the whole distance from Midford to Bath Junction.

Just before his van emerged from the tunnel, Wagner expected to feel the coupling closing up due to the application of the tender brake, but did not. He applied his brake gently at first and then harder when he realised something was amiss. After passing Bath Junction, knowing he could do no more and that a smash was inevitable, he jumped from his van. He never really recovered from his injuries and died on 25 March 1939. Maurice Pearce recovered and eventually became a driver at Saltley.

Unfortunately, everything had been against the enginemen that afternoon: with a heavy train they had to make a dead start from Midford; they had to endure smoke and fumes from three trains which had passed through the tunnel not long before, while weather conditions offered high humidity and absence of wind.

Colonel A. C. Trench said in his report of 28 February 1930 to the Ministry of Transport that it was the first instance in over 50 years that an engine crew had been overcome by fumes and 'under normal conditions the atmospheric conditions are not such as to involve any risk or anything more than a degree of discomfort'. He said that the obvious safeguard of a ventilation shaft or a fan would be too expensive, but a practical remedy would be a reduction of the load of up trains and that a longer turntable be installed at Bath to avoid tender-first working. Going in reverse meant the cab acted like a cup and scooped fumes in a tunnel. Trench recommended that if possible, a train be detained at Wellow rather than Midford, though appreciated that with the limitations of single-line working, this was not always possible.

On 29 July 1936, Driver C. W. Rawlings and Fireman Frank Parker were on Class 3F 0-6-0T No 7620 shunting Writhlington Colliery Sidings between Wellow and Radstock. They were standing on the up main line facing Radstock with eight empty wagons behind them. Suddenly Driver Rawlings was horrified to see Class 7F 2-8-0 No 13803 approaching on the same line with a train of 37 wagons. It was the 8.10am from Evercreech Junction to Bath and had run through protecting signals.

Rawlings noticed that there was no one on the footplate because Driver Brewer and Fireman Hiroms had jumped off to avoid the impending collision and were busily pinning down wagon brakes as the train passed them. Swiftly thinking how a collision could be avoided, Rawlings flung the reversing lever over and opened the regulator and when the eight wagons in front were safely buffered up, he opened it fully. By this time the two engines had almost met. Quick as a flash he jumped off No 7620 and as No 13803 lumbered by, swung on to the footplate, fully closed the regulator and brought the runaway to a halt within three engine lengths.

But pride comes before a fall. As he leapt from his side of the cab, his fireman, not hearing his driver's shout telling him to remain with his engine, jumped off the other side, so no-one was now on board No 7620 to close its fully open regulator. When he realised he had mistaken his driver's intentions, Fireman Parker ran after his escaping engine, but to no avail. The runaway roared through Wellow at a speed the signalman estimated at 50mph and continued on to Midford. Here the double track became single and seven of the eight wagons derailed felling signals, telegraph poles and Signalman Larcombe's box, luckily not harming him. Six wagons shot down the 40ft high retaining wall into a garden. The owner subsequently managed to secure the wreckage for firewood at a very reasonable figure. The debris fortunately missed a house, the roof of which was several feet below rail level. The stationmaster hearing the loud crash, lay on the floor of his office as the bits spread over 140yd.

No 7620 kept to the rails and careered on her way pushing before her like a coster's barrow the remains of a wagon running on only two wheels. Remarkably, this curious vehicle succeeded in negotiating the mile-long Combe Down Tunnel, but at Claude Avenue bridge about midway between the north portal of Devonshire Tunnel and Bath Junction, the end door of the wagon fell off, derailing the locomotive's rear wheels and bringing it to a halt. About the same time, owing to a shortage of water, the fusible plug on the firebox crown melted and the fire was put out.

Why did the goods run through the signals? The driver was instructing his 19-year-old mate in firing and missed seeing the distant signal at caution and noticed the home signal only when he was almost upon it. Unfortunately, the error was compounded by the fact that the Writhlington signalman had misunderstood his clearance point and accepted the goods when he should have refused due to the position of the shunting engine and wagons.

Driver Brewer immediately applied his steam brake, threw No 13803 into reverse and opened the regulator. In his panic he omitted to use the catch to secure the reversing handle which, owing to the weight of the valve gear, spun back into full forward gear. He tried to close the regulator, but it jammed. When he jumped, speed had been reduced to 10mph, a good reduction from 20mph on a falling gradient of 1 in 120.

The distorted track at Midford station, looking south towards the viaduct. The track here was on a ledge in the hillside rising steeply right, with a sheer cliff on the left.
Courtesy Bath Chronicle

The wrecked signalbox at Midford, 29 July 1936. The lineman sign hangs on the signalbox front.
Courtesy Bath Chronicle

Signalman Larcombe at Midford showed great presence of mind. The railway telegraph wires had been wrecked by the derailment, so he ran to a nearby house and used the telephone to warn Bath Control which then made arrangements with Bath Junction signalbox to direct the runaway into the goods yard. Staff in the Bath Locomotive office were ordered to leave immediately as the runaway would have been diverted beyond the yard down Boat Road only inches from the office wall.

Lt-Col E. Woodhouse believed the Writhlington signalman was primarily to blame for the incident, while Driver Brewer was also criticised for abandoning his locomotive, an act which he said was 'quite indefensible', failing to secure the reverse, and not closing the regulator before jumping. Woodhouse said it would have been better had Driver Rawlings stayed on his own engine and applied the brakes as soon as the engines made contact. Woodhouse's report concluded: 'The morale of enginemen is such that the contingency of an engine running away unattended with the regulator open is very remote, and therefore does not suggest that precautions should be taken against a recurrence of a similar accident'. It was fortunate indeed that the Midford crash occurred at 10.6½am – the time when the clock in the signalbox there stopped — because a Bath to Bournemouth passenger train was due out at 10.20am. Had the passenger and the runaway tank engine collided in Devonshire or Combe Down tunnels, the results would have been unthinkable. While the runaway was approaching, shunting was in progress at the Co-op siding, Oldfield Park, but fortunately work finished shortly before its arrival and the engine concerned had returned to Bath.

A Somerset Collieries wagon in a garden at Midford, 29 July 1936. *Courtesy Bath Chronicle*

On the afternoon of 13 March 1944, a down double-headed ten-coach troop train hauled by SR 'S11' class 4-4-0 No 402, piloting LMS '4F' 0-6-0 No 4523, was approaching Henstridge and passing below the A30, when a United States Army heavy transporter, negotiating the narrow bridge, demolished the parapet and crashed down on to the two locomotives, severing the coupling between them. The pilot engine remained upright and continued down the line until stopped by its driver.

The train engine was struck by the transporter and the tractor it was carrying. The smokebox of No 4523 was crushed and the engine diverted into a field. As the train passed through Henstridge station, debris struck a signal post on which Porter William Jackson was tending an oil lamp. Jackson was able to drop into the field unhurt as the post toppled. Driver Harold Burford and Fireman Ted Pauley emptied the firebox of No 4523 and administered first aid to some of the wounded. At least five soldiers were killed in the first coach and all casualties were in the first five coaches. Royal Engineers stationed near Shaftesbury and men from the Royal Naval station at Henstridge cut up the frames of the seriously damaged coaches. The line remained blocked for 24 hours. No 4523 spent 32 working days at Derby undergoing a heavy general repair and returned to traffic on 18 April 1944.

Circa 1963 a signalman at Bath Junction heard a goods train approaching sooner than expected and saw that it was running away. He directed it from the goods yard road to the main line to give its crew longer to get it under control. He phoned the station box to alert them to the runaway and suggested they give it as many crossovers as possible to slow it down before giving it a platform road. This plan proved successful and it struck the blocks fairly slowly. The fireman threw the tablet out by the Co-op siding and searching for it took quite some time.

Class 4F 0-6-0 No 44523, which was involved in the 13 March 1944 accident, climbs to Midsomer Norton with the 4.25pm from Bath to Bournemouth West on 26 June 1953. The siding to Norton Hill Colliery is in the foreground. *Rev Alan Newman*

Class 2P 4-4-0 No 40537 and Class 5 4-6-0 73019 tackle the 1 in 50 gradient out of Bath with the 'Pines Express' on 28 March 1959. No 40537 was the last MR '2P' 4-4-0 to remain active, not being withdrawn from service until the week ending 1 September 1962, having run a high mileage of approximately 1,800,000. It was the last Midland '2P' to pilot the 'Pines Express'. Transfer to Templecombe was seasonal, with each winter being spent in store at Gloucester before resuming duties at Templecombe each March. *Author*

Bibliography

The Somerset & Dorset Railway, R. Atthill, D&C 1967.

The Somerset & Dorset Railway, D. S. Barrie and C. R. Clinker, Oakwood 1948.

Somerset & Dorset Locomotive History, D. Bradley and D. Milton, D&C 1973.

Making Economies on the Somerset & Dorset Joint Line 1929-31, N. Burgess, *LMS Journal* 6, Wild Swan, N.D.

Alfred Whitaker and the Tablet Apparatus, P. E. Cattermole, S&D Trust 1982.

Track Layout Diagrams of the GWR and BR WR Section 18, R. A. Cooke, Author 1980.

The Somerset & Dorset— Aftermath of the Beeching Axe, T. Deacon, OPC 1995.

The Somerset & Dorset Railway, D. Harper, Millstream 1998.

LMS Engine Sheds Vol 4, C. Hawkins and G. Reeve, Wild Swan 1984.

Highbridge in Its Heyday, C. G. Maggs, Oakwood 1986.

The Mangotsfield to Bath Line, C. G. Maggs, Oakwood 2005.

Bath to Evercreech Junction, V. Mitchell and K. Smith, Middleton 1988.

Life on the Railway, J. Owen. Millstream 1989.

Footplate Over the Mendips, P. Smith, OPC 1978.

Newspapers

Bath & Cheltenham Gazette
Bath Chronicle